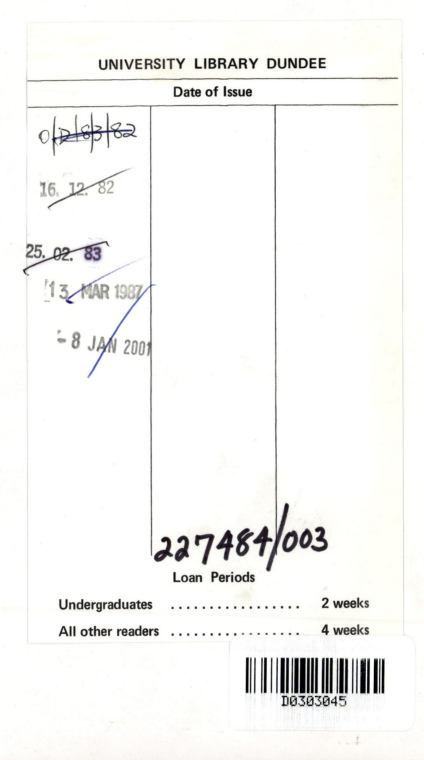

UNIVERSITY LIBRARY DUNDEE

Date of Issue

0 2 8 3 82

16. 12. 82

25. 02. 83

13 MAR 1987

- 8 JAN 2001

227484/003

Loan Periods

Undergraduates .... 2 weeks

All other readers .... 4 weeks

ANNUAL
ACCOUNTING
REVIEW

ANNUAL ACCOUNTING REVIEW

VOLUME 1 (1979)
VOLUME 2 (1980)
VOLUME 3 (1981)

Co-editors: Stanley Weinstein and Michael A. Walker
Mann Judd Landau–Hodgson Landau International
Coordinating Editor: Jacqueline J.M. Koziol

ISSN 0142-5897

ANNUAL ACCOUNTING REVIEW

Edited by Stanley Weinstein and Michael A. Walker
Mann Judd Landau–Hodgson Landau International

VOLUME 3
1981

 harwood academic publishers
chur· london· new york

Copyright © 1981 by OPA, Amsterdam, B.V.

Published under license by:

Harwood Academic Publishers GmbH
Poststrasse 22
7000–CH Chur, Switzerland

Editorial Office for the United Kingdom:
61 Grays Inn Road
London WC1X 8TL

Editorial Office for the United States of America:
Post Office Box 786
Cooper Station
New York, New York 10003

Printed in the United States of America

This book is dedicated to the high ideals of the accounting profession and the dream that it will someday achieve the recognition it deserves.

S.W.
M.A.W.

PREFACE

This annual publication was conceived to provide professional accountants, financial executives and educators with a perspective and prospective overview of some of the most important developments in accounting. We expect it to be a valuable tool for those individuals who find it increasingly difficult to keep abreast of recent developments and anticipated future changes in accounting and financial reporting.

The subjects and authors for each volume are selected by an editorial advisory board comprised of distinguished leaders in the profession.

Contributors are asked to present their views on selected matters of importance in the field thereby providing readers with a unique opportunity to obtain knowledge of the thoughts of a number of the most outstanding individuals in the profession.

"The third edition of Annual Accounting Review contains thirteen articles in which distinguished authors have covered matters of significant interest to the accounting profession. Four of the articles summarize developments during 1980 in specific areas. The other nine articles review particular subjects which are of continuing importance to the profession".

We hope that this publication will help individuals who find it increasingly difficult to keep up with the publication explosion in accounting and financial reporting and to place this information in useful perspective. We welcome comments from readers which may assist us in achieving this goal.

We owe a special debt of gratitude to the members of the editorial advisory board and to the coordinating editor, Jacqueline J.M. Koziol, who gave unsparingly of their time.

Stanley Weinstein
Michael A. Walker
Editors

TABLE OF CONTENTS

1980 REVIEW—FASB DEVELOPMENTS

Alex T. Arcady
Bruce J. Rosen

Ernst & Whinney
Cleveland, Ohio

CONTENTS

ABSTRACT

*Messrs. Arcady and Rosen review the accomplishments of the Finan-
cial Accounting Standards Board through October, 1980. The accounting standard-setting body of the private sector moved forward on the
conceptual framework project with the issuance of its second Statement
of Concepts as well as several proposals. It issued an exposure draft to
replace its controversial Statement No. 8 on foreign currency translation,
and two Statements on pension plans affecting the accounting by defined benefit plans and the disclosures made by employers who sponsor
such plans. The Board also addressed specific problems on various issues
relating to income taxes, capitalized interest, and the effects of inflation.*

INTRODUCTION

During 1980, the results of a survey conducted by Louis Harris and Associates, Inc. to find out how the Financial Accounting Standards Board
(FASB) is doing in the eyes of those most affected by its work were released. Respondents included chief financial and executive officers, top
officers of investment and brokerage firms, leading accounting educators,
partners from accounting firms, and key government officials. The survey
showed that, in assessing the output of the FASB to date, 24% of the respondents feel it has been "highly effective," 55% "somewhat effective,"
and only 12% "not very effective" or "not effective at all." A large majority of the respondents also said it is "highly important" to have the private
sector continue setting financial accounting and reporting standards.

As the focal point of accounting standard-setting by the private sector,
the FASB made significant progress on a number of projects during the
year. The Board continued to move forward on the conceptual framework
project—a constitution of accounting—issuing its second Statement of Concepts as well as several proposals relating to other phases of the project. It
released an exposure draft which would replace its controversial Statement
on foreign currency translation, and issued two Statements on pension plans
which affect the accounting by defined benefit plans and the disclosures
made by sponsors of such plans. The Board also addressed specific problems

on various issues relating to income taxes, capitalized interest, and the effects of inflation.

PENSION PLANS

During the year, the FASB issued Statement No. 35 on "Accounting and Reporting by Defined Benefit Pension Plans." In addition, the Board issued Statement No. 36 that expands the pension disclosures made by employers who sponsor such plans—pending completion of its reevaluation of APB Opinion No. 8, "Accounting for the Cost of Pension Plans" (discussed later).

Statement No. 35, "Accounting and Reporting by Defined Benefit Pension Plans"

Statement No. 35 covers companies' plans and those of state and local governments. It calls for using the accrual method of accounting and provides that most plan investments should be carried at market value. The emphasis is on plan participants' needs, in keeping with the Board's conviction that pension plan statements are primarily "to provide financial information that is useful in assessing the plan's present and future ability to pay benefits when due."

Statements of net assets available for benefits at the end of the plan year and changes therein for the year are required. Separate statements or footnotes should include the actuarial present value of accumulated plan benefits and certain annual changes therein; but this information may be measured as of either the beginning or end of the plan year. If the beginning of the year information is used, net assets available for benefits as of that date and changes for the previous year also should be disclosed.

Participants' benefits relate to service through the latest benefit valuation date. Current pay rates are to be used, but the accumulated benefits will be discounted by an "appropriate" interest rate and further adjusted by factors concerning payment probability (death, withdrawal, etc.).

The Statement is effective for plan years beginning after December 15, 1980, although earlier application is encouraged. If financial statements for earlier periods are presented for comparative purposes, they must be restated.

Statement No. 36, "Disclosure of Pension Information"

The FASB's long-standing project to reconsider APB Opinion No. 8 on accounting for pension cost is not scheduled for completion until 1982. The Board believes, however, that certain new disclosures are necessary now, and has issued Statement No. 36 which affects sponsors of defined benefit pension plans. For each set of complete financial statements, entities sponsoring such plans should disclose:

> Actuarial present value of accumulated plan benefits (including the vested portion) determined as of the most recent valuation date within each fiscal year.

> Fair value of the plan's net assets available for benefits determined as of the same date.

> Interest rate assumption used in the measurement of accumulated plan benefits.

> Valuation dates.

These disclosures should be determined in accordance with FASB Statement No. 35 (see above). The information may be aggregated for all pension plans sponsored. However, disclosure of significant unfunded amounts "...may be desirable if a significant number of participants in such an unfunded plan are employed by a subsidiary or division that is unprofitable or experiencing a continuous decline in business." The Statement does not change the present disclosure requirements of Opinion No. 8 relating to the nature of the plan, participants covered, the accounting and funding policies, provision for pension cost, and significant matters affecting comparability.

Effective for fiscal years beginning after December 15, 1979, the Statement does not require that comparative financial statements for earlier years contain the new disclosures. Plans for which the benefit information is not available (generally because it is not required under ERISA) should continue to follow the existing disclosure requirements of Opinion No. 8.

INCOME TAXES

The Board addressed specific issues on this topic, issuing a final Statement on the "Balance Sheet Classification of Deferred Income Taxes," and an Interpretation on how to apply percentage limitations in recognizing investment tax credit.

Statement No. 37, "Balance Sheet Classification of Deferred Income Taxes"

Statement No. 37 amends APB Opinion No. 11 to state that deferred income taxes *not* related to an asset or liability should be classified according to the expected reversal date of the timing difference. Deferred taxes that are related to an asset or liability should continue to be classified according to the provisions of Opinion No. 11 (i.e., the same as the asset or liability). And they are related, says the Statement, if reducing the asset or liability would cause the timing difference to reverse.

Most affected by the new FASB pronouncement are those contractors that use the completed-contract method for tax purposes and the percentage-of-completion method for financial reporting. The resulting deferred tax credits have generally been classified as current, but now they will be allocated between current and long-term based on the estimated completion date of the contract because reversal is not directly related to a reduction in any asset or liability.

The Statement also provides that deferred income taxes associated with changes in accounting methods for income tax purposes should be classified according to the expected reversal of the timing difference; and those on undistributed earnings of a consolidated foreign subsidiary should be classified according to the expected remittance date.

The Statement is effective for periods ending after December 15, 1980, although earlier application is encouraged. Reclassification in previously issued financial statements is permitted, but not required.

Interpretation No. 32, "Application of Percentage Limitations in Recognizing Investment Tax Credit"

The Revenue Act of 1978 increased the amount of federal income taxes otherwise payable that can be offset by investment tax credits (ITC). Previously, the limitation generally was 100% of the first $25,000 of federal income taxes payable and 50% of the remaining taxes. Under the Act, the limitation applicable to the remaining taxes was increased to 60% in 1979, and will rise incrementally up to 90% in 1982. Because of the revised percentage limitations, there had been some confusion as to which rate should be used for recognizing ITC in the financial statements—the rate currently in effect or the rate scheduled to be in effect when timing differences are expected to reverse.

Interpretation No. 32 provides that the percentage limitation companies should use in their "with-and-without" tax computations is the limitation that is in effect for the period for which the computation is being made. Additional amounts of ITC are to be recognized as reductions of previously recorded deferred tax credits based on percentage limitations scheduled to be in effect in the year timing differences are expected to reverse. Only net deferred tax credits that have not previously been offset and that will reverse during the ITC carryforward period can be offset. Net deferred tax credits offset in prior years should not be adjusted to reflect changes in the statutory percentage limitations.

The Interpretation is effective for fiscal years beginning after December 15, 1979.

CONCEPTUAL FRAMEWORK

During 1980, the FASB continued its efforts to develop a conceptual framework, considered by many to be the Board's most significant undertaking. In addition to a final Concepts Statement on "Qualitative Characteristics of Accounting Information" (see below), the Board issued proposed Statements on "Elements of Financial Statements of Business Enterprises," and "Objectives of Financial Reporting by Nonbusiness Organizations," and an Invitation to Comment on "Financial Statements and Other Means of Financial Reporting." These pending pronouncements are discussed later.

Statement of Financial Accounting Concepts No. 2, "Qualitative Characteristics of Accounting Information"

In May 1980, the FASB issued its second Statement of Financial Accounting Concepts. Theoretical in content, the Statement is designed to assist the FASB in making choices among accounting alternatives. In addition, the Board believes the qualitative characteristics will guide companies in selecting accounting and reporting alternatives (although many commentators on the exposure draft questioned this aspect).

The Statement defines accounting's goal as producing information that is "the most useful for decision-making" and says relevance and reliability should be given the most weight in setting accounting standards. Materiality also is discussed, but the Board does not offer any quantitative guidelines. Despite the difficulties, the Board acknowledges that in establishing a new standard, it must try to be satisfied that its benefits outweigh its costs.

OTHER MATTERS

Statement No. 38, "Accounting for Preacquisition Contingencies of Purchased Enterprises"

How to account for matters unresolved at the date of purchase of a business, such as pending litigation, has been an unsettled issue for some time. FASB Statement No. 38, which amends APB Opinion No. 16, will limit an often-used treatment—that of retroactively changing the purchase price allocation for any subsequent adjustments. The Statement says that contingencies are part of the cost of the acquired business only if they can be quantified within a given time period after the acquisition.

The time period allowed to identify and estimate the amount of a contingency, known as the "allocation period," can't exceed the time it takes the purchaser to obtain the information needed (e.g., appraisals, actuarial valuations) to identify and value the assets purchased and liabilities assumed. After this allocation period, which usually should not exceed one year, any adjustments made should be recorded in current income. The FASB elaborates that escrowed amounts should be recorded as part of the purchase price in the original allocation because such amounts ultimately will be paid either to the seller or to a third-party claimant.

The Statement becomes effective for business combinations initiated after December 15, 1980, so retroactive adjustment of the purchase price allocation for previous acquisitions still will be permitted. And, under certain circumstances, the Statement allows earlier combinations to be accounted for by the new method.

Interpretation No. 31, "Treatment of Stock Compensation Plans in EPS Computations"

As a result of Interpretation No. 31, some companies with compensatory stock option plans (including stock appreciation rights and similar arrangements) may have a different earnings per share (EPS) figure. This is because the Interpretation modifies the definition of "proceeds" in Interpretation No. 28.

EPS computations generally assume, in accordance with APB Opinion No. 15's "treasury stock method," that outstanding stock options, etc., are exercised and the resulting proceeds are used to buy common stock in the market. The Interpretation says proceeds means the sum of the cash to be received on exercise, the amount of measurable compensation ascribed to future services and not yet charged to expense, and any tax benefits ("windfall" benefits) to be credited to capital. Previously, proceeds could be assumed to include all related compensation accruals.

The Interpretation provides that stock appreciation rights and other variable plans payable in cash or stock are presumed to be common stock equivalents unless the presumption can be overcome (i.e., they are likely to be paid in cash).

The Interpretation is effective for fiscal years beginning after December 15, 1979. Retroactive application is permitted.

**Interpretation No. 33, "Applying FASB Statement No. 34
to Oil and Gas Producing Operations Accounted for by the
Full Cost Method"**

Interpretation No. 33 provides oil and gas producers guidance in capital-
izing interest costs. The Interpretation says that unusually significant investments in unproved properties and major development projects that are
accounted for by the full cost method and are not being depreciated, depleted, or amortized, and significant properties in cost centers with no
production, are assets that qualify for interest capitalization as long as
exploration or development activities are in progress. Conversely, assets
that are currently being depreciated, depleted, or amortized do not qualify
because those assets are deemed to be in use and contributing to the enterprise's earning activities.

The Interpretation is effective for fiscal years beginning after December
15, 1979. Restatement of previously issued financial statements and interim
financial data is encouraged, but not required.

PENDING PRONOUNCEMENTS

The Board has a number of other projects in process.

Proposed Statement, "Foreign Currency Translation"

The FASB has issued an exposure draft which would replace its controversial Statement No. 8, "Accounting for the Translation of Foreign Currency
Transactions and Foreign Currency Financial Statements." Under the proposal, companies would translate all assets and liabilities of a foreign entity
using the exchange rate in effect at the balance-sheet date (i.e., the current
rate). Revenues and expenses (including cost of goods sold and depreciation) generally would be translated using an average of the exchange rates
in effect during the reporting period.

The most significant change from Statement No. 8 is that most of the
volatility in reported earnings that often result from applying Statement
No. 8 would be eliminated. Adjustments resulting from translation of foreign subsidiary financial statements would be reported as a separate component of stockholders' equity, pending substantial or complete liquidation
or impairment of the investment in the foreign entity.

Adjustments due to settlement or translation of unsettled foreign currency transactions (e.g., a U.S. company's receivable denominated in a
foreign currency) would continue to be recognized currently in net income.

However, transactions intended to be an economic hedge of a net investment in a foreign entity or translation of intercompany foreign currency balances or transactions between a parent and its subsidiary or investee are exceptions to the general rule and would be reported like translation adjustments.

Chief among the proposed disclosures are:

> The aggregate exchange gain or loss included in determining net income for the period.

> An analysis, either in a separate financial statement, in the notes, or as part of the statement of stockholders' equity, of the separate component of stockholders' equity. It would include: beginning and ending cumulative amounts; aggregate translation adjustment for the period; any income taxes provided on translation adjustments; and any amounts transferred from equity to net income due to liquidation or impairment.

The proposal would be effective for fiscal years beginning on or after December 15, 1981, with earlier application encouraged. Restatement of prior periods' financial statements would be permitted, but not required. The effect of applying the current rate to an entity's assets and liabilities as of the beginning of the year in which the Statement is first applied would be reported as the opening balance in the separate component of stockholders' equity.

The Board is divided on the proposal—the four assenting Board members being solidly in favor and the three dissenting members, including Chairman Donald J. Kirk, solidly against it. The exposure draft devotes seventeen paragraphs to explaining the views of the dissenting Board members. Essentially, they would have preferred a few basic changes to Statement No. 8 (e.g., translating locally-sourced inventory at the current rate). They believe a complete reconsideration is not necessary—issuing a complete new pronouncement will only further confuse financial statement users. Based on the results of public hearings and comment letters, the Board may re-expose a proposed Statement.

Proposed Statement of Financial Accounting Concepts, "Elements of Financial Statements of Business Enterprises"

The exposure draft includes definitions of the "elements" of financial statements—assets, liabilities, revenues, expenses, gains, and losses. The

99-page draft painstakingly outlines how the Board believes the definitions would apply to present practice and future aspects of the conceptual framework project. The Board stresses that the definitions would not lead to "upheavals in present practice, although they may in due time lead to some changes in practice or at least in the ways certain items are viewed."

The definitions are broad enough to accommodate virtually any financial statement model, including the present historical cost accounting model. The proposal says: "The Board expects most assets and liabilities in present practice to continue to qualify as assets and liabilities under the definitions in the (proposed) Statement." To support that contention, and to refute critics of an earlier exposure draft who thought otherwise, an appendix to the proposal explains why the definitions would not rule out various deferred charges and credits that presently exist in order to match costs with related revenues.

The Board apparently sees itself as the primary user of the proposed definitions. However, just because an item meets one of those definitions does not guarantee its inclusion in financial statements—it still must meet measurement and recognition guidelines that will be developed later in the conceptual framework project. For example, the Board notes that research and development activities might meet its definition of an asset, but the high uncertainty of resulting future benefits might preclude including them as an asset in financial statements.

Unlike an earlier proposal, this one does not define earnings. Instead it uses "comprehensive income" (all changes in owners' equity from nonowner sources). The Board wants to reserve the term "earnings"for possibly identifying some intermediate measure or component.

Proposed Statement of Financial Accounting Concepts, "Objectives of Financial Reporting by Nonbusiness Organizations"

Because nonbusiness organizations are not judged by profit performance, their financial reporting objectives differ from those of businesses. This is a key conclusion of the FASB in a tentative Statement of Concepts on nonbusiness organizations. If this Statement is adopted, it will apply to nonprofit hospitals, colleges and universities, health and welfare organizations, and—perhaps most significantly—state and local government units.

The proposal recommends that financial statements provide information useful in making resource allocation decisions, assessing services provided and continued ability to provide them, and assessing management stewardship and performance. A final Statement would not establish accounting standards nor require any accounting changes, but would be a foundation for future standards in this area.

The Board emphasizes that this action does not mean it is assuming responsibility for setting government accounting standards. Who should— or would—do so remains an open question.

Invitation to Comment, "Financial Statements and Other Means of Financial Reporting"

What financial information should be required, who should provide it, and where it should be presented are issues basic to the FASB's standard-setting process. The Board's Invitation to Comment covers these matters. It encompasses what is often called the "big GAAP/little GAAP" and supplementary reporting issues.

According to the Board, decisions on what information to provide and who should provide it are interrelated and flow from the objectives and qualitative characteristics of financial reporting. Thus, the Board should require disclosure of information if it is useful to investors and creditors. Because useful information must be relevant, reliable, and cost-effective, the Board should apply these qualitative characteristics in deciding the "what" and "who" questions. This approach could result, for example, in a standard that affects only public enterprises because of its low relevancy to nonpublic or closely held enterprises, such as segment reporting.

Decisions on where information should be presented will be determined largely by other conceptual framework decisions on elements, measurement, and recognition. Once the content of financial statements is established, the information earmarked for footnotes would be that which completes the statement data, like accounting policies and maturity dates of debt.

Supplementary information, on the other hand, would contain data that presents an enterprise from a different perspective, such as under another measurement basis (e.g., current cost) or different level of aggregation (e.g., segment data). Such supplementary data could then be either required to accompany financial statements or available upon request, depending on the needs and sophistication of a particular class of users.

Proposed Statement, "Financial Reporting and Changing Prices: Specialized Assets"

FASB Statement No. 33 required the nation's largest public companies to disclose the effects of inflation. But four industries—oil and gas, mining, forest products, and real estate—were given special treatment because the Board needed more time to consider current cost measurement problems for unprocessed natural resources and income-producing real estate.

The FASB set forth proposed requirements for these industries in a supplement to Statement No. 33. It reflects the Board's view that the general guidelines for measuring and disclosing current cost data should apply to assets of the specialized industries. The proposal also considers certain "fair value" information, and contains guidance for determining both current cost and fair value.

The Board subsequently announced the following tentative decisions:

> Current cost information would be required for oil and gas producing activities and mining. In addition, mining operations would have to disclose quantities of proved reserves as well as the average market price for each significant mineral product, and quantities produced. Proposed disclosures of the estimated fair market value of proved oil and gas reserves would not be required, but the Board would continue to evaluate the usefulness of Reserve Recognition Accounting for oil and gas producers as applied under the SEC requirements.

> The Board would continue to review the disclosure provisions for income-producing real estate properties and forest products. In the meantime, these industries would use constant dollar amounts or an appropriate index of specific price changes for determining current cost in their 1980 financial statements.

Proposed Statement, "Accounting for Compensated Absences"

Companies that record "compensated absences" on a cash instead of an accrual basis may have to change. The FASB proposed a one-sentence standard that reads: "For each accounting period, employers shall accrue the liability for compensated absences for estimated probable future payments attributable to employees' service during that period." Compensated absences, the Board says, are not just vacations and holidays but also paid absences because of illness or for other personal reasons. Benefits need not be vested.

Some exceptions are specified, among them severance or termination pay, post-retirement and other long-term benefits, and disability pay; these are included in the Board's employer pension cost project. Also excluded are stock options and deferred compensation, which are already covered by existing accounting principles. Finally, state and local governments would not have to follow the standard because their overall accounting is currently under study.

The proposal provides that if the effects of the accounting change are material to net income, retroactive adjustment of those statements presented would be required; otherwise, only beginning retained earnings would have to be adjusted.

The Board subsequently announced certain tentative conclusions based on comments received:

> Existing interim reporting practices for compensated absences should not be changed.

> Accrual for a liability for compensated absences should be based on a constructive obligation basis. Employers would recognize a liability for rights that had been earned through services already rendered, can be carried forward and used in subsequent years, and are estimable and probable. Where estimates cannot be made, the minimum liability would be vested amounts.

> The liability should be based on current rates of pay without discounting.

Proposed Statement, "Disclosure of Guarantees, Project Financing Arrangements, and Other Similar Obligations"

Companies would be required to disclose additional information about off-balance-sheet financing arrangements if this proposed amendment to FASB Statement No. 5 is adopted. Examples of these obligations are project financing arrangements, take-or-pay contracts, throughput contracts, and working capital maintenance agreements.

Some believe these arrangements should be recognized in the balance sheet; others say no, on the grounds that they are only commitments or contingent liabilities. Pending further work on the accounting recognition phase of its conceptual framework project, the FASB has concluded that certain information should be required in the financial statement footnotes if the arrangements presently are not recognized as assets and liabilities. Proposed disclosures are: the nature, amount, and duration of the obligation or guarantee and, for commitments to pay certain amounts periodically, the amounts of payments required in each of the five succeeding years.

Proposed Statement, "Determining Materiality for Capitalization of Interest Cost"

According to FASB Statement No. 34, interest costs are to be capitalized if the effect is material. However, the Statement provides little guidance for determining materiality and, as a result, various approaches have been proposed. Some have proposed a pro forma prospective calculation whereby the projected future effects of interest capitalization would be used as a basis for determining materiality. Others have suggested a pro forma retroactive calculation based on an assumption that a company had always capitalized interest costs.

The Board has concluded that neither of these approaches is desirable and is proposing an amendment calling for the same materiality tests as those used for applying other accounting principles. For example, the after-tax effect of interest capitalization would be compared to what net income otherwise would have been in the year of adopting Statement No. 34. However, the Board is concerned about implementation costs. For this reason, and because retroactive application of Statement No. 34 was prohibited, the Board asked for input about the different approaches and whether the traditional materiality tests are sufficient.

The amendment would be applied at the same time the provisions of Statement No. 34 are first applied. Companies that have already issued annual financial statements that did not capitalize interest because the effect was not material based on a pro forma calculation would have the option of restating those financial statements.

.Proposed Interpretation, "Accounting by Oil and Gas Producing Companies for the Tax Benefits of Percentage Depletion"

How should the tax benefits arising from the use of percentage depletion be treated in the financial statements of oil and gas producers? The FASB addresses that question in a proposed Interpretation of FASB Statement No. 19, which states that any percentage depletion in excess of tax cost depletion be accounted for as a timing difference (and deferred taxes provided) until the cumulative amount of depletion deducted for income tax purposes equals the tax cost basis of the property. Thereafter, excess percentage depletion would be treated as a permanent difference.

The amount of percentage depletion used in computing the provision for income taxes would be limited to the amount allowable as a deduction

for income tax purposes for that year. Although unused percentage depletion may be carried over indefinitely, the Board believes it is not appropriate to recognize the tax benefits associated with the excess carryover.
   Retroactive application of this Interpretation would be permitted.

Discussion Memorandum, "Effect of Rate Regulation on Accounting for Regulated Enterprises"

An Addendum to APB Opinion No. 2 provides that enterprises whose rates
or prices are subject to government regulation may, in certain circumstances,
apply accounting standards differently because of the rate-making process.
Many questions and uncertainty as to the application of the Addendum
have prompted the FASB to reconsider regulated enterprises' accounting.
   While application to the Addendum generally has been limited to public
utilities, such as electric, gas, and telephone companies, the Board's project
has taken a much broader perspective. The Discussion Memorandum sweeps
health care organizations, insurance companies, motor carriers, and airlines
into the discussion, even though the effects or rate regulation on these entities' financial reporting may be limited.
   The DM states that the authority of regulatory agencies to either recognize, defer, or not recognize revenues and costs in establishing rates "adds
a unique consideration to the accounting and reporting of those enterprises." A key issue raised in the DM is whether the accounting prescribed
by regulatory agencies should be considered "generally accepted"for purposes of preparing financial statements for the general public. An affirmative answer would, in effect, make the regulatory agencies the standardsetting bodies for financial reporting purposes.

Agenda Topic—Reconsideration of Accounting by Employers for Pensions and Other Retirement Benefits

The FASB has on its agenda the reconsideration of APB Opinion No. 8 on
accounting by employers for pensions and other retirement benefits. As an
initial step, the Board has made available a twelve-page background paper
on the changing "pension environment" and the possible accounting implications. It discusses:

> The employer's pension obligation—what is it? What portion should
> be reflected as a liability?
>
> How should the obligation be recognized over time?

What measurement methods and assumptions are appropriate?

What are the unique accounting problems of multiemployer plans?

There will be no final Statement on this topic for some time; however, as an interim measure, the Board issued Statement No. 36 amending the pension disclosure rules.

AUDITING DEVELOPMENTS

James J. Leisenring

Bristol Leisenring Herkner & Co.
Battle Creek, Michigan

CONTENTS

ABSTRACT

From his perspective as Chairman of the Auditing Standards Board of the AICPA, James Leisenring reviews developments in auditing during 1980 with particular emphasis on the pronouncements of the Auditing Standards Board. Specifically this article reviews:

Reporting On Required Supplemental Information

Reporting On Internal Accounting Control

Audit Evidence

Reporting on Information Occupying The Basic Financial Statements

The Auditor's Considerations When A Question Arises About An Entity's Continued Existence

The Auditor's Standard Report

Review Of A Financial Forecast

INTRODUCTION

Activities of the Auditing Standards Board continue to reflect the impact of the recommendations of the Commission On Auditor's Responsibilities and a continued emphasis on expanding the services provided by the auditor.[1] Projects include consideration of the auditor's standard report, reports on internal accounting control, reviews of financial forecasts and reporting on required supplemental information.

The activities of other standard setting bodies, such as the Financial Accounting Standards Board, the Quality Control Standards Committee and on-going peer reviews conducted on behalf of the SEC Practice Section and the Private Companies Practice Section of the Division for Firms also impact the agenda of the Auditing Standards Board. The Board is especially concerned with the results of peer reviews that may indicate the need for additional or modified guidance for auditors to effectively meet their responsibilities.

Also of special concern is the impact of auditing standards on small entities and the auditor's responsible for such engagements. The Board has undertaken in this past year a significant research effort to determine if there are unique audit problems in engagements involving relatively small enterprises. Particularly, the research is designed to identify problems of implementing the existing auditing standards.

These activities are consistent with the responsibilities of the Board as identified in the charge of the Auditing Standards Board which has been reproduced as Appendix A.

Particular emphasis, in this article, is placed on projects of the Board that have resulted in Statements on Auditing Standards (SAS) or activities that are expected to result in such Statements. The Board also approves issuance of various audit guides typically oriented toward the audit problems of specific industries. Additionally, the staff of the Auditing Standards Division periodically issue interpretations of existing literature. Statements of Position are also issued which interpret the various audit guides.

The following Statements On Auditing Standards were issued by the Board in the fiscal year ending in October of 1980.

> SAS No. 27, "Supplementary Information Required by the Financial Accounting Standards Board"

> SAS No. 28, "Supplementary Information on the Effects of Changing Prices"

> SAS No. 29, "Reporting on Information Accompanying the Basic Financial Statements in Auditor-Submitted Documents"

SAS No. 30, "Reporting on Internal Accounting Control"

SAS No. 31, "Evidential Matter'

SAS No. 32, "Adequacy of Disclosure in Financial Statements"

SAS No. 33, "Supplementary Oil and Gas Reserve Information"

REPORTING ON REQUIRED SUPPLE- MENTAL INFORMATION

The Financial Accounting Standard Board has concluded that certain information is required for financial reporting though not required as a part of financial statements. This distinction, of information that is required but outside the financial statements, has extended the auditor's role to apply procedures and in certain circumstances, reporting on information not included in financial statements.

The auditor has assumed responsibility for other information in documents containing audited financial statements since the issuance in 1975 of SAS No. 8, "Other Information In Documents Containing Audited Financial Statements". That document concluded the auditor should read the other information for material misstatements of fact or material inconsistencies with the financial statements. In issuing SAS No. 27, "Supplementary Information Required by the Financial Accounting Standards Board", auditors were required to make inquiries and apply certain analytical procedures to information required as an essential part of financial reports.

The Board has concluded that SAS No. 27 should be considered a general statement of standards for supplemental information and has issued additional statements giving specific guidance on the nature of inquiries and analytical procedures to be applied in specific circumstances. To date two additional pronouncements have been issued which are to be considered in conjunction with the general standards established by SAS No. 27. The two pronouncements are:

SAS No. 28, "Supplementary Information On the Effects of Changing Prices"

SAS No. 33, "Supplementary Oil and Gas Reserve Information"

Under consideration at the close of the year is a pronouncement on supplementary mineral reserve information as required by Statement of Financial Accounting Standards No. 39. It is not assumed that all requirements for supplementary information will necessitate a separate Statement

On Auditing Standards as the general guidance of SAS No. 27 may be sufficient.

It should be noted that SAS No. 33 also applies to the oil and gas reserve information required by the Securities and Exchange Commission and amends SAS No. 27 to apply to that information, as well as information required by the Financial Accounting Standards Board. Similarly the Auditing Standards Board has exposed for comment, "Interim Information Required By SEC Regulation S-K". If adopted, the document would incorporate the concepts of SAS No. 24, "Review of Interim Financial Information", to apply to interim information presented outside the financial statements as required by the Securities Exchange Commission.

Reporting guidance is given in SAS No. 27 and concludes that the auditor's standard report should be expanded if:

(a)   the information that is required is omitted,
(b)   the auditor concludes that the measurement or presentation of the information departs materially from established guidelines, or
(c)   the auditor is unable to complete the required procedures.

The Auditor's opinion on the basic financial statements is not, however, affected by the three circumstances described. The information is presented outside financial statements and is thus not required by generally accepted accounting principles in the basic financial statements opined on by the auditor.

The Auditing Standards Board continues to study whether it would be preferable to explicitly report on required supplemental information in all circumstances rather than expand the auditor's report for the three exceptions. This issue cannot be resolved until uncertainties concerning the location of the information (outside or inside basic financial statements), whether Section 11a of the Securities Act of 1933 applies to a report on supplemental information, and the nature of the types of information that may become required is somewhat better defined. Some would conclude that the limited procedures required by SAS No. 27 and additional pronouncements do not warrant inviting reliance on the work of the auditor by an explicit report on the information. Other would suggest that absent an explicit report, indicating the responsibility assumed by the auditor, the user may be mislead as to the nature of the auditor's involvement. Resolution of these reporting questions is anticipated in 1981.

REPORTING ON INTERNAL ACCOUNTING CONTROL

Auditors have long reported, in various circumstances, on internal accounting controls. Interest in reports on internal accounting control increased by passage of the Foreign Corrupt Practice Act of 1977 and recent proposals of the Securities Exchange Commission (the SEC). The SEC had proposed that auditors publicly report on internal accounting controls. Significant criticism of the proposals, particularly for cost-benefit reasons, led, in part, to withdrawal of the proposals. Withdrawal of the rule proposals was done acknowledging that the private sector efforts to increase management reports on internal control had been significant. The SEC intends to monitor for three years the experimentation with public reports on internal control, including auditor association with those reports.

The Auditing Standards Board issued in 1980, SAS No. 30, "Reporting On Internal Accounting Control". The Statement provides guidance to auditors when engaged to report on internal accounting controls. The Statement also modifies the definition of a material weakness in internal accounting control by amending Statement On Auditing Standards No. 20, and SAS No. 1, section 320.68.

The SAS distinguishes between the form of report based on a review of the system of internal accounting control for purposes of reporting on the system and a report on internal accounting controls based solely on a study and evaluation of internal accounting control made as part of an audit of the entity's financial statements. The latter report is not a public report and is restricted to use by management, specified regulatory agencies, or other specified third parties. Guidance is also provided for reporting based on a regulatory agencies pre-established criteria and certain other special purpose reports, such as on the design of a system.

It is acknowledged that the study and evaluation of internal accounting control for the purpose of expressing an opinion on the system and the study and evaluation made as a part of an audit of financial statements involve similar procedures. Generally, however, the study and evaluation of a system of internal accounting control in an audit is more limited because in an audit the auditor may decide not to rely on certain controls and thus not test compliance with those controls.

The report used to express an opinion on a system of internal accounting control as illustrated in paragraph 39 of the SAS is as follows:

We have made a study and evaluation of the system of internal accounting control of XYZ Company and subsidiaries in effect at (date).

Our study and evaluation was conducted in accordance with standards established by the American Institute of Certified Public Accountants.

The management of XYZ Company is responsible for establishing and maintaining a system of internal accounting control. In fulfilling this responsibility, estimates and judgments by management are required to assess the expected benefits and related costs of control procedures. The objectives of a system are to provide management with reasonable, but absolute, assurance that assets are safeguarded against loss from authorized use or disposition, and that transactions are executed in accordance with management's authorization and recorded properly to permit the preparation of financial statements in accordance with generally accepted accounting principles.

Because of inherent limitations in any system of internal accounting control, errors or irregularities may occur and not be detected. Also, projection of any evaluation of the system to future periods is subject to the risk that procedures may become inadequate because of changes in conditions, or that the degree of compliance with the procedures may deteriorate.

In our opinion, the system of internal accounting control of XYZ Company and subsidiaries in effect at (date), taken as a whole, was sufficient to meet the objectives stated above insofar as those objectives pertain to the prevention or detection of errors, or irregularities in amounts that would be material in relation to the consolidated financial statements.

It is important to note that the opinion relates to meeting the objectives of internal accounting control and to the prevention or detection of errors or irregularities in amounts that are material to the entities' financial statements. The report would be modified if the study and evaluation discloses a material weakness. "A material weakness in internal accounting control is a condition in which the specific control procedures or the degree of compliance with them, do not reduce to a relatively low level of risk that errors or irregularities in amounts that would be material in relation to financial statements being audited may occur and not be detected within a timely period by employees in the normal course of performing their assigned functions".[2]

This definition results in the identification and reporting of a material weakness irrespective of whether management believes the weakness can be justified by cost-benefit analysis.

If weaknesses that are not considered material are reported together with material weaknesses, the SAS concludes the communication should separately identify any material weakness.

AUDIT EVIDENCE

In August of 1980, the Auditing Standards Board superseded Statement On Auditing Standards No. 1, Sec. 330, "Evidential Matter" with the issuance of Statement On Auditing Standards No. 31, "Evidential Matter". The Statement introduces to auditing literature the broad categories of assertions embodied in financial statements. Acknowledged as assertions are the following:

- Existence or occurrence, Re whether assets or liabilities of the entity exist at a given date and whether recorded transactions have occurred during a given period.
- Completeness, Re whether all transactions and accounts that should be presented in the financial statements are so included.
- Rights and obligations, Re whether assets are the rights of the entity and liabilities are the obligation of the entity at a given date.
- Valuation, Re whether asset, liability, revenue, and expense components have been included in the financial statements at appropriate amounts.
- Presentation and disclosures, Re whether particular components of the financial statements are properly classified, described and disclosed.

The Statement concludes that the auditor, in obtaining evidential matter in support of financial statement assertions, must develop specific audit objectives with respect to each assertion. Additionally, audit procedures are designed to meet each of the audit objectives.

As previously discussed in Sec. 330 of SAS No. 1, the Statement discusses the nature, competence and sufficiency of evidential matter. An auditor, in evaluating evidential matter, considers if specific audit objectives have been met. Thus, the SAS establishes in the literature the relationship between financial statement assertions, specific audit objectives and the related audit procedures. An illustration of this relationship utilizing inventories of a manufacturing company is provided in an appendix to the SAS.

REPORTING ON INFORMATION ACCOMPANY-
ING THE BASIC FINANCIAL STATEMENTS

Different types of information may accompany basic financial statements and the statements may be included in client prepared or auditor submitted documents. Required supplemental information is discussed elsewhere in this article. The distinguishing characteristic of that information, is, however, that it is required to accompany the financial statements. Other information may accompany financial statements that is not required and the form of the document is then of importance. In a client prepared document, SAS No. 8, "Other Information In Documents Containing Audited Financial Statements", provides guidance to the auditor. In auditor submitted documents, SAS No. 30, "Reporting On Information Accompanying the Basic Financial Statement In Auditor Submitted Documents", is applicable.

SAS No. 30 was issued in July of 1980 and supersedes SAS No. 1, Section 610, "Long-Form Reports". When an auditor submits a document containing audited financial statements to his client or others, he has the responsibility of reporting on all information included in the document. The objective of a report on other information is to clearly describe the character of the auditor's examination and the degree of responsibility assumed.

An auditor has no obligation to apply auditing procedures to information presented outside the basic financial statements. However, he may, in certain circumstances, audit such information or may choose to modify the procedures applied in the audit of the basic financial statements to permit expressing an opinion on the information in relation to the basic financial statements taken as a whole. When reporting in the latter circumstances, the measure of materiality is the same as determined for the basic financial statements taken as a whole and procedures would not be as extensive as would be required to express an opinion on the information taken by itself.

An example of a report on information accompanying the basic financial statements in an auditor submitted document is illustrated in SAS No. 29 in paragraph 12 as follows:

> Our examination was made for the purpose of forming an opinion on the basic financial statements taken as a whole. The (identify accompanying information) is presented for purposes of additional analysis and is not a required part of the basic financial statements. Such information has been subjected to the auditing procedures applied in the examination of the basic financial statements and, in our opinion, is fairly stated in all material respects in relation to the basic financial statements taken as a whole.

The auditor would modify that report when he disclaims an opinion on all or part of the additional information. In addition, if the auditor concludes the accompanying information is materially misstated in relation to the basic financial statements taken as a whole, he would modify his report on the accompanying information or refuse to include the information in the document.

If the auditor has modified his report on the basic financial statements he should assess the impact that modification should have on the report on accompanying information. In no circumstances should the report on accompanying information negate or contradict a disclaimer or adverse opinion on the basic financial statements.

THE AUDITOR'S CONSIDERATIONS WHEN A QUESTION ARISES ABOUT AN ENTITY'S CONTINUED EXISTENCE

At the end of 1980, work was concluding on a document which will be issued as a Statement On Auditing Standards giving guidance when a question is raised concerning an entity's ability to continue in existence. When the continued existence of the entity is in question, the auditor is particularly concerned about the recoverability and classification of recorded asset amounts and amounts and classification of liabilities.

A proposed Statement On Auditing Standards, "The Auditor's Considerations When A Question Arises About An Entity's Continued Existence", was exposed for comment in March of 1980. As proposed, the statement reaffirms the presumption that an entity's continued existence is usually assured absent evidence to the contrary. An auditor would not search for evidence supporting the presumption the entity would continue in existence, but may become aware of information that would be contrary to the presumption of continued existence.

In forming an opinion on financial statements, the auditor would consider any contrary information, factors that would mitigate the contrary information, and the plans of management for dealing with the conditions faced by the entity. Contrary information would include information that might indicate potential solvency problems or other types of contrary information not necessarily related to solvency.

After considering the contrary information, the factors that mitigate such conditions, as well as discussing the plans of management for dealing with alternative courses of action, the auditor may conclude that a substantial doubt remains about the entity's ability to continue in existence. When such doubt exists, the auditor must consider whether the recoverability of recorded asset amounts, and the amount and classification of liabilities constitute an uncertainty requiring modification of the standard auditor's report.

When the auditor concludes his report should be modified for such an uncertainty, the report may be illustrated as follows:

> As shown in the financial statements, the Company incurred a net loss of $..... during the year ended December 31, 19X1 and, as of that date, the Company's current liabilities exceeded its current assets by $..... and its total liabilities exceeded its total assets by $..... These factors among others, as discussed in Note X, indicate that the Company may be unable to continue in existence. The financial statements do not include any adjustments relating to the recoverability and classification of recorded asset amounts or the amounts and classification of liabilities that might be necessary should the Company be unable to continue in existence.
>
> In our opinion, subject to the effects of the financial statements of such adjustments, if any, as might have been required had the outcome of the uncertainty about the recoverability and classification of recorded asset amounts and the amounts and classification of liabilities referred to in the preceding paragraph been known, the financial statements referred to above present fairly the financial position of X Company as of December 31, 19X1 and the results of its operations and the changes in its financial position for the year then ended, in conformity with generally accepted accounting principles applied on a basis consistent with that of the preceding year.

When reporting on comparative financial statements, there is disagreement as to whether modification of the report on the current year financial statements should also result in modification of the previously issued opinion on the preceding year. Some would conclude that a substantial doubt about the entity's ability to continue in existence that becomes apparent in the current period should not indicate that such doubt also existed in the prior period and accordingly the previously issued report should not be changed. Others would conclude that the uncertainty concerning the recoverability and classification of recorded asset amounts, or the amounts and classification of liabilities, in the financial statements for the current period because of a substantial doubt about an entity's ability to continue in existence also should extend to the same assets and liabilities in the financial statements of the prior period.

Ultimate resolution of this disagreement will allow for issuance of a final document as there is little other controversy or disagreement with the conclusions in the exposure draft.

THE AUDITOR'S STANDARD REPORT

The Report of the Commission on Auditor's Responsibilities recommended that the form and content of the auditor's standard report be revised. The summary of conclusions and recommendations in the Report stated:

> Evidence abounds that communication between the auditor and users of his work—especially through the auditor's standard report—is unsatisfactory. The present report has remained essentially unchanged since 1948 and its shortcomings have often been discussed. Recent research suggests that many users misunderstand the auditor's role and responsibilities, and the present standard report only adds to the confusion. Users are unaware of the limitations of the audit function and are confused about the distinction between the responsibilities of management and those of the auditor.[3]

The auditing standards board formed a task force in 1978 to study revision of the auditor's standard report. In October, 1979 an issues paper was developed which requested comments on the following five issues.

1) Who is the user of the standard report on audited financial statements?
2) How knowledgeable should we assume the user to be?
3) What should be the format and language of the auditor's report?
4) What topics should the auditor's report cover?
5) What steps other than revision of the report could be taken to improve users' understanding of the auditor's report, the nature of financial statements, and the auditor's role concerning them?

The issues paper also served to announce a public hearing concerning the auditor's standard report which was held in December of 1979. Results of the hearing and comments received from a variety of respondents reaffirmed a basic conclusion of the Commission On Auditor's Responsibilities. Users of the auditor's report do not understand the implications of the auditor's report, the role of the auditor, or the auditor's responsibilities.

In an attempt to improve user understanding of the auditor's report and thus better communicate the role and responsibility of the auditor, modification of the standard report has been proposed in an exposure draft dated September 10, 1980, "The Auditor's Standard Report". In modifying the report as proposed, the following changes would be made to the current form of the report.

- It would add a title containing the word *independent.*
- It would add an assertion that the financial statements are the representations of management.
- It would add a statement that "an audit is intended to provide reasonable, but not absolute, assurance as to whether financial statements taken as a whole are free of material misstatements."
- The word *audited* would replace the word *examined.*
- The scope paragraph would state, "Application of [generally accepted auditing standards] requires judgment in determining the nature, timing, and extent of tests and other procedures and in evaluating the results of those procedures."
- The word *fairly* would be deleted from the opinion.
- It would delete the reference to consistency of application of accounting principles.

It is important to recognize that the seven changes, while they may modify a reader's perception of the auditor's responsibility when reporting on financial statements, have not changed the basic responsibilities of auditors. Auditing standards remain as before and only the vehicle used to report on the financial statements has been modified. The form of the standard report as proposed in the exposure draft is as follows:

(Title-to include the word independent)

(Scope paragraph)
The accompanying balance sheet of X Company as of [at] December 31, 19XX, and the related statements of income, retained earnings, and changes in financial position for the year then ended are management's representations. An audit is intended to provide reasonable, but no absolute, assurance as to whether financial statements taken as a whole are free of material misstatements. We have audited the financial statements referred to above in accordance with generally accepted auditing standards. Application of those standards requires judgment in determining the nature, timing, and extent of tests and other procedures and in evaluating the results of those procedures.

(Opinion paragraph)
In our opinion, the financial statements referred to above present the financial position of X Company as of [at] December 31, 19XX,

and the results of its operations and the changes in its financial position for the year then ended in conformity with generally accepted accounting principles.

The comment period of the exposure draft does not expire until early in 1981 and a final decision on whether the report should be changed, and what changes may be acceptable, will not be made until sometime in 1981. It is apparent, however, that the proposal has prompted significant debate and controversy.

Of the seven proposed modifications, deletion of the word "fairly" from the opinion paragraph is probably the most controversial. The board concluded in proposing the modified report that removal of the word was justified. The document concludes: "The Board believes that it is appropriate to remove the word *fairly* from the phrase "present fairly ... in conformity with generally accepted accounting principles" in the current form of the opinion. The word is subjective and is interpreted differently by different users of the auditor's report. The board believes that the word is unnecessary since the quality of fairness is encompassed in adherence to generally accepted accounting principles and in the qualities about financial statements that are listed in paragraph 4 of SAS No. 5."[4] In addition, "The removal of the word *fairly* from the report does not change the types of judgments that the auditor should continue to make in forming his opinion on the financial statements. Thus, its removal does not change auditors' responsibilities or the level of assurance intended by the opinion."[5] Certain comments received have indicated that this conclusion is not considered acceptable. Some have felt that removal of the word implies an unwarranted level of absoluteness with respect to the financial statements. Still others have concluded that omisson of fairly weakens the opinion as the auditor would appear to only be concerned with the application of accounting rules with no regard to any concept of fairness. In exposing the document for comment, the Board had concluded, however, that, "in forming an opinion that financial statements present financial position, results of operations, and changes in financial position in conformity with generally accepted accounting principles, the auditor does more than determine that there is compliance with accounting pronouncements. He is concerned with the appropriateness of the principles selected in the circumstances, and he must be satisfied that the financial statements are informative and reflect the substance of the conditions or events they purport to represent."[6]

Deletion of a reference to consistency has also met disagreement by people who believe the auditor needs to offer a "red flag" in the auditor's report to help identify changes in the application of accounting principles.

It would be inappropriate for me to speculate on whether the Board will ultimately change the standard auditor's report or if changed what form will be approved. There is a high level of interest by users and preparers of financial statements in this particular project in addition of course to the significant interest of auditors. The comments of all parties will be studied and the final decision on a change will be responsive to concern expressed in the comment letters.

REVIEW OF A FINANCIAL FORECAST

Accountants have long provided a variety of services with respect to prospective financial information. There are also many types of prospective information including forecasts, projections, feasibility studies and budgets. This past year the AICPA Auditing Standards Division issued guidance on one form of service, a review; for a type of information, a forecast. The document issued as a "Guide For A Review of A Financial Forecast" was prepared by the Financial Forecast and Projection task force, but deliberated at length by the Auditing Standards Board. At one point in time the document was considered as a Statement On Auditing Standards, but ultimately it was decided to issue the pronouncement as a guide.

It is important to recognize the significance of the point raised above concerning the applicability of the document. It applies to a financial forecast as defined in "Statement of Position On Presentation and Disclosure of Financial Forecasts, Statement of Position 75-4." A forecast is therein defined as, "an estimate of the most probable financial position, results of operation and changes in financial position for one or more future periods." Also, the document applies only to a review of the forecast and no degree of responsibility assumed by the accountant, other than as a reviewer having applied the procedures required in the document, is acceptable to report as illustrated.

Procedures to be applied in a review of a forecast are acknowledged to be effected by factors, such as, the accountant's knowledge of the business, management's forecasting experience, the forecast period and the forecasting process. Inherent in a review of a forecast is the accountant's satisfaction that key factors effecting financial results have been identified and included in the significant assumptions. The accountant is charged with performing those procedures he considers necessary in the circumstances to enable him to report on whether he believes the assumptions are a suitable basis for management's forecast.

Recognizing that a forecast is defined as "most probable," management must not only conclude what it feels are the most likely set of conditions, but determine what its most likely course of action will be given the conditions. Guidance is provided to assist the accountant in concluding whether significant assumptions are suitably supported. An accountant cannot determine, however, if future results are most probable in part because management's intentions cannot be reviewed.

The form of report for a review of a financial forecast as illustrated on page 22 of the Guide is as follows.

The accompanying forecasted balance sheet, statements of income, retained earnings, and changes in financial position, and summary of significant forecast assumptions of XYZ Company as of December 31, 19XX, and for the year then ending, is management's estimate of the most probable financial position, results of operations, and changes in financial position for the forecast period. Accordingly, the forecast reflects management's judgment, based on present circumstances, of the most likely set of conditions and its most likely course of action.

We have made a review of the financial forecast in accordance with applicable guidelines for a review of a financial forecast established by the American Institute of Certified Public Accountants. Our review included procedures to evaluate both the assumptions used by management and the preparation and presentation of the forecast. We have no responsibility to update this report for events and circumstances occurring after the date of this report.

Based on our review, we believe that the accompanying financial forecast is presented in conformity with applicable guidelines for presentation of a financial forecast established by the American Institute of Certified Public Accountants. We believe that the underlying assumptions provide a reasonable basis for management's forecast. However, some assumptions inevitably will not materialize and unanticipated events and circumstances may occur; therefore, the actual results achieved during the forecast period will vary from the forecast, and the variations may be material.

The report is to be modified and an adverse report issued when the forecast departs from presentation guidelines or the accountant believes one or more significant assumptions are unreasonable. The Guide also provides for reports that indicate scope limitations and concludes you cannot review a forecast when an accountant is not independent.

The Auditing Standards Division continues to work on guidelines for reporting on and presentation of other forms of prospective financial information. Many comment letters on the exposure draft of the guide expressed particular concern for the need to provide guidelines on compilation of projections.

CONCLUSIONS AND A LOOK TO 1981

The Board has a very full and interesting agenda to be completed in 1981. Work must continue on revision of the Standard Auditor's Report and recently, the Board has agreed to consider the implications of reporting on contingencies and uncertainties. Other reporting concerns include involvement with prospective financial information other than forecasts as well as reports on prospective information other than those based on reviews.

Late in 1980 an exposure draft on Audit Sampling was released for comment and work continues on a project concerned with audit risk and materiality. These two efforts portentially will have a significant impact on certain conceptual aspects of auditing.

Results of peer reviews to date indicate that additional guidance is necessary in the standards to require workpapers. An exposure draft on "Workpapers" is expected to be issued early in 1981.

Auditor involvement with information accompanying financial statements remains a concern of the Board. The responsibility for information in management reports will be considered, as well as explicit reporting on required supplemental information.

There has been significant changes in the role of the auditor these past few years. The profession has positively responded to demands for change and a much expanded role. The next few years would appear to be equally challenging if the demands of user groups and clients are to be met.

REFERENCES

1. The Commission on Auditor's Responsibilities: Report, Conclusions and Recommendations, The Commission on Auditor's Responsibilities, New York, New York, 1978.

2. Statement on Auditing Standards No. 30, Reporting on Internal Accounting Control, AICPA, New York, New York, 1980.

3. The Commission on Auditor's Responsibilities: Report Conclusions and Recommendations, page XXIV.

4. Proposed Statement on Auditing Standards, the Auditor's Standard Report, AICPA, New York, New York, 1980.

5. Ibid.

6. Ibid.

APPENDIX A

The Charge of the Auditing Standards Board

The Auditing Standards Board shall be responsible for the promulgation of auditing standards and procedures to be observed by members of the AICPA in accordance with the Institute's rules of conduct.

The Board shall be alert to new opportunities for auditors to serve the public, both by the assumption of new responsibilities and by improved ways of meeting old ones, and shall as expeditiously as possible develop standards and procedures that will enable the auditor to assume those responsibilities.

Auditing standards and procedures promulgated by the board shall:

a. Define the nature and extent of the auditor's responsibilities.
b. Provide guidance to the auditor in carrying out his duties, enabling him to express an opinion on the reliability of the representations on which he is reporting.
c. Make special provision, where appropriate, to meet the needs of small enterprises.
d. Have regard to the costs which they impose on society in relation to the benefits reasonably expected to be derived from the audit function.

The Auditing Standards Board shall provide auditors with all possible guidance in the implementation of its pronouncements, by means of interpretations of its statements, by the issuance of guidelines, and by any other means available to it.

THE INTERNATIONAL FEDERATION OF ACCOUNTANTS: OPERATING PROCEDURES AND CURRENT PROGRESS

Robert N. Sempier

International Federation of Accountants, New York

CONTENTS

ABSTRACT

Mr. Sempier reviews the background of the formation of the International Federation of Accountants (IFAC). He describes its basic objectives and indicates that its overall objective is "the development and enhancement of a coordinated worldwide accounting profession with harmonized standards." He also summarizes IFAC's organizational structure and comments on each of its seven committees—auditing, education, ethics, international congress, management accounting, planning, and regional organization. Primary emphasis is on the International Auditing Practices Committee including a summary of the pronouncements that have been issued and the exposure drafts that were outstanding at the beginning of 1981.

The International Federation of Accountants (IFAC) was formed at the time of the XI International Congress of Accountants held at Munich, Germany in October 1977. It is a new and exciting organization of great significance to the accounting profession worldwide. Progress can be made on a planned basis in an international organization of this type. However, expectations must not be unduly high, since any organization representing seventy-six accountancy bodies from fifty-eight countries must take time to settle and adjust in a variety of ways.

As a result, a work program has been designed for IFAC that is both reasonable in terms of expected accomplishments and at the same time sufficiently aggressive to demonstrate to our membership and other interested organizations that IFAC is moving steadily forward in fulfilling its objective—the development and enhancement of a coordinated worldwide accountancy profession with harmonized standards.

BASIC OBJECTIVES OF IFAC

The basic objectives of IFAC are, in general terms:

1. To work towards international, technical, ethical, and educational guidelines—and towards reciprocal recognition of practice qualifications—through committees and subcommittees of IFAC;
2. To promote and assist in the development of new regional organizations; and
3. To arrange International Congresses of Accountants which will allow members of the profession worldwide to exchange ideas, to keep informed, and to reach broad conclusions on desired common aims.

BASIC OBJECTIVES OF IFAC'S PROGRAM OF WORK

IFAC has developed a twelve-point work program to serve as a guide to IFAC committees and staff over the first five years.
The basic elements of this program are to:

1. Develop statements which can serve as guidelines for international auditing practice;
2. Establish the basic principles which should be included in the code of ethics of any member body of IFAC and to refine or elaborate on such principles as deemed appropriate;
3. Determine the requirements and develop programs for the professional education and training of accountants;
4. Collect, analyze, research, and disseminate information on the management of public accounting practices to assist practitioners in more effectively conducting their practices;
5. Evaluate, develop, and report on financial management and other management techniques and procedures;
6. Undertake other studies of value to accountants, such as a possible study on the legal liability of auditors;
7. Foster closer relationships with users of financial statements including preparers, trade unions, financial institutions, industry, government, and others;
8. Maintain good relations with regional organizations and explore the potential for establishing other regional organizations, as well as assisting in their organization and development;
9. Establish regular communications among the members of IFAC and other interested organizations, principally through an IFAC Newsletter;
10. Organize and promote the exchange of technical information, educational materials and professional publications, and other literature emanating from member bodies.
11. Organize and conduct an international congress of accountants approximately every five years; and
12. Seek to expand the membership of IFAC.

IFAC has established the following committees in an attempt to deal with the foregoing work program:

1. Auditing;
2. Education;
3. Ethics;

4. International Congress;
5. Management Accounting;
6. Planning; and
7. Regional Organizations.

THE INTERNATIONAL AUDITING
PRACTICES COMMITTEE (IAPC)

The aims of this committee are to develop and issue, on behalf of the Council of IFAC, guidelines on generally accepted auditing practices and the form and content of audit reports. It also seeks to promote, with the support of the Council, the voluntary acceptance of such guidelines.

IAPC comprises one nominated member from each of the following countries: Australia, France, India, Mexico, Philippines, the United States of America, Canada, the Federal Republic of Germany, Japan, the Netherlands, and the United Kingdom and Republic of Ireland.

It is my belief that auditing is potentially an international language to a greater extent than are taxation and accounting which tend to be influenced to a greater extent by national legislation. This view was supported by the review of the standards already in force in member countries, for it was apparent that most of the differences were historical in nature with little technical justification.

While it was easy to reach agreement that the committee in its work should aim to use existing literature wherever possible and not seek to "reinvent the wheel," this policy provides difficulties in practice as it remains to be determined which of the differing statements is to be chosen as the basis for drafting the international model.

INTERNATIONAL AUDITING GUIDELINES

Within each country, local conditions govern to a greater or lesser degree the auditing of financial information. Such regulations may be of a statutory nature or take the form of auditing standards or statements issued by professional or regulatory bodies, or possibly a combination of both.

AUTHORITY

It is important to recognize that the International Auditing Guidelines issued by IAPC do not and cannot override regulations governing the audit of financial information in any member country. To the extent that International Auditing Guidelines conform with local regulations on a particular subject, the audit of financial information in that country in accordance with local regulations will automatically comply with the International Auditing Guideline in respect to that subject. In the event of local regulations differing from, or being in conflict with, International Auditing Guidelines on a particular subject, member bodies, in accordance with the constitution of IFAC, should work towards the implementation of the Guideline issued by IAPC, when and to the extent practicable.

SCOPE

International Auditing Guidelines apply whenever an independent audit is carried out, that is, in the independent examination of financial information of any entity, whether profit oriented or not, and irrespective of size, or legal form, when such an examination is conducted with a view to expressing an opinion thereon. International Auditing Guidelines may also have application as appropriate to other related activities of auditors. Any limitation of the applicability of a specific International Auditing Guideline is made clear in the introductory paragraph to that Guideline.

WORKING PROCEDURES

The agreed working procedure of IAPC is to select subjects for detailed study by a subcommittee established for that purpose. IAPC delegates to the subcommittee the initial responsibility for the preparation and drafting of auditing guidelines. The subcommittee studies background information in the form of statements, recommendations, studies or standards issued by member bodies, regional organizations, or other bodies, and as a result of that study, an exposure draft is prepared for consideration by IAPC. If approved by at least three-quarters of the total voting rights of IAPC, the exposure draft is widely distributed for comment by member bodies of IFAC, and to international agencies as IAPC may determine. Adequate time is allowed for each exposure draft to be considered by the persons and organizations to whom it is sent for comment.

The comments and suggestions received as a result of this exposure are considered by IAPC and the exposure draft revised as appropriate. Provided that the revised draft is approved by at least three-quarters of the total voting rights of IAPC, it will be issued as a definitive International Auditing Guideline becoming operative from the date specified in the guideline.

IAPC WORK PROGRAM

The committee is proceeding on schedule with its agreed program of work. To date the committee has issued the following definitive international auditing guidelines.

● *Objective and Scope of the Audit of Financial Statements—* The Guideline describes the overall objective and scope of the audit of financial statements of an entity by an independent auditor.

● *Audit Engagement Letters—*The Guideline takes the position that an auditor's engagement letter to his client is designed to document and confirm his acceptance of the appointment, the scope of his work, and the extent of his responsibilities and the form of any reports.

● *Basic Principles Governing an Audit—*This Guideline describes the basic principles governing an auditor's professional responsibilities which should be exercised whenever an audit is carried out. The basic principles identified involve: integrity, objectivity and independence, confidentiality, skills and competence, work performed by others, documentation, planning, reviewing accounting systems and internal control, obtaining evidence, reviewing financial information, and reporting. It is intended that these basic principles will be the cornerstone in the development of in-depth international auditing guidelines on specific auditing practices.

● *Planning—*This Guideline is the first in a series to amplify on the basic principles governing an audit. It states that adequate audit planning helps to ensure that appropriate attention is devoted to important areas of the audit, potential problems are promptly identified, utilization of assistants is optimized, and the work is completed expeditiously.

Five exposure drafts of proposed International Auditing Guidelines have been distributed to the member bodies for their review and comment.

● *Using the Work of an Other Auditor—*The draft guideline describes procedures a principal auditor should perform when he intends to use the work of an other auditor.

● *Study and Evaluation of the Accounting System and Internal Control in Connection with an Audit—*The draft guideline describes the components of internal control and the audit procedures necessary for the study and evaluation of internal control.

• *Control of the Quality of Audit Work*—The draft guideline provides guidance as to the procedures to be followed with respect to delegation, direction, supervision and review of audit work performed by assistants to control the quality of the audit work performed.

• *Audit Evidence*—The draft guideline describes the nature and sources of audit evidence as well as the methods of obtaining it.

• *Documentation*—The draft guideline describes the form and content of working papers that are needed to support an auditor's opinion. It recognizes that the extent of documentation is a matter of professional judgement, and also provides examples of working papers that are normally obtained or prepared by the auditor.

IAPC also released for exposure a proposed *Standard Inter-Bank Confirmation Request*. The exposure draft is being issued jointly by IAPC and the Committee on Banking Regulations and Supervisory Practices of the Group of Ten major industrialized countries and Switzerland (the Basle Committee). The proposed confirmation request is for use by banks and their auditors when they wish to obtain confirmation of balances or other information with other banks. It is in two parts: a discussion of the audit confirmation process, and the confirmation request which also includes definitions of selected banking terms. The confirmation request is available in English, French, German and Spanish. This project was undertaken by IAPC at the request of the Basle Committee.

Subcommittees have been formed to develop proposed guidelines on the following subjects:
Fraud and Error
Use of the Work of an Internal Auditor
Related Parties
Auditor's Report

RELATIONSHIP WITH IASC

IAPC hopes that it will be able to match the progress made by IASC since its formation in 1973. IFAC has established a close working relationship with IASC and are liaising on a regular basis. It is likely that a substantial part of the future work of IAPC will be interdependent with that of IASC. There will be close cooperation and collaboration to ensure that there is harmony in approach and output.

IAPC–THE FUTURE

It is likely that a period of from three to five years will elapse before the IAPC guidelines match auditing standards already on issue in most developed countries. This period should therefore be regarded as one of establishment and consolidation of its acceptance as the international authority on auditing matters. This acceptance can be achieved only by professional performance by IAPC, with the support of its member bodies and, in turn, by individual members of those bodies.

EDUCATION COMMITTEE

This committee has as its terms of reference the preparation of a survey of the entry requirements, examination or alternative educational requirements, and practical experience requirements, and on the basis of this information to develop guidelines on prequalification, training, and education. It will also review developments with respect to continuing professional education.

On the basis of the information obtained in its initial work the committee has developed two proposed international educational guidelines as follows:

> ● *Prequalification Education and Training*—This proposed guideline sets out in general terms the framework of education and training for all accountants. It recommends that the minimum educational standard for a person to commence a course of study leading to membership of an accountancy body should be equivalent to that which enables entry upon a university degree or equivalent tertiary education course.

> ● *Continuing Professional Education*—This proposed guideline has its purpose to encourage and assist member bodies to develop and evaluate existing CPE programs and to provide them with general guidance in this area. The proposed guideline also recommends that in adopting the concept of CPE for their members, member bodies should have as their objective, the acceptance, as a norm for each member, a minimum of 30 hours per annum, or 90 hours in every three year period, of structured learning activity. The proposed guideline also recommends that in the early years of development member bodies introducing CPE should do so on a system of voluntary monitoring.

In process are guidelines on practical experience, the core of knowledge and tests of professional competence for the qualifying accountant.

ETHICS COMMITTEE

It is well established that ethics and independence are of vital concern to the accounting profession worldwide. This committee has as its terms of reference to develop a suggested minimum code of professional ethics and to promote understanding and voluntary acceptance of such code.

The committee has issued an ethical guideline entitled "Professional Ethics for the Accountancy Profession" which sets forth the principles which should form the basis of detailed ethical requirements by which members of the profession should be guided in the conduct of their professional lives. In addition, the committee is in the process of developing statements of guidance on each of the matters covered in the basic principles for use by the member bodies in preparing or modifying their own ethical requirements.

To date the committee finalized two proposed Statements of Guidance which were approved by Council for distribution to the member bodies for their review and comment. The proposed Statement of Guidance on *Advertising, Publicity and Solicitation* takes the position that advertising by professional accountants is not desirable and that the direct uninvited solicitation of a potential client is contrary to the fundamental principle on ethical behavior set forth in the Ethical Guideline "Professional Ethics for the Accountancy Profession." The proposed Statement of Guidance on *Professional Competence* deals with both the attainment and maintenance of professional competence.

Under development are proposed Statements of Guidance dealing with:

- Confidentiality
- Conditions for acceptance of an assignment previously carried out by another accountant
- Condition for acceptance of an assignment when another accountant is already carrying out work for the same client
- Payment and receipt of commissions and the basis on which fees are to be charged
- Ethics across the border

INTERNATIONAL CONGRESS COMMITTEE

The International Congress Committee has oversight of the plans and arrangements for the XII International Congress of Accountants. The technical program will allow each participant to elect to participate in three discussion groups from among six technical subjects. The following technical subjects will be considered:

    (1)   Image of the Accountant before Society;
    (2)   Education and Training of the Accountant;
    (3)   Accounting Principles;
    (4)   Auditing;
    (5)   Management Accounting; and
    (6)   What can the Accounting Profession do for Government?.

Now that there is a formally constituted international organization, IFAC's committees are expected to take a leading role in the preparation of the background papers to be used as a basis for discussion by participants in small discussion groups.

The XII International Congress will be held in Mexico City from October 10-13, 1982 and will have as its theme "The Accounting Profession—Leadership Opportunities in a Changing World."

MANAGEMENT ACCOUNTING COMMITTEE

It is well recognized that in many countries, management accountants—those not in public practice—equal approximately half of the total members of accounting bodies. IFAC recognizes that those who practice management accounting in industry, government, and elsewhere are vitally affected by auditing and accounting standards. It is for these reasons that IFAC has given significant recognition to this particular area of our membership. As such, preparers and users of financial statements are asked to contribute to the work of the Management Accounting Committee and to assist in advancing standards of management accounting in both developed and developing countries.

The Council of IFAC has placed the onus on this committee to encourage the development of management accounting and to undertake studies of direct concern to management accountants, as well as to stimulate an increased level of competence and thereby improve the standing and recognition of management accountants.

The committee has released to the member bodies, for their review and comment, a paper setting forth the Definition of Management Accounting, the Responsibilities of Management Accountants and Their Interface with External Auditors. The committee has also developed an occasional paper on Management Accounting Concepts for Non-Profit Organizations. A report has been submitted to the Council of IFAC on the responses to a questionnaire sent to the member bodies to determine the extent of involvement by management accountants in their activities. The committee also has in process a bibliography for management accountants and has issued a summary of research projects on management accounting published or in process in selected countries.

REGIONAL ORGANIZATIONS COMMITTEE

The Regional Organizations Committee has developed guidelines for the structure and constitution of new regional organizations. In addition, the committee has finalized a paper outlining the criteria to be used by IFAC for recognition of new regional organizations.

IFAC recognizes three regional organizations:

1. Confederation of Asian and Pacific Accountants (comprises twenty-eight member accounting organizations in twenty-one countries in Asia and the Pacific);
2. Interamerican Accounting Association (comprises twenty-eight member accounting organizations in twenty-two countries in the Americas); and
3. Union Europeenne des Experts Comptables Economiques et Financiers (comprises twenty-seven member accounting organizations in twenty-one countries in Europe).

The committee's terms of reference also require it to see that the recognized regional organizations are invited to:

(1) provide advice on and participate in the program of work of IFAC;
(2) comment on draft guidelines;
(3) make available to each other and to IFAC for their information and use, all studies or statements which they issue;
(4) adopt, as appropriate, and publish to their own members, IFAC's guidelines, statements and studies; and
(5) develop recommendations on communications between IFAC and

regional organizations concerning their respective programs of work.

COUNCIL AND PLANNING

The Council is responsible for implementing the objectives of IFAC and overviews the work of the committees to satisfy itself that IFAC is moving steadily forward in fulfilling its objective—the development and enhancement of a coordinated, worldwide accountancy profession. A Planning Committee composed of six members of Council maintains relevance of IFAC's continuing objectives and contributes to their advancement by reviewing strategy plans and constitutional matters prior to discussion by the Council.

RELATIONSHIP WITH OTHER ORGANIZATIONS

The membership of IFAC now stands at seventy-six accountancy bodies in fifty-eight countries representing over 700,000 accountants in public and private practice, education, and government service. As an organization, we have the capability and responsibility of assuming a greater role on the world scene as initiatives developed by other world organizations that have an impact on the profession. In this regard, considerable emphasis is being given to increasing the visibility and involvement of IFAC in such activities.

CONCLUSION

IFAC's program will be considered by many to be ambitious but with goodwill and effort, IFAC can strengthen and enhance the significance of the role played by the accounting profession worldwide.

1980 REVIEW—SEC DEVELOPMENTS

James J. Doyle

Ernst & Whinney
Chicago, Illinois

Bruce J. Rosen

Ernst & Whinney
Cleveland, Ohio

CONTENTS

ABSTRACT

Messrs. Doyle and Rosen review significant activities of the Securities and Exchange Commission. They address the major efforts aimed at achieving an integrated and simplified registration and reporting system, including changes in the requirements for the annual shareholders report and Form 10–K, and proposals to introduce new registration forms and modify Form 10–Q. And, among other matters, they discuss the SEC's decision not to require management reporting on internal control, releases aimed at helping smaller issuers, the simplification of filings on Form S–8, amendments affecting bank disclosures, and proposed revisions to proxy disclosures of management remuneration.

INTRODUCTION

During 1980, a major thrust of activities by the Securities and Exchange Commission centered on achieving an integrated and simplified registration and reporting system. Sweeping revisions were made to the reporting requirements for the annual shareholders report and Form 10–K to improve disclosures and encourage integration of filings. And proposals were issued to introduce new registration forms that would, in many instances, revise 1933 Act disclosures to permit greater use of previously filed information, and change Form 10–Q to make certain interim disclosures consistent with annual reports.

The SEC decided not to adopt its controversial proposal to require that management and auditors report on the adequacy of a company's systems of internal control, and, for the time being, will rely on the private sector for further initiatives in this area. To help smaller issuers, it adopted rules exempting certain securities sales from registration, and considered requiring less disclosures and reporting for "small" companies. And filings on Form S–8 were made easier by providing for "automatic updating."

Various other matters were addressed, including amendments to rules affecting disclosures by banks and bank holding companies, proposed revisions to proxy disclosures of management remuneration, and postponement of a requirement that oil and gas reserve information be audited.

RULES AND PROPOSALS FOR INTEGRA-
TION OF DISCLOSURE REQUIREMENTS

Major Revisions to Reporting Rules

The SEC has issued Releases 33–6231 through 33–6234 called by Chairman Harold M. Williams "the single most important advance toward achieving the Commission's longstanding goals of an integrated and simplified disclosure system." They were originally proposed in January 1980, and are intended to simplify the registration process by integrating filings under the 1933 and 1934 Acts and further link the annual shareholders report and Form 10-K. The rules are effective for fiscal years ending after December 15, 1980.

Annual report to shareholders. The consolidated financial statements in the annual shareholders report must now comply with Regulation S-X. However, a proposal to require portions of the shareholders report to be incorporated by reference into Form 10-K was dropped, although incorporation by reference still is permitted and, in fact, encouraged.

The shareholders report must include a table of "Selected Financial Data" for five years, replacing the current summary of operations. The table lists such income statement and balance sheet amounts as revenues, income from continuing operations, and total assets. A proposed requirement to state working capital was dropped.

Management's discussion and analysis is now required to focus on financial condition as well as the income statement, and include discussion of liquidity, sources of capital, and results of operations. To encourage more meaningful discussion, the percentage tests have been replaced with general guidelines. All companies also must discuss the impact of inflation. Those not subject to FASB Statement 33 must provide a narrative discussion of the impact of inflation on revenues and income from continuing operations. The safe harbor rules have been expanded to cover any forward-looking information included in management's discussion.

An often-criticized proposal to require that the principal executive, financial, and accounting officers, as well as a majority of the board of directors, sign Form 10-K has been adopted. Chairman Williams stated that "directors will be encouraged to devote the needed attention to reviewing the 10-K, and to seek the involvement of other professionals to the degree necessary to give themselves sufficient comfort."

Uniform financial statement requirements. In annual shareholders reports and most SEC filings, income statements and statements of changes in financial position now are required for three years and balance sheets for two years. Industry segment information has been reduced from five to three years, but differences between the FASB and SEC requirements remain. However, segment data now may be presented in either the financial statements or description of business, and cross-referenced.

In most cases, interim financial information included in registration statements should be in the same detail as that required in Form 10-Q reports.

Regulation S-X. "Compliance notes"—footnote disclosures formerly required in Form 10-K but not in annual shareholders reports—have undergone considerable change. Some have been eliminated altogether. Some will now be included in shareholders reports and thus become *de facto* GAAP. And a few are moved to the Form 10-K schedules (e.g., short-term debt borrowing information and weighted average interest rates). Supplementary income statement information was not moved to a footnote as proposed; it stays in a schedule.

Among the disclosures required by Regulation S-X that now will be included in shareholders reports:

> Reconciliations of tax expense to statutory rates, details of the deferred portions of tax provisions, and foreign and domestic pretax income. (However, the SEC did not adopt most of a proposed expansion of these disclosures.)
>
> Compensating balance information.
>
> Debt maturities for the next five years.

For the time being, the financial statements in annual shareholders reports of banks, insurance companies, and investment companies are not required to include the "compliance notes" required by special articles of Regulation S-X for their respective industries. The SEC will review the special articles in the Regulation dealing with these industries to see what changes, if any, are necessary.

Proposed changes to the property, plant and equipment schedules to show assets by depreciation method, major classification, and weighted average lives were deferred. The presently required information on lives and depreciation methods has been moved from a compliance footnote to a schedule, and the SEC expects to issue a revised proposal in the near future. A number of schedules have been deleted: Bonds, Mortgages, and Similar Debt; Capital Shares; and Warrants or Rights.

Form S-15. This new Form for registering securities issued in connection with certain business combinations was adopted substantially as proposed. It may be used if the issuer qualifies to use Form S-7 and the transaction will have less than a 10% effect on the issuer's sales, net income, assets, and equity. The advantage of Form S-15 is that most of the business and financial information about the issuer can be provided by attaching the annual shareholders report to the prospectus.

Proposed New Registration Forms

As a further step in its efforts to integrate the registration and reporting requirements of the 1933 and 1934 Acts, the SEC, in Release 33–6235, is proposing three new registration forms called, for the time being, Forms A, B, and C. Specific criteria which attempt to measure a company's financial stability and following in the market have been proposed for the use of these forms.

Form A is analagous to Form S-16 and is intended to be used for the same primary and secondary offerings as Form S-16 by companies that are widely followed in the market. It would go beyond Form S-16, which restricts primary offerings to firm commitment underwritings, to include those underwritten on an "all-or-none" basis.

Form A incorporates by reference information in previously filed Forms 10-K, 10-Q, and 8-K (but not proxy materials), but this information need not accompany the prospectus. Although the Form has no general financial statement requirements, statements and other financial information may be required for business combinations, substantial changes in accounting principles, or material dispositions of assets.

The basic Form A prospectus would require only information about the securities being registered, plus such summary information as a brief description of the business and material features of the offering, a five-year table of selected financial data, and disclosure of any material dilution to shareholders' interests involved.

Form B is intended to be used by a second tier of financially stable companies that already report under the 1934 Act. The basic Form B prospectus would be much the same as Form A, except that financial statements and other information similar to that in the annual shareholders report and

Form 10-Q would have to be included or else the latest copies of those two documents should accompany the prospectus.

Form C would be basically a simplified Form S-1, available to first-time registrants and other companies not eligible for Forms A or B. It would require the basic information called for by Form A, plus all that required by all Items of Regulation S-K. All financial statements required by Regulation S-X also would be required. Under certain circumstances, information on directors and executive officers, beneficial owners and management, and management remuneration could be incorporated by reference from Form 10-K.

Proposed Revisions to Form 10-Q

Form 10-Q is used to report a company's quarterly financial results to the SEC. As an adjunct to its integrated disclosure project, the SEC, in Release 33-6236, now is proposing a number of changes in Form 10-Q. The objectives of these changes are: incorporation in Regulation S-X of uniform instructions governing interim financial statements; consistency of certain disclosures as between interim and annual reports; and encouraging integration of Form 10-Q with quarterly reports sent to shareholders.

The requirements for the form and content of interim financial information, which will also apply to "stub periods" in registration statements, would appear in a new Article 10 of Regulation S-X. They are essentially the same as the current Form 10-Q rules, except for the specifying that footnote disclosures of material uncertainties and contingencies be repeated even without any significant change since the last annual report.

Management's discussion in quarterly reports would be expanded to parallel the recent changes to annual report rules by covering material changes in the company's financial condition as well as in operations. Deleted would be the requirement to compare current-quarter with previous-quarter operations. At their option, companies could incorporate by reference in Form 10-Q the financial information section of their quarterly shareholder reports. The safe-harbor rules would be expanded to cover forward-looking information in Part I.

Part II would delete present Items 3, 5 and 6 (Changes in Security for Registered Securities; Increase in Amount Outstanding of Securities or Indebtedness; and Decrease in Amount Outstanding of Securities or Indebtedness).

If there is a review of interim financial information by independent accountants, and the registrant states that it was made, the accountants' report is required as an exhibit. No longer required, however, would be a statement on adjustments and disclosures proposed by the independent accountants.

Adoption of Uniform Exhibit Requirements

One result of the standardization of exhibit filing requirements for the SEC's most frequently used registration and reporting forms is to eliminate some exhibits. Others are revised, and requirements for all of them are consolidated in a new Item 7 of Regulation S-K. The requirements, adopted in Release 33-6230, cover 1933 Act Forms S-1, S-2, S-7, S-8, S-11, S-14, S-15 and S-16; and 1934 Act Forms 10, 8-K, 10-Q and 10-K.

One new exhibit is required, relating to so-called "SAS 24 reports" (an accountants' report on a review of unaudited interim financial information). As it is no longer necessary for an accountant to file a consent when a SAS 24 report accompanies or is incorporated into a registration statement (because rules were adopted in ASR 274 which excluded accountants from Section 11 liability for a SAS 24 report), there must now be a letter from the accountants acknowledging use of the report in the statement. Also, if there is a fourth-quarter change in accounting principles, a letter from the independent accountants must be filed as an exhibit with Form 10-K, commenting on the preferability of the change. This letter was previously not required until filing of the first Form 10-Q of the next fiscal year.

RELEASES RELATED TO THE FOR- EIGN CORRUPT PRACTICES ACT

Withdrawal of Proposed Rules for Management Reporting on Internal Control

The SEC has decided not to adopt rules for public reporting on internal controls. Chairman Williams cited "the responsiveness of the private sector" as the key reason for withdrawing the proposal. He said he expects this voluntarism to continue, and he will look to registrants and independent auditors to further develop means of reporting on and monitoring systems of internal control. During the next three years, the SEC will review the private sector's progress and reconsider the need for rules.

Last year, the Commission proposed that companies report on whether they had adequate internal accounting controls—one of the key requirements of the Foreign Corrupt Practices Act (FCPA). Also, independent auditors would have had to review and report on management's statement.

Approximately 950 comment letters were received, most in strong opposition because they felt the proposed reporting would not be cost effective and for a variety of other reasons.

In contrast to its original proposal, the SEC, in ASR 278, now recommends that voluntary management reports cover more than internal accounting controls (e.g., management's responsibility for the financial statements). While management reports would include an assessment of the internal control system, they would not have to discuss whether the company is in compliance with the FCPA. The SEC also recommends reporting as of a point-in-time, such as the fiscal year end, rather than for the entire year as originally proposed.

Chairman Williams believes reviewing internal controls "will almost necessarily involve the participation of the outside auditor," and the SEC supports the concepts of the recently adopted Statement on Auditing Standards No. 30 on auditor reporting on internal control, which does not extend to immaterial weaknesses.

ASR 278 also includes a discussion of the Commission's views about compliance with the internal control provisions of the FCPA.

Impact of Anti-Bribery Provisions

In Release 34-16593, the SEC asked registrants and other interested parties what impact the anti-bribery provisions of the FCPA have had on overseas operations of American businesses. Those provisions prohibit registrants from paying or promising to pay anything of value to a foreign official, political party, or any candidate for foreign political office in order to wrongfully obtain or retain business.

Specifically, the business community and its professional advisors were asked to provide details of experiences which might substantiate the claim that U.S. corporations are having difficulty conducting their business as a result of the anti-bribery provisions. The SEC was not seeking comments on the impact of the Act's accounting and recordkeeping provisions.

Policy on Enforcement Actions

The Department of Justice has initiated a review procedure where, in response to a request setting forth the facts and circumstances of a proposed transaction, it will state its enforcement intentions under the anti-bribery provisions of the FCPA. Release 34-17099 announces that the SEC, although not participating in this review procedure, will not bring an enforcement action alleging violations of the anti-bribery provisions with respect to a transaction cleared with the Justice Department before May 31, 1981. The Commission hopes this policy will encourage companies to avail themselves of the Justice Department review procedure, and help compile data to permit an assessment of the law's impact.

RELEASES AIMED AT SMALLER ISSUERS

Exemption of Certain Securities Sales from Registration

Primarily directed to helping small businesses raise capital, but applicable to all qualifying offerings, is a new SEC rule, issued in Release 33–6180, exempting certain securities sales from 1933 Act registration requirements. Rule 242 allows offerings of up to $2,000,000 in a six-month period, reduced by securities sales under other exemptions such as Regulation A. Purchasers are limited to 35 in number, except for certain "accredited persons." That category includes institutional purchasers (banks, insurance and investment companies, and most employee benefit plans), executive officers and directors of the issuer, and persons who invest $100,000 or more and pay with cash or a note due within 60 days.

No specific information need be supplied to these accredited persons. Other purchasers should be given information similar to that required in Form S-18 (includes description of the securities being offered, brief description of the business, financial statements for two years, and remuneration for executive officers and directors), except that only the most recent fiscal year's financial statements need be audited. If the company files periodic reports under the 1934 Act, this provision of the Rule may be met by furnishing the latest Form 10-K and any subsequent reports filed under the Act (e.g., Forms 10--Q, proxy statements, Forms 8-K), plus the information on the use of proceeds and distribution required in Form S-18.

An initial filing of Form 242 (notice of sale) should be made within 10 days after the sale begins and a final filing within 10 days after it ends. There are resale limitations, including a two-year holding period. Rule 242 applies only to U.S. and Canadian companies. It cannot be used by investment companies or those primarily engaged in oil and gas or mining operations.

Reduced Reporting for Smaller Issuers

In addition, the SEC, in Release 34-16866, asked for views on whether less disclosure and reporting should be required of small registrants—and, if so, how "small" should be defined. No specific changes have been proposed pending study of comments on this "concepts" release.

The Commission acknowledges that the cost of complying with periodic reporting requirements (e.g., Forms 10-K, 10-Q, and 8-K) is relatively much higher for smaller companies than for larger ones. It notes, too, that these reports may have only limited value. Analysts, the principal users of Forms 10-K and 10-Q, do not generally follow small companies, and individual investors get their information chiefly from annual shareholders reports.

So the SEC is considering a classification system for small companies that would reduce disclosure requirements. The chief concerns are whether the small companies would benefit from such a system; whether it would sufficiently protect investors; and by what criteria "smaller" issuers should be defined (e.g., by total assets, revenues, net worth, number of shareholders, or any combination of those). The Commission suggests an initial category of companies in the $2- to $3-million asset range (about 1,000 companies in this range are SEC registrants). It points out that the $1-million asset threshold for registration under the 1934 Act was established back in 1964, and inflation alone could justify raising that figure to between $2 and $3 million.

Other questions the SEC asked are: Should the nature and frequency of periodic reports be modified? How might reduced reporting requirements affect small companies' ability to gain interest in their securities? And what changes should be made in the proxy requirements for small companies?

NEW RULES FOR FILING ON FORM S-8

The SEC announced in Release 33-6190 that original filings on Form S-8 —the registration used for security offerings under employee stock option, stock purchase, and similar benefit plans—will now become effective automatically 20 days following filing and post-effective amendments will become effective immediately upon filing. Affirmative action by the SEC is no longer required.

Release 33-6202 provides that "automatic updating" of Form S-8 will now be available for many companies. Only general information about the benefit plan that usually does not change (e.g., how to purchase securities) is to be included in Form S-8 itself. Filing required periodic reports (Forms 8-K, 10-K, 10-Q, 11-K, proxy statements) would provide the updated financial information about the sponsoring company and the plan.

For many companies, this new SEC procedure eliminates annual post-effective amendments to Form S-8, provided they include all the necessary data in their other periodic reports. In particular, this may mean expanding the table of outstanding options, in either the annual report to shareholders or the proxy statements.

Annual post-effective amendments of Form S-8 still will be required where the plan must provide annual data to employees to evaluate available investment choices—a not uncommon feature.

REVIEW OF REGISTRATION STATEMENTS GUIDES

The SEC, in response to a recommendation from its Advisory Committee on Corporate Disclosure, is evaluating the effectiveness of the Guides for Preparation and Filing of Registration Statements and Reports under both the 1933 and 1934 Acts. While the Commission requested comments in Release 33-6163 on all aspects of the Guides, the following are among the points singled out for special consideration:

Ways of making the Guides more useful to registrants and the resulting disclosures more meaningful for investors.

The cost of compliance.

Any portions no longer necessary because of changes in laws, Commission rules or regulations, financial practices, or securities market requirements.

NOTIFICATION OF LATE FILING

Companies thinking they might miss an SEC filing deadline should take note that extensions no longer are available for most Exchange Act reports, such as Forms 10-K and 10-Q. Rather, amended rules announced in Release 33-6203 require a registrant to notify the Commission, no later than one business day after the due date of the report, why the report or any part of it will not be filed on time. Extensions could still be requested for 8-K filings of financial statements of acquired businesses.

Relief is available if the registrant's notification discloses that the late filing cannot be avoided without unreasonable effort or expense. Provided such notification and necessary exhibits were properly filed, the report will be considered timely if it is filed within prescribed time limits after the normal due date (15 days for annual reports; five days for quarterly reports).

Companies failing to file timely reports (or notifications under the new rules) are not eligible to use Forms S-7 or S-16 (short-form registrations).

Other possible consequences for violations are enforcement actions or suspension of trading.

AMENDMENTS AFFECTING DISCLOSURES BY BANKS

Article 9 of Regulation S-X for banks and bank holding companies has been amended by ASR 276 to reduce the details required about loans to directors and to require more disclosure about deposits of $100,000 or more.

Disclosure of ordinary course of business loans which otherwise meet materiality criteria (generally $500,000 or 2½% of stockholders' equity, whichever is less, per "person") to directors (and their affiliates) who are not executive officers or principal holders of equity securities may now be limited to the aggregate amounts of loans.

Disclosure is now required of the aggregate amount of time certificates of deposit and other time deposits in denominations of $100,000 or more, in both domestic and foreign categories. Interest expense on time certificates of deposit exceeding $100,000 remains a disclosure requirement, but a proposal to disclose interest expense for other time deposits in these denominations was not adopted.

In addition, in Release 33-6221, the SEC has amended its Guides 61 and 3, "Statistical Disclosure by Bank Holding Companies." The result, the Commission believes, will be to reduce the volume of disclosure, improve the quality, and lower the cost of compliance. Although the Guides are not Commission rules, they specify statistical disclosures expected by the Division of Corporation Finance in the "description of business" portion of registration statements, Form 10-Ks, and certain other filings by banks and bank holding companies.

Significant is a general reduction in the number of years covered from five to three, except for disclosures about loan portfolios and related loss experience. The period is even shorter—two years—for small banks or bank holding companies (those with assets under $200 million or net worth of $10 million or less). And the disclosures are no longer required for interim periods subsequent to the latest fiscal year—unless the information or the trends it suggests change materially.

Among other amendments adopted are certain clarifications, such as the SEC staff's position that these Guides apply to foreign registrants and their policy of allowing registrants to present a narrative discussion of the risk elements in loan portfolios instead of a breakdown of the allowance for loan losses. "Non-accrual loans" will be a new category in the disclosure of nonperforming loans, and only loans 90 days past due, rather than

60, will require disclosure. And other requirements have been modified to conform to, or eliminate duplication of, Article 9 of Regulation S-X.

RECONSIDERATION OF RATIO OF
EARNINGS TO FIXED CHARGES

The SEC is considering changing—or even dropping—the ratio of earnings to fixed charges that it requires in various filings when significant amounts of debt are being offered or are outstanding. It is used, with variations, by bond rating agencies, financial analysts and some investors to judge a company's ability to meet interest or preferred dividend payments and to identify trends.

When a pro forma ratio is required, it usually is computed conservatively. That is, a proposed debt offering would be assumed to have been outstanding during the past fiscal year, and interest thereon incurred, but no benefits from the proceeds are assumed. Making the pro forma ratios consistently lower than actual results was cited as misleading by an AICPA task force a few years ago.

While no specific proposals are made at this time, comments were requested in Release 33-6196 on a number of issues including:

Should the ratio be cash-oriented so investors could judge whether principal payments would be made on time? If so, how?

What additional items should be included in fixed charges?

In what ways could the pro forma ratio be improved?

PROPOSED CHANGES IN FORMAT
FOR REMUNERATION DATA

After a major revision and several interpretations, the SEC, in Release 33-6210, has again proposed to revise the information included in companies' management remuneration tables in proxy statements. The most important change would affect employee stock option and similar plans. Currently, the difference between the fair market value and the option price of securities received under these plans is included in the remuneration table. This causes year-to-year compensation to fluctuate widely because such amounts are reported when the options are exercised. The proposal would remove amounts related to stock options from the table. And information on stock options that accompanies the table would be expanded to include information for stock appreciation rights and phantom stock plans.

Other changes to the table would involve defined benefit pension plans and future compensation. Contributions to defined benefit plans would no longer be reported as part of compensation (they may now be excluded if the portion related to individuals in the table cannot be readily computed and that fact is disclosed). And the rules would clarify that the terms of future compensation payment plans have to be described, supplementing the amounts in the table, such as vested contributions to a profit sharing plan.

REVIEW OF INTERNAL CONTROL IS AN AUDIT SERVICE

An accounting firm's review of a company's system of internal accounting control for adequacy, or of the company's own procedures for determining the adequacy of its system, is an audit service for purposes of computing the proxy statement disclosures required by ASR 250. This is the position now taken in SEC Staff Accounting Bulletin 38, which says these reviews need not be done "in conjunction with the examination of financial statements" to be so classified. But services provided with a view to designing new internal control systems or redesigning existing ones remain nonaudit services.

POSTPONEMENT OF AUDIT REQUIREMENT
FOR OIL AND GAS RESERVE INFORMATION

The SEC, in ASR 277, has postponed the audit requirement for oil and gas reserve information. The postponement covers both reserve quantity and reserve value disclosures. It will continue until the SEC decides whether oil and gas producers' primary financial statements should reflect Reserve Recognition Accounting.

In addition, companies now may present the reserve information outside of the financial statements, rather than in an unaudited note or integral schedule as previously required. This, in effect, gives the Regulation S-X reserve disclosures the same status as the FASB-required disclosures of reserve quantities and changing prices.

INCLUSION OF FASB STATEMENT 33 DISCLO-
SURES IN REGISTRATION STATEMENTS

In Release 33-6201, the SEC proposes that companies required to provide supplementary inflation disclosures under FASB Statement 33 would include such data in registration statements. The FASB rule extends only to the annual shareholders report and Form 10-K.

The existing safe harbor rule for projections would be expanded to cover these changing prices disclosures, including voluntary presentations of the Statement 33 data and descriptions of the effects of changing prices as part of management's discussion and analysis. The proposal makes clear that the SEC does not intend to extend the Statement 33 disclosures to those registrants not otherwise covered.

AUDITOR REPORTING ON FASB
SUPPLEMENTARY INFORMATION

Auditors now are required to report only when they are aware that the supplementary information required by the FASB on oil and gas reserves and changing prices is wrong or when they have not been able to apply certain procedures to it. However, the SEC wants the accounting profession to develop standards for independent auditors to explicitly report on unaudited supplementary information. This request met earlier resistance because of uncertainty about whether such reports, resulting from a review but not an audit, would be subject to "experts" liability under the 1933 Securities Act. Now, under proposed SEC rule amendments issued in Release 33-6208, auditors would be protected from that liability with respect to reports on reviews of supplementary information on oil and gas reserves and changing prices.

SEC STAFF REPORTS ON CORPO-
RATE ACCOUNTABILITY STUDY

The SEC's staff, after studying corporate accountability and governance issues for three years, has issued a "Staff Report on Corporate Accountability." It calls on corporations to strengthen their accountability through a wide range of actions and warns that if they do not, new SEC rules or legislation may be necessary.

One recommendation is for more companies to adopt formal procedures for considering shareholder nominations to boards of directors. The staff also urges the SEC to seek comments on issues related to corporate political activities and the shareholder proposal process, including whether special requirements are needed for disclosure of political expenditures. The staff opposes requiring more disclosure of "socially significant information," but says the SEC should rule that shareholders must be told where to obtain copies of significant environmental compliance reports filed by the company.

SEC REPORTS ON THE ACCOUNTING PROFESSION

The SEC's third annual Report on the Accounting Profession should be read, according to Chairman Harold M. Williams, "as an interim assessment and endorsement of the profession's current activities and commitment for the future." Besides focusing on initiatives of the profession to establish meaningful self-regulation, it covers certain corporate governance issues, as well as the accounting and auditing standard-setting processes.

Most public companies have established audit committees to strengthen auditor independence, the report acknowledges. But it expresses concern that some committees may not be reviewing the scope and results of outside auditors' work—a function the Commission regards as essential. Also, the Commission reaffirms its belief that management should report on a company's internal accounting controls, and that auditor involvement may be needed.

The Commission continues to believe that accounting and auditing standards should be established by the private sector, subject to Commission oversight. In particular, it supports the FASB's conceptual framework project and its Statement No. 33 on changing prices, although noting that progress has been slow.

FORECASTS BY MANAGEMENT AND THE INDEPENDENT ACCOUNTANT'S REVIEW

Philip E. Fess

Arthur Andersen & Co., Alumni Professor of Accountancy,
University of Illinois, Urbana-Champaign

CONTENTS

ABSTRACT

Professor Fess reviews the present state of the art in 1) the prepara-
tion of financial forecasts by management and 2) the independent ac-
countant's review and reporting on such forecasts. He comments on
practices presently being followed by management in the preparation
of forecasts and discusses the SEC's prior and current position with re-
spect to the presentation of forecast data in documents filed with it. He
then covers the AICPA's pronouncements dealing with the presentation
of financial forecasts, discusses the difference between management's
and the independent accountant's responsibilities with respect to such
data and concludes by reviewing the "Guide for a Review of a Financial
Forecast" which deals with the independent accountant's procedures in
the review of a forecast as well as the appropriate reporting thereon.

INTRODUCTION

Over the past decade there has been increasing interest by analysts, investors, potential investors, and others in the financial community in financial

forecasts prepared by the management of public corporations. Although independent accountants have traditionally resisted reviewing and reporting on these financial forecasts, there is growing pressure on them to do so to enhance their reliability and usefulness.

The purpose of this chapter is to present a resume of the present state of the art in (1) the preparation of financial forecasts by the management of public corporations and (2) the independent accountant's review and reporting on such forecasts.

MANAGEMENT'S CURRENT PRACTICES
IN PRESENTING FORECAST DATA

Many companies regularly prepare financial forecasts for internal use. However, there is no current requirement for this type of forecast data to be made available to the public by the management of public corporations nor on the dissemination of this data.

Traditionally projected data made available to the public has varied widely from company to company. In many cases, forecast data released by management to the public has been restricted to revenues, net income, and earnings per share—the three items considered to be of prime interest to analysts and others. Very few companies have made public complete statements of financial forecasts. In addition, the dissemination of forecast information has not been uniform. Some companies have divulged such data publicly on a formal basis, for example, in their annual reports, while others have made the forecast data available on an informal basis, usually to security analysts and to selected investors.

Although not all accountants and users agree, many believe that the general purpose external financial statements could be made more useful if reliable and complete financial forecasts of financial position and income and changes in financial position were made available to all interested parties on a uniform basis. To this end, more and more companies are experimenting with complete financial forecasts and seeking means to overcome the problems associated with their preparation.

The problems associated with the preparation of financial forecasts involve many considerations including the possible competitive damage that might accrue to issuers from the disclosure of management projections; the concern that the user will place undue reliance on the forecasts in making decisions; the fear that inaccurate financial forecasts might damage the company's image, or perhaps worse, lead to legal liability; the ability of management to prepare reliable forecasts; the fear that pressure for management to achieve target forecast figures could adversely affect management performance; etc. Of the concerns, perhaps the primary concern centers on the issue of forecast reliability.

A number of research studies have examined management forecasts in an attempt to determine their accuracy. Although these studies have been too few to serve as the basis for drawing definite conclusions about forecast accuracy, "empirical studies consistently reveal that forecast accuracy does not appear to be impressive."[1]

Without debating the problems that have been raised in connection with the preparation of forecasts, "There is an increasing demand for forecasted information."[2] Even the Securities and Exchange Commission, which historically has prohibited the inclusion of forecast data in reports filed with it, has recently taken steps to encourage companies whose securities are publicity-traded to report financial forecast data. The S.E.C.'s current position is to encourage management to provide forecast data to the public on a timely and uniform basis. Such a position reflects the Commission's concern that currently not all parties have equal access to forecast data.

The American Institute of Certified Public Accountants neither advocates nor discourages the publication of financial forecasts. However, because such forecasts are being disseminated, the AICPA has provided authoritative guidelines for their preparation. In addition, it recently issued an audit guide covering the independent review and reporting on financial forecasts.

The Financial Accounting Standards Board considered the desirability of including financial forecasts as part of the published financial statements at a public hearing on December 3 and 4, 1979 on its conceptual framework project on "Reporting Earnings." The views expressed at that hearing supported the Board's statement made in its discussion memorandum, that served as a basis for the hearing, that there would be no requirement for forecast data at this time.

THE S.E.C. POSITION

Perhaps the main stimulus for the current trend in providing more forecasts by management can be traced to the efforts of the S.E.C. Prior to 1972, the Commission's policy had been to prohibit the presentation of forecasts in reports filed with it. In late 1972 the Commission announced that it was reassessing that policy. Public hearings were held on the subject late in 1972 and on February 2, 1973, the Commission released a "Statement by the Commission on the Disclosure of Projection's of Future Economic Performance." The statement set forth the S.E.C.'s conclusion that, while it did not intend to require registrants to disclose forecast data, it would propose to permit companies that meet certain standards to include projection data in its filings with the Commission. In Securities Act Release No. 5581, dated April 28, 1975, the Commission proposed amendments to its filing procedures that would implement its February 2, 1973 statement.

The Commission received several hundred letters from businessmen, independent accountants, and users of financial information opposing its April 28, 1975 release. These comments, which raised legal, disclosure, and technical issues, contributed in great measure to the Commission's withdrawal of many of its proposals in Securities Act Release No. 5699, dated April 23, 1976. However the Commission indicated that it would not object to disclosure of projections in filings with it if they were made in good faith and on a reasonable basis, and provided that they were presented in an appropriate format and were accompanied by sufficient disclosures for users to make their own judgments. In other words, although the S.E.C. made the filing of forecast data voluntary, those who choose to do so should meet certain standards.

In November 1978 the Division of Corporation Finance of the S.E.C. issued a guide on the disclosure of projections in Commission filings. The Commission, in addition to indicating that it was encouraging companies to disclose management projections in its filings, stated that it was encouraging companies to make such disclosures in other public reports.

To further encourage the issuance of projections, the S.E.C. adopted a safe-harbor rule effective for projections published after July 29, 1979. The rule limits a company's liability for cases when the forecast turns out to be wrong provided the forecast was made in good faith and on a reasonable basis. The rule also places the burden of proof on the plaintiff for assertions that the forecast was not prepared on a reasonable basis and in good faith. Both the guide and the safe-harbor rule require the company to correct forecasts that become inaccurate because of subsequent events or discoveries that the company knows or should know about as long as the forecasts continued to be relied upon.

The safe-harbor rule does not relate to a complete set of forecast statements. Instead, the rule covers the reporting of the following projected financial data: revenues, income or loss, earnings or loss per share, and other financial items such as dividends, capital expenditures and capital structure. However, some accountants have expressed the opinion that complete statements may be necessary to meet the S.E.C.'s good faith disclosure standards.[3]

The S.E.C. has thus taken several positive steps, ranging from the issuance of guides to adopting a safe-harbor rule, to encourage the reporting of financial forecasts by the management of public corporations. The Commission is closely monitoring the results of its current policy in an effort to improve the financial forecast information that is made available to investors and the public.

THE A.I.C.P.A. POSITION

The American Institute of Certified Public Accountants has issued two documents containing guidance on the preparation of financial forecasts: (1) *Guidelines for Systems for the Preparation of Financial Forecasts,* Management Advisory Services Guideline 3, March 1975, issued by the AICPA Management Advisory Services Division and (2) *Statement of Position on Presentation and Disclosure of Financial Forecasts,* Statement of Position 75–4 August 1975, issued by the AICPA Accounting Standards Division.

While neither advocating nor discouraging the publication of financial forecasts, the MAS guide was prepared because forecasts are being issued and accordingly there was a need for authoritative guidelines for the development of a system for their preparation. The guide sets forth the following ten formal recommendations for developing forecasting systems:

1. *Single most probable result.* A financial forecasting system should provide a means for management to determine what it considers to be the single most probable forecasted result. In addition, determination of the single most probable result generally should be supplemented by the development of ranges or probabilistic statements.
2. *Accounting principles used.* The financial forecasting system should provide management with the means to prepare financial forecasts using the accounting principles that are expected to be used when the events and transactions envisioned in the forecast occur.
3. *Appropriate care and qualified personnel.* Financial forecasts should be prepared with appropriate care by qualified personnel.
4. *Best information available.* A financial forecasting system should provide for seeking out the best information, from whatever source, reasonably available at the time.
5. *Reflection of plans.* The information used in preparing a financial forecast should reflect the plans of the enterprise.
6. *Reasonable assumptions suitably supported.* The assumptions utilized in preparing a financial forecast should be reasonable and appropriate and should be suitably supported.

7. *Relative effect of variations.* The financial forecasting system should provide the means to determine the relative effect of variations in the major underlying assumptions.
8. *Adequate documentation.* A financial forecasting system should provide adequate documentation of both the forecast and the forecasting process.
9. *Regular comparison with attained results.* A financial forecasting system should include the regular comparison of the forecast with attained results.
10. *Adequate review and approval.* The preparation of a financial forecast should include adequate review and approval by management at the appropriate levels.

The MAS guide did not include recommendations on the format for the forecast nor address itself to the disclosures required for the financial forecast statements. The guidelines for the preparation and disclosure of forecast data are set forth in A.I.C.P.A. Statement of Position 75–4. The statement requires the presentation of certain minimum information—revenues, gross profits, net income or loss, gains and losses from disposal of segments and from extraordinary items, earnings or loss per share, and other significant anticipated changes in financial positions. An illustration of the format indicating this minimum data is presented in the statement and is as follows:

XYZ Company, Inc.

Summarized Financial Forecast
Year Ending December 31, 19X3
(in thousands)

	Forecasted	Comparative Historical Information	
	(19X3)	*(19X2)*	*(19X1)*
Sales	$101,200	$91,449	$79,871
Gross Profit	$ 23,700	$21,309	$19,408
Income tax expense	$ 3,400	$ 3,267	$ 2,929
Net income	$ 4,500	$ 3,949	$ 3,214
Earnings per share (in dollars)	$ 4.80	$ 4.14	$ 3.37
Significant anticipated changes in financial position Working capital provided by operations	$ 7,300	$ 6,371	$ 5,395

Proceeds from long-term borrowing	$ 6,000	$ 4,100	$ 2,000
Dividend payment (per share 19X3: $1.50; 19X2: $1.35; 19X1: $1.00)	$ 1,400	$ 1,288	$ 954
Additions to plant and equipment	$ 4,400	$ 2,900	$ 2,114
Increase in working capital	$ 2,700	$ 1,876	$ 1,944

See accompanying Summary of Significant Forecast Assumptions and Summary of Significant Accounting Policies.

It should be noted that the summarized financial forecast data includes a summary of significant forecast assumptions and a summary of significant accounting policies (not illustrated here, but illustrated on pages 72–75). Also the illustration includes, in addition to data for the forecast year, comparative historical data for the past two years.

Although the guidelines require only certain minimum specified data, they *recommend* that a financial forecast be presented in the format of the historical statements and that all significant assumptions should be disclosed. In other words, the recommended forecasts would include a balance sheet and statements of income and changes in financial position. The guide includes an illustration of these statements as follows:

XYZ Company, Inc.

Forecasted Statement of Income and Retained Earnings
Year Ending December 31, 19X3
(in thousands)

	Forecasted (19X3)	Comparative Historical Information	
		(19X2)	(19X1)
Net sales	$101,200	$91,449	$79,871
Cost of sales	77,500	70,140	60,463
Gross Profit	$ 23,700	$21,309	$19,408
Selling, general and administrative expenses	$ 15,100	$13,143	$11,014
Operating income	$ 8,600	$ 8,166	$ 8,394
Other income (deductions):			
Miscellaneous	$ 1,700	$ 964	$ (308)
Interest expense	(2,400)	(1,914)	(1,943)

	(700)	(950)	(2,251)
Income before income taxes	$ 7,900	$ 7,216	$ 6,143
Income taxes	3,400	3,267	2,929
Net income for the year	$ 4,500	$ 3,949	$ 3,214
Retained earnings at beginning of year	$ 10,500	$ 7,803	$ 5,543
Dividend (per share 19X3: $1.50; 19X2: $1.35; 19X1: $1.00)	(1,400)	(1,288)	(954)
Retained earnings at end of year	$ 13,600	$10,464	$ 7,803
Earnings per share (in dollars)	$ 4.80	$ 4.14	$ 3.37

See accompanying Summary of Significant Forecast Assumptions and Summary of Significant Accounting Policies.

XYZ Company, Inc.

Forecasted Statement of Changes in Financial Position
Year Ending December 31, 19X3
(in thousands)

	Forecasted	Comparative Historical Information	
	(19X3)	(19X2)	(19X1)
Sources of working capital			
Net income	$ 4,500	$ 3,949	$3,214
Depreciation which does not use working capital	2,800	2,422	2,181
Working capital provided by operations	$ 7,300	$ 6,371	$5,395
Proceeds from long-term borrowings	6,000	4,100	2,000
	$13,300	$10,471	$7,395
Uses of working capital			
Dividend	$ 1,400	$ 1,288	$ 954
Current installations and repayment of long-term debt	2,600	3,800	2,300
Additions to plant and equipment	4,400	2,907	2,114
Increase in other assets	2,200	600	83
Increase in working capital	2,700	1,876	1,944
	$13,300	$10,471	$7,395

Changes in components
of working capital
Increase (decrease) in
current assets

Cash	$ 1,500	$ (334)	$1,017
Accounts receivable	2,500	1,430	483
Inventory	100	3,995	1,431
Other	1,700	350	62
	$ 5,800	$ 5,441	$2,993

Increase (decrease) in current
liabilities

Notes payable bank	$ 1,500	$ 100	$ (300)
Accounts payable and accrued expenses	1,100	1,686	846
Current installments of long-term debt	400	958	342
Other	100	811	161
	$ 3,100	$ 3,565	$1,049
Increase in working capital	$ 2,700	$ 1,876	$1,944

See accompanying Summary of Significant Forecast Assumptions and Summary of Significant Accounting Policies.

XYZ Company, Inc.

Forecasted Balance Sheet
December 31, 19X3
(in thousands)

	Forecasted	Comparative Historical Information	
	(19X3)	*(19X2)*	*(19X1)*
Assets			
Current assets			
Cash	$ 3,300	$ 1,862	$ 2,196
Accounts receivable (net)	14,900	12,438	11,008
Inventory	27,000	26,932	22,937
Other	3,500	1,813	1,463
Total current assets	$48,700	$43,045	$37,604

Property, plant and equipment	$30,900	$26,915	$22,832
Less accumulated depreciation	17,300	14,912	11,314
Net property, plant and equipment	$13,600	$12,003	$11,518
Other assets	5,000	2,714	2,114
	$67,300	$57,762	$51,236

Liabilities and Stockholders' Equity
Current liabilities

Notes payable to bank	$ 4,600	$ 3,100	$ 3,000
Accounts payable and accrued expenses	12,300	11,193	9,497
Current installments of long-term debt	4,400	3,968	3,010
Other	900	925	114
Total current liabilities	$22,200	$19,186	$15,621
Long-term debt, excluding current installments	$20,100	$16,700	$16,400
Stockholders' equity:			
Capital stock	$11,400	$11,412	$11,412
Retained earnings	13,600	10,464	7,803
Total stockholders' equity	$25,000	$21,876	$19,215
	$67,300	$57,762	$51,236

See accompanying Summary of Significant Forecast Assumptions and Summary of Significant Accounting Policies.

XYZ Company, Inc.

Summary of Significant Forecast Assumptions
for the Year Ending December 31, 19X3

This financial forecast is management's estimate of the most probable financial position, results of operations and changes in financial position for the forecast period. Accordingly, the forecast reflects management's judgment based on present circumstances of the most likely set of conditions and its most likely course of action. The assumptions disclosed herein are those which management believes are significant to the forecast or are key factors upon which the financial results of the company depend. Some assumptions inevitably will not materialize, and unanticipated events and circumstances may occur subsequent to February 17, 19X3, the date of this forecast. Therefore, the actual results achieved during the forecast period will vary from the forecast and the variations may be material. The comparative historical information for 19X1 and 19X2 is extracted from the company's financial statements for those years, presented on pages xx to xx. The financial statements should be read for additional information.

a. **Sales.** The overall market for the company's products has grown over the past five years at an average rate of 2 percent above the actual increase in gross national product, and the company's market share has remained steady at 14 to 16 percent. Selling prices generally increase in line with cost of manufacturing, and gross margins are not expected to vary from experience over the past five years. Sales are forecasted to increase 5 percent from 19X2 (which is 2 percent above the Department of Commerce Bureau of Economic Analysis estimate of the rise in gross national product in the forecast period), with a market share of 15 percent and unit prices increased to cover forecasted increased cost of manufacturing.

b. **Cost of Sales**
Materials. Materials used by the company are expected to be readily available, and the company has generally used producer associations' estimates of prices in the forecast period to forecast material costs. A significant exception is copper, a major raw material whose market has been disrupted by political events in certain principal producer countries. The company expects to be able to assure sufficient supplies, and estimates that the cost of copper will increase by 22 percent over 19X2. However, due to the uncertainties noted above, industry estimates of copper prices in the forecast period range from 15 to 30 percent above 19X2 prices. A variation of five percentage points in the actual increase above or below the assumed increase would affect forecasted net earnings by approximately $485,000.
Labor. The Company's labor union contract, which covers substantially all manufacturing personnel, was negotiated in 19X2 for a three-year period. Labor costs are forecasted based upon the terms of that contract.

c. **Plant and Equipment and Depreciation Expense.** Forecasted additions to plant and equipment, $4,430,000, comprise principally the regular periodic replacement of manufacturing plant and vehicles at suppliers quoted estimated prices, and do not involve any significant change in manufacturing capacity or processes. Depreciation is forecasted on an item-by-item basis.

d. **Selling, General and Administrative Expenses.** The principal types of expense within this category are salaries, transportation costs, and sales promotion. Salaries are forecasted on an individual-by-individual basis, using expected salary rates in the forecast period. Pension cost is planned to be funded and is forecasted based upon its direct relationship to payroll cost. Transportation costs comprise principally the use of contract carriers; volume is forecasted based upon the sales and inventory forecasts (including forecasts by sales outlet), and rates are forecasted to rise by 16 percent over 19X2, based upon trucking industry forecasts. Sales promotion costs are expected to increase in line with the consumer price index (assumed to rise 9 percent based on the mean of [several widely-used estimates]) and, except for a special campaign budgeted at $750,000, are expected to remain at a level similar to 19X2. The level of other expenses is expected to remain the same as in 19X2, adjusted for the assumed inflation rate of 9 percent.

e. **Bank Borrowing and Interest Expense.** The forecast assumes that the company will obtain an extension of existing short-term lines of credit at terms comparable to those in effect in 19X2 (2 percent over prime rate). The company used the arithmetic mean of [three widely used estimates] of bank prime rate during the forecast period (ranging from 8 percent to 10 percent) to estimate prime rate at 9 percent. The company forecasted additional long-term borrowings of $6,000,000, and has entered into preliminary negotiations with its bankers for this financing. The borrowings are principally to fund purchases of plant and equipment and additions to other long-term assets and will be secured by such additions. Based upon the preliminary negotiations, the company has assumed that the additional long-term financing will bear interest at 10 percent.

f. **Income Taxes.** The provision for income taxes is computed using the statutory rates in effect during 19X2, which are not expected to change, and assuming investment tax credit on qualifying investments at rates in effect in 19X2.

g. **Dividend.** The company's normal dividend policy is to pay out the previous year's dividend increased to the extent of at least one-third of any increase in profits over the previous year, provided the board of directors considers that the company's cash and working-capital position will not be adversely affected. The dividend has been forecasted at $1.50 per share, assuming an increased payout over 19X2 of one-third of the excess of forecasted net earnings for the year ending

December 31, 19X3, above those of 19X2. The board of directors wishes to emphasize that the actual payment of the forecasted dividend is contingent both on the achievement of the forecasted net earnings and on the company's future cash position and, accordingly, is not assured.

Summary of Significant Accounting Policies

The financial forecast has been prepared on the basis of the generally accepted accounting principles expected to be used in the historical financial statements covering the forecast period, which are the same as those used to prepare the historical financial statements for the year ended December 31, 19X2, as described in the Summary of Significant Accounting Policies on page xx.

It should be noted that the A.I.C.P.A. guidelines require the disclosure of more data than do the S.E.C. guidelines and recommend the presentation of a complete set of forecasted statements.

MANAGEMENT VS. INDEPENDENT ACCOUNTANT'S RESPONSIBILITIES

Since management controls and directs the operations of the business, it is in the best position to develop the underlying assumptions for the forecast, to install the system, and to take responsibility for the preparation of the forecast itself. However, management may enlist the assistance of outside parties in preparing the forecast. In many cases, the independent accountant may provide such assistance; but management must assume the responsibility for the forecast data.

It should be noted that the A.I.C.P.A. Code of Professional Ethics prohibits the independent accountant, who has assisted management in the preparation of the forecast, from permitting his name to be used in conjunction with the forecast in a manner that may lead to the belief that he vouches for the achievability of the forecast.

THE INDEPENDENT ACCOUNTANT'S REVIEW AND REPORT ON FINANCIAL FORECASTS

In October 1980 the A.I.C.P.A. Financial Forecasts and Projections Task Force of the Auditing Standards Board issued "Guide for a Review of a Financial Forecast." Although the issuance of the guide is not to be interpreted to mean that the A.I.C.P.A. is recommending an independent review and report on the forecast, the guide does provide guidance in these areas.

The guide indicates that the objective of a review is to provide the independent accountant with a basis for reporting (1) whether the forecast was prepared in accordance with the recommendations in A.I.C.P.A. Statement of Position 75–4 and (2) whether the underlying assumptions provide a reasonable basis for management's forecast. The guide sets forth procedures for the independent accountant to consider in evaluating the forecast assumptions and the forecast itself.

The guide indicates that the independent accountant's standard report on a review of a financial forecast should include:

1. An identification of the forecast information presented by management and a description of what it is intended to represent.
2. A statement that the review was made in accordance with applicable AICPA guidelines for a review of a financial forecast and a brief description of the nature of such a review.
3. A statement that the accountant assumes no responsibility to update the report for events and circumstances occurring after the date of the report.
4. A statement regarding whether the accountant believes that the financial forecast is presented in conformity with applicable AICPA guidelines for presentation of a financial forecast and whether the underlying assumptions provide a reasonable basis for management's forecast.
5. A caveat regarding the ultimate attainment of the forecasted results.

The form of the standard report suggested in the guide is as follows:

The accompanying forecasted balance sheet, statements of income, retained earnings, and changes in financial position, and summary of significant forecast assumptions of XYZ Company as of December 31, 19XX, and for the year then ending, is management's estimate of the most probable financial position, results of operations, and changes in financial position for the forecast period. Accordingly, the forecast reflects management's judgment, based on present circumstances, of the most likely set of conditions and its most likely course of action.

We have made a review of the financial forecast in accordance with applicable guidelines for a review of a financial forecast, as established by the American Institute of Certified Public Accountants. Our review included procedures to evaluate both the assumptions used by management and the preparation and presentation of the forecast.

We have no responsibility to update this report for events and circumstances occurring after the date of this report.

Based on our review, we believe that the accompanying financial forecast is presented in conformity with applicable guidelines for presentation of a financial forecast, as established by the American Institute of Certified Public Accountants. We believe that the underlying assumptions provide a reasonable basis for management's forecast. However, some assumptions inevitably will not materalize and unanticipated events and circumstances may occur; therefore, the actual results achieved during the forecast period will vary from the forecast, and the variations may be material.

It should be noted that the S.E.C. does not require the report of an independent accountant for forecasts filed with it. However, to encourage the independent accountant to review and report on forecasts, the safe-harbor rule mentioned previously applies to the independent accountant's report.

CONCLUSION

Practices for management reports on financial forecasts and the review of such forecasts by the independent accountant are in a state of evolution. The past few years can be characterized as ones of increasing experimentation. As more experience is gained with the disclosure of forecasts and their review by independent accountants, a more standard reporting and review practice is likely to appear.

NOTES

1. Davis L.S. Chang, "Measuring and Disclosing Forecast Reliability," *The Journal of Accountancy*, May 1977, p. 77.

2. Alvin J. Mentzel and Leonard J. Proscia, "Financial Forecasts—State of the Art", *The CPA Journal*, July 1980, p. 12.

3. *Ibid*, p. 16.

THE CASE FOR INTERNATIONAL
ACCOUNTING STANDARDS

J.A. Burggraaff

Chairman,
International Accounting Standards Committee

CONTENTS

ABSTRACT

In this article the author, chairman of International Accounting Standards Committee, reviews current international developments in the area of accounting standards.

He concludes that the question what should be the contents of company reports is still open-ended. The author examines the various purposes accorded to financial statements, and concludes that a common base can be found in the assumption of public accountability.

This public accountability requires financial statements to be understandable for outsiders, which in its turn requires accounting standards. The author examines some problems in developing standards both nationally, and internationally, and the merits of standardsetting by law and in the private sector.

After a discussion of the efforts made by E.E.C., O.E.C.D. and U.N.O., an outline is given of some recent developments in I.A.S.C., designed to broaden its base and to liaise with supranational bodies.

> *Compliance with statements of I.A.S.C. cannot be achieved by the accountancy profession alone. Support from others is needed, especially from international enterprise.*

When looking around in the world, and analysing addresses of distinguished individuals, a lot of confusion about the subject of Company Reporting becomes apparent. Evidently, there are different schools of thought on the subject, heavily influenced by national environments, national customs, national legal systems.

PURPOSE OF COMPANY REPORTING

When trying to abstract from any preconceived ideas, I think that company reports can be looked upon as a vehicle for communication. They convey information, provided by the preparer to the reader (or user) either on a voluntary basis or because of obligations by law or contract. By communicating facts, and at times policies or ideas behind the facts, the preparer enables the reader to make his own assessments in connection with whatever his interests are. At the same time, by communicating information, the preparer may expose himself to disadvantages. He may elicit criticisms on his behaviour; he may adversely affect the attitudes of customers or of suppliers of merchandise, labour and money; he may harm his competitive position. The fundamental problem of reporting is, what information should be included in order to enable the reader to make proper assessments without causing undue damage to the enterprise.

Clearly, there is no single answer to this question, to-day or in the near future. Factors influencing the contents of company reports are amongst others:

— Economic or social importance of the enterprise. The smaller a business is, the less likely that outsiders are interested in its operations. In general, insiders have other means to acquire information and do not have to rely on the annual report. But concerning a large business there may be many interested outsiders. Apart from size the field of operations may be important. Multinational enterprises often are considered to have an impact that is different from that of a company, operating within its own country only.

— The groups of users identified as having a legitimate interest in the enterprise. Usergroups which exist in one society may be absent in another society. This is the case e.g. with environmentalists, whose prominence is increasing in the industrialized western world, but have no strong voice in many developing countries.

    — The perceived needs of user groups. Having identified user groups as "stakeholders" does not mean that their information needs have been identified. It depends largely on circumstances, in what respect they wish to make assessments, and what data are relevant to those assessments.

    — The need of the enterprise to gain public confidence. For some enterprises it is essential, that the public perceives them as operating with due regard to the interests of all concerned. This confidence is enhanced by openness in supplying information, and by being responsive to demands for more. On the other hand, some enterprises may be operating in an environment, in which public confidence is considered to be of minor importance.

    — The power structure in a society. It is natural for everybody, including preparers of company reports, to supply information to the extent he feels will be beneficial to his own ends. This observation is not meant to cast a doubt on the honesty of reporting, it only points to the limitation an individual is inclined to apply on disclosures. Users, on the other hand, may wish to receive information, that enterprise is not inclined to provide voluntarily. In that situation it depends on the balance of power between preparers and users, in political and in other terms, whether information will be supplied or withheld. If users are relatively strong, enterprise will have to provide more information than if users are relatively weak.

The question what the contents of company reports should be, therefore is in my opinion open-ended. In different environments, at different times, the answer is different for different enterprises. Maybe this will be one of the conclusions which come out of the studies on a Conceptual Framework, currently undertaken in U.S.A. and in other countries.

PURPOSE OF FINANCIAL STATEMENTS

Financial statements, or annual accounts, form part of the company report. In virtually all countries there is a requirement, or a custom, to prepare such statements. Format and contents have been influenced strongly by national traditions that may vary widely from one country to another. At closer examination it appears that these variations stem from differences in view what the primary purpose of financial statements is.

Of these differences in view the following have some relevance to this study.

— Primary purpose is to protect creditors. In most countries it is customary for enterprises to be organised as a legal entity with limited liability. That implies that claims from creditors can be satisfied only by the proceeds of assets, and the financial statements should show to what extent liabilities are covered by assets. Often the law requires financial statements to be published, in order to be available for creditors. In many countries the law contains rules on format, disclosure and valuation in order to prevent misleading of creditors. The intention to protect creditors puts solvency into focus, and encourages conservatism in the preparation of financial statements.

— Primary purpose is to protect shareholders. Management employs funds provided by the shareholders, and runs the business at their risk. By submitting financial statements, management should account for its stewardship, and report what profit, if any, became available for distribution. In many countries the law requires submission of financial statements to shareholders, and gives shareholders the right to approve or disapprove. The intention to protect shareholders puts distributable profit into focus, and encourages prudence instead of conservatism in the preparation of financial statements, so as to present a "true and fair view."

— Primary purpose is to serve the taxcollector. Although in no country it is stated bluntly that way, it is a fact that in many countries the interest of the revenue service is considered to be overriding by requiring that financial statements are prepared in conformity with income-tax-regulations. In case tax-regulations require or allow accounting treatments which are at variance with treatments considered to be appropriate for reporting purposes, one cannot but expect that financial statements will be prepared in the best interest, taxwise, of the enterprise, irrespective of whether the financial statements are misleading for reporting purposes or not. In other countries it is accepted that financial statements for reporting purposes are not identical to those for tax purposes, and that accounting treatments adopted for reporting purposes may vary from those adopted or prescribed for tax purposes.

The intention to serve the taxcollector encourages accounting policies that subordinate information-needs of other users to the desire to avoid paying taxes in excess of what is strictly necessary.

— Primary purpose is to protect investors on securitymarkets. In order to enable individuals to make proper investment decisions, reliable and timely information on financial position and results should be made available. This implies that financial statements should be published in a higher frequency than annually. It implies too a strong demand for information to be comparable between one enterprise and another.

The intention to protect investors encourages the application of uniform accounting policies, established by an authoritative body; the question whether or not that application results in a true and fair view for the individual enterprise, moves into secondary position.

In more recent studies of the subject[1] the primate of any single user-group is rejected. Instead, it is contended that there is a public accountability: the purpose of financial statements is to provide information on financial position and performance of an enterprise to all who have, or may have, a stake in the enterprise. This contention—which I personally endorse—raises two questions.

— Do the different user groups have something in common to such an extent that financial statements are equally useful to all of them? Clearly, the answer is "no" as far as the tax collector is concerned. As said before, tax considerations may render financial statements useless for all other users. Therefore, tax authorities should be convinced that their needs can, and should be, satisfied by financial statements prepared for tax purposes only, and that they should abstain from interference with financial statements prepared for reporting purposes. As to all other users I believe the answer is "yes," although it may occur that a detail of special interest to a specific user group is not appropriate for inclusion in a general purpose report. The reason for my belief is, that all user groups have in common the need to know the real facts, to the extent accounting is capable of presenting reality in financial statements. By including details in the financial statements, user needs can be met that may exist in the various groups with various degrees of urgency. Adequate information therefore will answer all needs that are common, and several needs that are felt by some but not by all users.

— Does this contention of public accountability provide a sufficiently clear basis to determine how financial statements should be drawn up, and what their contents should be? In my view the answer is affirmative. The subject of accountability is defined: the position and performance, in financial terms, of the enterprise. And basically there is sufficient clarity as to type and detail of information to be supplied: the information required to enable a reader with reasonable skills to make a fair assessment of that position and performance. This is not to say that there are no problems left. On the contrary, many issues both of measurement and of disclosure still have to be solved, and debates on those issues may continue for a considerable period of time. But the terms of reference for such debates have been established.

NEED FOR ACCOUNTING STANDARDS

In the preceding paragraphs I did not discuss for what reasons readers want to be informed about financial position and performance of the enterprise. Those reasons may be very different, and depend upon the type of relationship between the reader and the enterprise. But whatever the reasons are, the common interest is to know what financial position and performance really are, and general purpose reports should be directed to that common interest.

As said before, company reports, and thus financial statements, are meant to be a vehicle of communication. They should be prepared in such a way that they are understood properly. Whoever wants to make himself understood, has to express himself in a common language. And in preparing financial statements that means that both in measurement and in disclosure common rules, that is: standards, should be applied.

As a matter of fact, no accountant can prepare financial statements unless he has standards at his disposal, either acquired during his professional education, or developed by himself, or derived from other sources. To a certain extent the standards of every professional are identical. Examples are found in the less sophisticated or controversial areas, such as accounting for cash or for accounts receivable. But in quite a few situations different accountants may come up with different answers. Reasons for such differences are, amongst others:

— Conditions of economic life, and consequently business practices, are not the same in all parts of the world. Some practices which are fairly frequent at one place, are unknown at another place or have in that environment a quite different meaning.

— Even in the same environment certain economic phenomena may be viewed upon and interpreted in different ways, resulting in different accounting treatments.
— Traditions have a strong influence on practice. Many preparers, and their accountants, look to tradition for guidance, and are hesitant to respond to new demands or to take a fresh look at existing or emerging types of business transactions.

Differences in accounting treatments, for whatever reason, are confusing the reader, and make financial statements unintelligible even when the accounting policies applied are spelled out in detail. Distrust or even suspicion of deceit, may be aroused in this way. What the public needs is information that is clear, understandable and straightforward.

The need is there within a country, but internationally as well. Today many companies have an impact on capital markets, on commodity markets, on labour, on prosperity in other countries. Readers of the financial statements of a company may be found in other countries, with different environments than prevailing in the country of the company's domicile. The existence and application of accounting standards, national and international, will enhance the understandability of financial statements for all readers.

On the side of the preparers there is a need for international standards as well, because of their wish to communicate information that is properly understood everywhere. But there is a second reason. Companies that are operating in several countries, or that have their shares quoted on foreign stock-exchanges, have to comply with the accounting standards prevailing in those countries. Since more and more countries are in the process of formulating accounting standards, more and more often we meet situations in which national standards show differences in requirements, or even are in conflict with each other. These divergences are most unfortunate for internationally operating enterprises, especially if standards of measurement are concerned.

PROBLEMS OF STANDARDSETTING

In the view of many, the primary purpose of accounting standards is to reduce the number of options for the accounting-treatment of a certain transaction, event or condition. I do not share that view. Differences in accounting treatment may stem from tradition, or from arbitrary choices, or from personal preferences. Clearly, if that is the case, there is no reason for different treatments, and standardsetters should opt for one single treatment. On the other hand, differences may stem from differences in economic meaning. The form of transactions or events may be identical, but that does not necessarily imply that their substance is identical as well. An overseas operation may have the form of a subsidiary. But that does not mean that all subsidiaries have the same economic meaning for the parent, and therefore should be accorded the same accounting treatment. Their substance may be an extension of the parent's operation, or alternatively an independent operation.

All timing differences between accounting income and tax income are identical in form. But their economic significance may vary with the number of years which will elapse before they are expected to reverse.

Therefore in my view, accounting standards should be designed in such a way that:

— differences in accounting treatment which are not founded on differences in economic significance are eliminated;

— circumstances which require different accounting treatments are specified in sufficient detail to give guidance to preparers and users, what treatment is appropriate under what circumstances.

Inevitably the process of setting standards is performed in a field of tension between on one hand the ideals of excellent reporting in the minds of sophisticated accounting theorists and on the other hand the necessity to recognize the views of preparers in order to get sufficient acceptance in practice. Neither of them is unequivocal. There are disagreements between accounting theorists as to what constitutes ideal reporting. And there are diverging views amongst preparers as to what is useful and practical. Standards therefore have a tendency to come out somewhere in between: somewhat ahead of current practice, and somewhat behind ideal practice. Because of this field of tension it is contended by some that standardsetting is a political exercise. There may be a point in this contention, when the issue is debated what information a company should disclose to what interestgroups. But as far as financial statements are concerned, I do not support that contention. What we are after is a reliable presentation of reality, to the extent accounting is capable of providing such presentation. There may be different, and well-founded opinions how truth can best be achieved or approximated. But debating these issues is not a political process, in which the interests of certain groups, or political aims, have a role to play.

In the field of setting international standards there is an additional problem: how to harmonize the requirements, formulated by national standardsetting bodies, into international standards. Obviously this effort for harmonisation will be slow and difficult. Study is needed in order to recognise the specific conditions prevailing in different countries and environments. Discussions are needed in order to develop solutions which properly respond to those conditions. A willingness to compromise is needed in order to agree upon the solution to be adopted as international standard.

The willingness to compromise can only be hoped for, if the process of setting international standards is truly international. It would be wrong if some countries would try to impose their own standards on the whole world. Such an effort would ignore the national differences in business environments and economic conditions, and is bound to come up with the wrong answers. International harmonisation requires exchange of views and a mutual understanding of the economic and social environment in different countries.

Probably it will not be possible to achieve world-wide uniformity in standards of measurement and disclosure at one stroke. It is more probable that the process will run through a number of levels, being:

— Compatibility. National standards should not prohibit an accounting treatment, which is required in another country. As long as national standards are not identical, compatibility would mean, that all national standards should allow options. In the international field this may be seen as an advantage, but in the national field it certainly is not.

— Comparability. National standards should be in harmony to such an extent that the outcome would not be significantly different, whether the standards of country A or of country B are applied. This level requires, that in measurement-issues national standards are substantially the same, whereas standards of disclosure may vary. Some argue that comparability can be achieved by supplementary statements. In that view the primary statements are prepared in accordance with national standards, and supplementary information is submitted on the base of international standards. Although in certain cases this may be an acceptable solution for a transitional period, it is my opinion that this practice would not achieve the goal of international accounting standards.

— Uniformity. National standards should be the same in all countries. This would require, that all specific circumstances which may prevail in various countries or types of industry are properly dealt with in international standards.

WHO SHOULD SET ACCOUNTING STANDARDS?

There are two traditions in the world to be found. One is, that the law specifies what rules have to be applied in preparing financial statements. The other is, that professional accountants, or the accountancy profession does so.

The advantage of enactment is, that compliance with regulations is mandatory, and that all subjects have to comply. The disadvantages of standardsetting by legislation are:

- Legislation is a slow process. It takes considerable time to change laws. And change are necessary in order to respond to new developments in business and in environment.
- Legislation is inflexible. The law is not a proper instrument to reflect the shades in conditions which may require a different accounting treatment.
- Legislation has a tendency to set requirements at a minimum level, since compliance is mandatory for all companies. Therefore, legislation is not encouraging the improvement of reporting practices.
- Political and tax considerations may influence the legislative process.

The advantages of standardsetting by the profession are:

- Professional accountants are experts on the subject. They have a thorough knowledge of business environment, of business practices, and of accounting treatments to deal with them.
- Professional accountants are independent from both preparers and users. They can express an unbiased opinion how transactions, events and conditions can be best accounted for in order that financial statements give a true reflection of financial position and performance.

As a disadvantage of standardsetting by the profession it is sometimes pointed out that the interested parties, preparers and users, are not involved in the process. Accounting standards, so the argument is, are too important to be left to the experts; either they pursue unrealistic ideals, or their thinking is suspected to be too closely associated with that of business.

In some countries this argument has caused a change in the structure of the standardsetting machinery. Sometimes the standardsetting process has been transferred from the profession to a separate and independent body. Sometimes the machinery has been enlarged so as to include representatives of preparers and users either on a consultative basis or as participants on the decisionmaking level.

It is my view that—without endorsing the argument—we have to recognise that involvement of preparers and users is beneficial to the acceptance of and compliance with standards, and that therefore such involvement should be welcomed.

Although there are, between countries, marked differences in the machinery of setting standards, I believe gradually a pattern is emerging. That is, that the law provides a broad framework, concentrating on minimum-requirements of disclosure. And that a standardsetting body, in which professionals, preparers and users play a role, elaborates how the requirements of the law should be met, and how measurement-issues should be dealt with.

WHO SHOULD SET INTERNATIONAL ACCOUNTING STANDARDS?

At this level too, there is the alternative: law or profession. In order to set international standards by law, there has to be a supranational authority.

So far, there is only one supranational authority with powers in the area of company reporting, the European Economic Community, comprising Belgium, Denmark, France, Ireland, Italy, Luxemburg, Netherlands, United Kingdom, Western Germany, and as from January 1st 1981: Greece. The objective of the Community is to create a common market, with a free flow of merchandise, capital and labour within its boundaries. In pursuing this objective, company-law is being harmonised, and that includes harmonisation of legislation on company-reporting.

In 1978 the E.E.C. issued the 4th directive,[2] which has to be incorporated in national law of the memberstates before a certain date. This 4th directive deals with company accounts. A 7th directive, dealing with consolidated accounts, is in preparation. These directives will have a tremendous impact on company reporting, within and outside the E.E.C., and contribute considerably to harmonisation. At the same time, it must be noted that these directives do not achieve complete uniformity:

— The 4th directive remains silent on a number of pressing issues, especially in the field of measurement, e.g. translation of foreign currencies, retirement-benefits, deferred taxation, leasing.
— The 4th directive leaves options on a number of issues, either to the memberstates or to the companies.

>   – The 4th directive had to accept that in some memberstates the
>   financial statements are affected by tax-regulations.

The E.E.C.-directives will result in more detailed laws in the memberstates. But supplementary work by standardsetting bodies has not become
superfluous and, since there is no standardsetting body on Community-
level, the bodies in the memberstates will have to continue their exercise.

Another supranational body is the Organization for Economic Cooperation and Development (OECD), consisting of 24 countries, and comprising
virtually all industrialized Western nations. OECD is addressing issues of
international investment, and in that context formulated, for voluntary
adoption, guidelines for the conduct of multinational enterprises. This
document,[3] published in 1976, and slightly modified in 1979, contains
guidelines on disclosure of information, for the enterprise as a whole.
It does not deal with issues of measurement.

In 1979 a working-group evaluated what had been achieved by these
guidelines. The group concluded, that clarification was needed, how
certain terms (such as sales, or operating results or new capital expenditure) should be interpreted. The group further concluded, that OECD
should energise the process of international harmonisation of accounting
standards, without becoming a standardsetting body in itself.

A new working group is now in the process of preparing clarifications,
after consultation with representatives of business, labour and the accountancy profession. As far as known, the group did not yet come up with
solutions how to energise international harmonisation.

A third supra-national body is United Nations Organisation (U.N.).
One of the commissions, that on Transnational Corporations, is examining
practices of multinational enterprises in host countries, especially in
developing countries. A group of experts, appointed by the Commission,
reported in 1977 on accounting and reporting by transnational corporations. The Report[4] contains lists of minimum items to be disclosed in
general purpose reports, financial and non-financial, for the enterprise as
a whole, and for the individual member-company. The Report does not
deal with issues of measurement. In that respect reference is made to the
work being carried out by IASC. In his introduction the U.N. Secretary-
General proposed "to work towards an intergovernmental agreement on
international reporting standards. Under such an agreement each Government would commit itself to take legislative and other action which would
make mandatory the application of the relevant international reporting
standards, by transnational corporations domiciled in its country and by
individual member companies domiciled in its country even though the
parent company of the group is domiciled in a different country."

The Commission received the report, and recommended the establishment of an ad-hoc governmental group of experts. The mandate of the group is, amongst other things, to consider appropriate further steps to be taken in the field of international standards of accounting and reporting for transnational corporations, taking into account the Report of the previous group, as well as other relevant activities in the field.

The ad-hoc group met twice in 1980. As far as the Report of the previous group is concerned, it made a beginning with discussions on the list of minimum-items, but so far did not address the question what further steps should be taken in the field of international standards of accounting and reporting.

It should be noted, that the ad-hoc group is discussing the reporting issues in the wider context of the objectives of the Commission on Transnational Corporations. The discussions are not primarily focused on what constitutes proper company reporting, but rather on what information should be made available by transnationals to host countries, especially developing countries. Divergences in economic and social interests, which may exist between developing and developed countries, are in this way transplanted into accounting and reporting practices. One has to recognise that modern accounting has been developed in the Western industrial world. There is no prima facie case for the contention that modern accounting would properly reflect the economic effects of transactions and conditions in different environments, and thus would have universal validity. On the other hand, it is unclear in what respects accounting requirements in developing countries would differ from those in developed countries. More research in this field is needed in order to make progress.

A fourth body is International Accounting Standards Committee (I.A.S.C.). It is not an intergovernmental body, but purely private. Its members are professional accountancy bodies in more than 40 countries, and its business is conducted by a Board, consisting of representatives of those bodies in 11 countries. Statements of IASC are prepared in steering committees, consisting of 3 or 4 member bodies. In the process of preparation all member-bodies have the opportunity for input and comment. Before making a definitive statement the Board publishes an exposure-draft, for public comment. At the end of 1980 IASC had promulgated 13 standards; 7 documents have been approved for publication as exposure draft.

DEVELOPMENTS IN I.A.S.C.

The structure of I.A.S.C. in its present form has attracted some criticism, and the Board has been considering how to respond.

One criticism is, that IASC is too narrowly based, since it consists of professional accountants only. This criticism is voiced by governments and intergovernmental bodies and, in a number of countries, by enterprise as well.

In order to enhance the acceptance of international accounting standdards the Board of IASC decided to approach international organisations of preparers and users with the proposal to become involved in the process of developing standards. Firm responses to these approaches have not yet been received, but preliminary reactions give the impression that there is a willingness to cooperate, provided that no deep involvement in the detailed technical work would be required. Current aim of the Board is to form a consultative group, comprising representatives of enterprise, labour, stock exchanges, financial analysts, financial executives and international finance. This group would receive all technical agenda-papers put before the Board, and have the opportunity, prior to the Board-meeting, to express views on the papers submitted.

Another criticism refers to the composition of the Board, which gives too much influence to the developed countries (especially the 9 founder members) and not enough influence to the developing countries, which occupy at the present time two seats. This criticism has been voiced by several developing countries, by the U.N., and by the International Federation of Accountants (IFAC).

The Board feels, that the demand of developing countries for more influence can be satisfied by increasing the number of Board-members to 13, the additional 2 seats being available for developing countries. Under the rules of IASC's constitution, this would give developing countries 4 votes on the Board, enough to prevent the adoption of a standard, in case they would feel that standard to be inadequate. This enlargement of the Board will be entered into the Constitution in November 1982. It has been noted, that Boardmembership requires from the professional body involved a considerable contribution, both in effort and in money. Not all developing countries can afford the monetary part of that contribution. Recently, a proposal has been submitted to council of IFAC, that IFAC will bear partly or wholly the expense of Board-membership falling upon developing countries with limited financial resources.

As to the position of the 9 foundermembers in the Board, there are different schools of thought. Some believe, that the acceptance of international standards would be enhanced if Boardmembers would be subjected to some electoral process, and that no country should enjoy a privileged position. Others firmly believe, that active participation of the founder members is indispensable to the success of the exercise. Recently, agreement was reached between representatives of IFAC and IASC, which satisfies both views. After this agreement has been ratified by the governing bodies, all Boardmembers will be appointed by IFAC-Council for a 5 years' term, but Council will see to it, that at all times the Board will comprise a substantial representation of those countries in which the accountancy-profession is highly developed or that are of predominant importance in international commerce and trade.

A third criticism refers, again, to the composition of the Board, being representatives of national professional bodies instead of national stand-ardsetting bodies. In a number of countries the professional body, or a committee of that body, is engaged in setting accounting standards. In other countries that task falls on others: the government, or a government agency, or an independent private body, or a joint body consisting of preparers, users, professionals and sometimes government. The status, terms of reference, and authority of the various standardsetters are very dissimilar, and that makes it virtually impossible, at least at the present stage, to organise them into a worldwide body. To overcome this criticism the Board recommended to its members to send as their representative at least one person that is involved in national standardsetting, or alternatively to liaise closely with the national standardsetting body. Several countries were able to achieve this.

A fourth criticism refers to both IFAC and IASC. To the eye of many it is confusing that—apart from regional organisations—there are two world-wide organisations of professional accountants, with almost identical membership. For the sake of clarity they urge the two bodies should be integrated. Concerning this issue there are different views. Some argue that IASC should remain a separate entity, because IASC needs a structure that permits participation of non-professionals in the standardsetting process; even if they do not participate in fact at the present time, IASC should be seen as a body prepared to share responsibilities with other interested parties. Others argue that accounting standards are of vital importance to the profession, and that, although the participation of others is highly welcome, the profession should make it clear that it accepts the primary responsibility for the setting of international account-ing standards; therefore IASC should be seen as an integral part of IFAC. This issue has been solved by a document on the interrelationship and the mutual commitments of the two bodies, prepared by a working-party. The document states, that both IFAC and IASC operate within the frame-work of the internationally organised accountancy profession, and that

IFAC-Council will appoint all professional Boardmembers. At the other hand, the document recognises, that IASC will continue to be autonomous, and will seek the involvement of other interested parties. The document makes clear, that IFAC and IASC are not competing with, but rather supplementary to each other, and that close liaison is beneficial to their objectives.

Last but not least is the relationship between IASC on one hand, intergovernmental bodies such as OECD and UN on the other hand. OECD expressed its wish not to become a standardsetting body. However, within the UN, it would appear from the recommendations of the Secretary General that a different view exists.

Clearly, it would be most unfortunate if different bodies would promulgate different, or even conflicting standards since this would bring enterprise into an untenable position. What is required is mutual coordination between the various bodies, in order to achieve common statements and to avoid duplication of work. IASC has, as a basis for further discussion, made the following proposals to both OECD and UNO:

- Let the working-group review the work of IASC, including:
  - suggestion of topics for future study by IASC;
  - provision of comments on proposed exposure-drafts at an early stage;
  - consideration of a periodic progress report on IASC's technical programme.
- Let the working-group examine a number of the most basic IASC-standards and, when found acceptable, endorse them.
- Let the working-group give public encouragement to support the adoption of all IASC-standards, where circumstances permit.
- Let IASC assist the working-group in developing subjects, identified as priorities by the working group.

These proposals show that IASC is willing to cooperate with other bodies, to assist them in the technical work, and to have its own statements scrutinised by those other bodies.

COMPLIANCE WITH INTERNATIONAL
ACCOUNTING STANDARDS

In order to achieve harmonisation in and improvement of financial statements, standards should not only be written, but effectively applied as well. Recent reviews give evidence, that there is an increasing awareness of international standards, but that their introduction into reporting practices is not prompt. This raises the question, what authority can be accorded to international standards, and who is going to supervise compliance with them.

As to the directives of the European Economic Community, these will become part of legislation of the memberstates. Compliance with these directives is ensured to the extent compliance with national law is ensured. With some exceptions an independent auditor's opinion will be required, specifying that the law has been complied with, or alternatively, specifying in what respects the law has not been complied with.

The guidelines on disclosure of information, promulgated by OECD, have been issued as recommendations. It is up to enterprises to decide to what extent it would be appropriate for them to follow OECD's guidance. Still, many multinationals do comply, either because the guidelines do not go beyond their present practice, or because they feel it is sensible to toe the line as drawn in OECD's guidelines for the conduct of multinationals.

As far as the UN are concerned, a code of conduct has not yet emerged from the Commission on Transnational Corporations, and it is still unclear, what status will be accorded to this document when it emerges. All papers, so far produced by UN in the field of accounting and reporting, are drafts for discussion. Therefore, the issue of compliance could not yet arise.

When the International Accounting Standards Committee was established in 1973 it was envisaged that the accountancy profession would ensure compliance with standards. When applying for membership of IASC a professional body had to subscribe to the obligations, detailed in the founding-agreement:

— to support the standards of IASC;
— to use its best endeavors:
- to persuade all parties concerned that financial statements should comply with the standards of IASC;
- to ensure that auditors satisfy themselves that financial statements do comply with the standards of IASC, or in case of non-compliance that this fact is disclosed either in the financial statements or in the audit report;
- to ensure that, as soon as practicable, appropriate action is taken in respect of auditors who neglect these duties.

It now appears, that it does not work out that way, at least not as fast as was presumed in 1973. Obviously, enterprise is hesitant to adopt international standards as long as they have not been incorporated into national ones. And in a number of countries the profession is not, or no longer, in control of the standardsetting process. In some countries the professional body has no power to prescribe what auditors should examine in the course of an audit, or should state in their report. In some countries the power to discipline members is accorded not to the professional body but to others.

The conclusion can be drawn, that auditors can only supervise compliance with international standards after those standards have been accepted as a proper requirement in the national or international environment of an enterprise. IASC can point out, through its standards, what is good practice but it has no effective power of enforcement; compliance depends upon endorsement by bodies that do have power of enforcement, and/or upon the willingness of enterprise to adopt standards voluntarily. This emphasises heavily the first and second commitment of member-bodies: to give support and to persuade other interested parties. At the same time, it indicates the importance of close liaison with representatives of preparers and users, with national standard-setting bodies, and with inter-governmental organisations such as OECD and UN.

The acceptance of the standards of IASC would be promoted tremendously if international enterprises would give full and public support to IASC. If enterprises want to avoid conflicting standards, national or international, they should come out in favour of IASC and say so in their financial statements. Now is the time for enterprise to realise that international standards are underway, and to decide what is the most effective machinery to get good ones. If prominent enterprises all over the world would endorse and apply IASC's statements, it would be a stimulating example to all self-respecting business-men in many countries. International standards are beneficial for mutual understanding by preparers and users all over the world. In trying to develop such standards, IASC has a promising case. But it needs support in order to get acceptance for its statements within a reasonable period of time. It is up to others to decide, whether it deserves that support.

NOTES

1. A.o. The Corporate Report, Accounting Standards Steering Committee, London, 1975. Corporate Reporting: its future evolution. Canadian Institute of Chartered Accountants, Toronto, 1980.

2. 4th Directive of the Council, E.E.C., Brussels, 1978.

3. Declaration on International Investment and Multinational Enterprises, OECD, Paris, Revised edition 1979.

4. International Standards of Accounting and Reporting for Transnational Corporations, E/C.10/33, U.N., New York 1977.

PEER REVIEW IN THE
ACCOUNTING PROFESSION

George J. Frey and John F. Barna
Peat Marwick Mitchell & Co.

CONTENTS

ABSTRACT

Messrs. Frey and Barna discuss the evolution of peer review in the accounting profession. They trace the sequence of events which contributed to the process as it exists today, both those which formed the basis of how the reviews are carried out, and the outside pressures which were influential in peer reviews coming to pass. They describe the structure of the AICPA's Division for CPA Firms, with particular emphasis on the peer review committees. They comment particularly on such matters as the need for quality control review panels, the question of including the work performed by offices outside the U.S. in the scope of the U.S. peer reviews, the SEC's desire for access to peer review working papers, and the approach that will be taken when a peer reviewer concludes that because of a significant failure in the application of generally accepted auditing standards, the firm lacked a reasonable basis for the opinion expressed.

Peer review in the accounting profession is now an accepted fact. It is an integral part of the profession's program of self-regulation. But it was not always so, nor was it readily accepted by most when it was first presented. Like many other new ideas that cause a change in the way of doing things and have an impact on the extent to which one can control his circumstances, it was initially met with widespread resistance. Some are still resisting.

Only after it became apparent to leaders of the profession that the consequences of not adopting peer review could be greater than the perceived objections to it, was there a concerted effort to bring it into being. As the issue became more a question of whether the profession should be regulated by government or be left basically as a self-regulating profession, peer review evolved as a key element—a prerequisite—to the concept of credibility in a self-regulating environment.

Thus, peer review became accepted in a somewhat crisis atmosphere as the profession rallied with remarkable speed to thwart efforts to bring the profession under legislatively mandated supervision and control.

The background leading up to the now existing program for peer reviews of firms which are members of the practice sections of the AICPA evolved over nearly a decade. This article will review some of the significant events in that process, as well as discuss the programs for peer review as they exist today.

SEQUENCE OF DEVELOPMENTS

Some of the more significant developments in the evolution of peer review discussed in this historical account are summarized in approximate chronological order:

Mid 1960s	— Several state societies of CPAs offered programs for the cross-review of working papers by practitioners.
Late 1960s	— AICPA Planning Committee recommended a program that provided practitioners an opportunity to have objective cross-reviews of their work. (A member of the

planning committee was John C. Burton, a Columbia University professor who later became Chief Accountant of the SEC.)

1971 — Quality Review Program for local firms commenced with practitioners performing cross-reviews.

Early 1970s — Public pressure was mounting on the profession as a result of well publicized business failures, frequently reported lawsuits against auditors alleging failures, SEC criticism of the profession and numerous articles on the profession, some suggesting government regulation of the profession as the answer.

1973 — Based on publicity given the local firm quality control program, the SEC requested the AICPA to develop a program for review of a firm's quality control procedures. (A document entitled "Tentative Program for an Inspection of the Quality Control Standards and Procedures of an Accounting Firm Pursuant to Rule 2(e) of the SEC Rules of Practice," was developed by the AICPA.)

Late 1973 — The AICPA appointed a Special Committee to Study Quality Control Review of Multi-Office Firms. (This committee, generally referred to as the Holton Committee, was chaired by Thomas L. Holton.)

April 1974 — The Holton Committee issued a Plan for Implementation of the AICPA Voluntary Program for Reviews of Quality Control Procedures of Multi-Office Firms which was accepted by the AICPA Board of Directors on April 26, 1974. (This plan identified nine elements of quality control which have come to be the benchmark of quality control reviews.)

1974 — The AICPA formed a Committee on Self-Regulation in response to SEC disciplin-

	ary actions, civil litigation and criminal actions by the Justice Department.
December 1974	— Statement on Auditing Standards No. 4, "Quality Control Considerations for a Firm of Independent Auditors" was issued as a professional standard incorporating nine elements of quality control based on those included in the Holton Committee report.
1975	— The Committee on Self-Regulation, recognizing that the existing system of self-regulation covered only individuals, proposed a plan for the registration of CPA firms.
1975	— The AICPA formed groups representing large, medium sized and small firms, designated as A, B, C firms to address self-regulation and other needs of varied sized practices.
February 1976	— The Committee on Self-Regulation revised its registration plan to a proposed plan for a voluntary quality control review program for firms with SEC practices.
Early 1976	— Special Committee on Proposed Standards for Quality Control Policies and Procedures (Burmester Committee) was formed and was assigned the tasks of providing guidance in the establishment of quality control policies and procedures by a CPA firm and developing standards for making and reporting on compliance reviews under the voluntary program.
May 1976	— The AICPA Council approved the Voluntary Quality Control Review Program for CPA Firms with SEC Practices and recommended that consideration be given to expanding it to cover all CPA firms.
July 1976	— Quality Control Review Committee (Robinson Committee) was formed to establish policies and to supervise the operations of the voluntary program.

October 1976	— AICPA Council adopted a revised plan for voluntary quality control reviews which included all CPA firms associated with financial statements. (It also provided for the addition of consulting reviews.)
December 1976	— U.S. Congressional concern was demonstrated as Metcalf Subcommittee Staff Study on the "Accounting Establishment" was issued.
Spring 1977	— Congressional hearings on the accounting profession were held by the Metcalf Subcommittee.
1977	— The Division for Firms concept with an SEC Practice Section and a Private Companies Practice Section, each with membership requirements was developed. (The formation of the Division for Firms and the two sections was approved by the AICPA Council in September of 1977.)
September 1977	— The AICPA Council approved the formation of the Quality Control Standards Committee as the senior technical committee designated to issue pronouncements on quality control standards.
October 1977	— The Special Committee on Proposed Standards for Quality Control Policies and Procedures issued a Guide to Quality Control Policies and Procedures for Participating CPA Firms.
November 1977	— Metcalf Subcommittee issued its report entitled "Improving the Accountability of Public Owned Corporations and their Auditors" which indicated a preference for self-initiated action by the private sector as the means to reform but threatened mandatory reforms if meaningful progress was not made on a timely basis.
July 1978	— SEC issued its first report to Congress on the Accounting Profession and the Commission's Oversight Role. (This report endorsed the profession's efforts toward

self-regulation but clearly conditioned that endorsement on continued progress toward the Commission's expectations and its future judgments as to the effectiveness of self-regulatory efforts.)

THE SEEDS OF PEER REVIEW

Commencing about the mid-60s, some state societies became involved in the cross-review of working papers of practitioners. These reviews were all made on a voluntary basis but in some cases were follow-up actions recommended by various committees in response to findings of post-issuance review programs. The scope of these reviews was largely engagement oriented and the recommendations that resulted from those reviews related mainly to suggestions for improvements in audit effectiveness or reporting practice.

In the late 60s the AICPA appointed a planning committee, chaired by David Culp from Indiana, to consider the need for inter-firm review of professional accounting and auditing practices. That committee recommended a program of review that provided local firm practitioners an opportunity to have objective cross-reviews of their work. This new program was first offered by the AICPA in 1971. A member of that planning committee, John C. (Sandy) Burton, was later named Chief Accountant of the SEC and in that role had considerable influence on the implementation of peer review.

The AICPA local firm review program was more structured than programs offered by various state society groups. Committees involved in the AICPA program developed rather detailed checklists that were used in the review process and as technical aids for firms in their self-review activities. The AICPA program was designed as an education or practice improvement program. Fees generally were set at levels designed to provide only cost reimbursement to the firms providing the review service, generally with an understanding that a reviewed firm would make its partners available to perform similar reviews of other practitioners who also wished to be reviewed. These reviews generally did not result in the issuance of a report but rather in the informal communication of findings and recommendations at the conclusion of a relatively short review. No particular effort was made to reach sample objectives or to obtain representative coverage of the accounting and auditing practices of the reviewed firm.

Reviews conducted mainly in the late 60s and early 70s did not reach a significant penetration of public practice. In recent years the extent of such review activity has diminished to the point where it may well have been supplanted by other programs which have become available. In the evolutionary process of peer review, however, the contribution of those involved in this initial local firm review program should not be underestimated.

SEC Involvement in Peer Review

Commencing in the early 70s, the SEC began to use peer review in conjunction with enforcement actions against firms involved in specific cases under investigation. From 1974 thru 1979, thirteen such reviews were reported under Accounting Series Releases of the Commission. In another four cases, practitioners avoided such review by resignation, thus giving up their right to practice before the Commission. The scope of these mandated reviews generally covered the nine elements of quality control described by AICPA literature supplemented by other areas of interest prescribed by the SEC that related more to the motivation and behavioral aspects of the practice. While reports on such reviews were directed by the review teams to the reviewed firms, copies of the reports were made directly available to the SEC. Under terms of the agreements between the SEC and the reviewed firms the Commission also retained the right of access to working papers of the review team.

While the SEC mandated reviews left audit judgments and reporting conclusions to the review teams, the SEC maintained a significant role in those reviews. Although the AICPA generally was requested to provide reviewers to staff the SEC mandated reviews, the SEC retained the right of selection of team captains or committees from nominees of the AICPA. While a reviewed firm generally has had a right of challenge for cause, final approval of review team or committee appointments rested with the Commission.

For the mandated reviews the review teams or committees were charged with responsibility for developing a program of review following the outline prescribed by the SEC. To the extent that such programs related to specific review procedures, the teams' decisions were generally unchallenged by the SEC. However, in terms of scope of review, for example, number and size of engagements to be reviewed or number of offices to be visited, review team plans were subject to review and approval by the SEC before the review was undertaken. Also, a conference with the reviewed firm and SEC representatives were generally held at the conclusion of a mandated review.

While it may be presumptuous for an outsider to explain the interest of the SEC in peer review, it seems more than coincidental that the initiation of this activity closely paralleled the activist role of the Commission's Chief Accountant during the period of this development. Sandy Burton was appointed Chief Accountant of the SEC in 1972. His prior involvement in both the professional practice of accounting and auditing, as a CPA, and as a member of the AICPA Planning Committee referred to previously, and his more recent identification with academia appeared to give him greater interest in combining remedial with punitive actions in the enforcement activities of the Commission. While the enforcement division of the SEC had general responsibility for imposing peer review on a particular firm, the continuing involvement in those actions by the Chief Accountant and the important role of Sandy Burton in the administration of mandated peer reviews by the SEC very closely link him with the development of peer review.

Underlying the actions of the Commission and its Chief Accountant in promoting peer review was a directed effort to encourage more effective self-regulation by the profession. Sandy Burton also spoke publicly of the need for peer review within the accounting and auditing profession. His interest in peer review seemed to be two pronged. He may have been interested primarily in the remedial aspects of this process and the prospect for general improvement in the audit practices of firms that demonstrated potential deficiencies in particular cases, but it appears that he was also very interested in this opportunity to obtain greater insight to the practice of the profession and to the audits of public companies. This insight was probably perceived as useful to the Commission in its regulatory role as well as a benefit to the growing body of practitioners who would be involved in the review process. Sandy Burton has made reference to the "bumble bee effect" of peer review reflecting both the effect of the review on a reviewed firm and the extraction or learning opportunity provided the participating reviewers.

While the profession cooperated with the SEC in administering the mandated review program, it was sensitive to the threat this approach had on self-regulation within the profession. Practitioners, likewise, were concerned with the involvement of a regulatory agency and the duplication of effort of the internal and external review programs. Perhaps the greatest sensitivity was the identification of a government regulatory agency with the practice of auditing in relation to specific engagements. While effective measures have generally been taken to safeguard the highly valued confidentiality standards of the profession, even the appearance of a breach of this confidentiality sent tremors of concern through the profession.

AICPA PROGRAM FOR REVIEWS OF MULTI-OFFICE FIRMS

One of the early efforts of the AICPA in the development of peer review was the appointment of a special committee to study quality review for multi-office firms. In 1973, this committee, known as the Holton Committee, was appointed to make a recommendation to the Board regarding the feasibility of peer review and if the committee concluded that such reviews were feasible to submit a plan for implementation. That committee presented its findings and recommendations to the Board in a report in April 1974. Rarely has a committee within the short period of time taken by that committee published a work product with more profound effect on the profession.

The quality control considerations identified by the Holton Committee were very similar to those later included in Statement on Auditing Standards No. 4 and now included in Statement on Quality Control Standards No. 1. Those considerations, now referred to as elements of quality control, were the subject of considerable scrutiny by other committees charged with responsibility for recommending policy and procedures to implement quality controls. Those committees have found the described areas of quality control to be comprehensive and appropriate. Of the nine considerations first identified, *Conduct of an Engagement*, was later replaced by *Assigning Personnel to Engagements* which appears to be a somewhat more limited but related element of quality control. These nine elements today represent the principal elements of a quality control system to which a peer review is directed.

The Holton Committee recommended that the Institute appoint a supervisory committee to be responsible for the program. The committee would draw review panels from groups of individuals nominated by their firms. Initially only partners were to be used as reviewers. The committee would be required to revise review procedures as appropriate, schedule reviews, select review team captains and generally keep itself available for consultation with representatives of review teams and reviewed firms when and as necessary.

Under the plan recommended by the Holton Committee, review teams would issue reports on reviews to the reviewed firms. No copy of that report would be given to any other person or organization. The supervisory committee responsible for administering this program obtained information regarding the scope of the review, but even this committee did not receive a copy of the report issued to the reviewed firm. This rather severe limitation on communication of reports was later determined to be imposed on the reviewed firm as well as on the reviewers.

Much controversy evolved from restrictions on the reviewed firms' ability to disseminate reports on reviews. Those advocating severe restriction on distribution felt that reviewed firms, at least in the initial years of the program, would be given undue competitive advantage if they were permitted to hold themselves out as having successfully completed a peer review. This type of recognition was sometimes referred to as the "good housekeeping seal of approval" on reviewed firms. One major firm that volunteered for review under the program decided against proceeding with such review because of the restriction imposed on later distribution of review results. It was that firm's contention that credibility of the program would be impaired and the reviewed firm could be subject to undue public criticism for refusal to disclose the results of its review.

While the controversy over publication of review findings resulted in the early demise of this program, it did serve as the basis for much of the peer review programs that followed. It dealt with the scope of review and provided for disclosure to the supervisory committee of any scope limitations imposed by a reviewed firm. It established administrative procedures relating to proposal letters, mediation of differences and other issues that would be common to any review program. It established guidelines for the number of offices in a multi-office environment and the number of engagements to be reviewed in relation to the accounting and auditing practices of a reviewed firm. It described the nature of the report to be issued which was a long form report addressing each of the elements accompanied by an overall opinion as to whether the quality control procedures described in the firm's quality control document are appropriately designed to provide the reviewed firm reasonable assurance that its audit practice is being conducted in accordance with generally accepted auditing standards. Much of this guidance has survived the evolving peer review programs and related guidance material that has been developed by the AICPA.

Another important aspect of the peer review program during the development stage has related to the stated objective of the program. The early programs including the program recommended by the Holton Committee appear to have placed greater emphasis on the educational aspects of the review. That program provided for an initial review of a firm's quality control policies and procedures followed by a delay in actual review of implementation of the firm's policies and procedures to permit implementation of recommended changes. Accordingly, the firm was provided an opportunity to correct identified potential deficiencies in its practice before subjecting itself to a compliance review with regard to those policies and procedures.

The *documentation* of a firm's quality control policies and procedures has been an issue of importance and an occasion for delay in implementation in many instances. The first effort toward a comprehensive review program as recommended by the Holton Committee did provide for preparation of a quality control document by the reviewed firm. From the beginning it was considered essential that a review team be provided criteria against which it could conduct a review. Since there were no standards for quality control at the time this committee made its recommendations, the reviewers would have to come to some understanding with the reviewed firm of the quality control policies and procedures against which it would conduct its review. Accordingly, it was of paramount importance at this stage that each reviewed firm have a well documented set of policies and procedures against which a review could be made. While reviewers could make an evaluation of the appropriateness of a firm's policies and procedures in relation to the elements of quality control identified by the committee, the test of compliance by a review team was necessarily directed to specific policies and procedures identified in the reviewed firm's document. While the accomplishments of the first special committee cannot be measured in terms of reviews completed, the resource its product provided to other committees in the development of quality control standards and in the development of review programs has been very significant.

VOLUNTARY QUALITY CONTROL
REVIEW PROGRAM FOR CPA FIRMS

In May 1976, the AICPA Council responded to the continuing call for progress in the development of peer review by authorizing a voluntary quality control review program for firms with SEC practice. This action was met with rather severe criticism by a large number of practitioners who felt the exclusiveness of this program would be damaging to their stature in practice. Accordingly, in October 1976, Council extended the voluntary quality control review program to all CPA firms. In the fall of 1976, a quality control review committee (the Robinson Committee) was appointed to implement and administer this voluntary program. While it was immediately recognized that considerable development effort was required before such a program could be offered to the members, a high priority was given to getting a review program off the ground.

The purpose of the voluntary program was stated as one that is educational and preventive in nature designed to assist firms in developing and implementing adequate systems of quality control in their audit practices, as well as assuring firms with existing systems that their quality control meets, in all material respects, the standards of the profession. It was expected that such a program would provide direct benefits to the participating firms through the application of objective, outside reviews to their quality control policies and procedures.

The voluntary program provided two types of reviews, consulting reviews and compliance reviews. Consulting reviews were expected to assist in organizing their quality control procedures and to provide a review service for quality control documents. Also the consulting reviews would offer a preliminary quality control review to firms that needed such help in preparing for participation in the quality control review program. Technical standards review, previously offered under the Institute's program of assistance to practitioners, was also incorporated in this program as a consulting review. The second type of review provided under the voluntary program was a compliance review which was a comprehensive review of the firm's quality controls and application of those controls to its accounting and auditing practice.

Of the consulting review services available under the voluntary program, the quality control document review was the most generally used service. While all firms necessarily had at least informal policies and procedures relating to quality control of their accounting and audit practices, most had not documented their policies and procedures. Considering the importance of documented policies and procedures in relation to an outside review, it is understandable that firms were concerned that such documents should be appropriate in relation to those needs. The AICPA subsequently published documents that provided assistance in the development of quality control documents. With the passage of time and development of better understanding of documentation requirements the call for consulting service in this area has diminished.

Compliance reviews under the voluntary program were designed to provide evaluation of the appropriateness of a firm's quality control policies and procedures in relation to its practice and review of audit working papers to determine whether the firm's quality control policies are in compliance with professional standards. This program established qualifications of reviewers and described procedures to be followed by reviewed firms desiring to have such reviews performed under the program. This program provided at the election of the firm to be reviewed either (a) a review team appointed by the committee, (b) a CPA firm engaged by the firm under review, or (c) some form of independent review satisfactory to the committee, such as an acceptable plan administered by a state society of CPAs. This compliance review program was not intended as a means for taking disciplinary action. However, it did provide that in the event serious violations of technical standards were encountered and the reviewed firm failed to take appropriate corrective action, the reviewers would not be precluded from referring such information to the Institute's Professional Ethics Division.

The results of field reviews under the voluntary program were to be reported to the reviewed firm in a short form report. That short form report included an illustration of an unqualified opinion that described the system of quality control with respect to the accounting and auditing practice of the reviewed firm as "appropriately comprehensive and suitably designed for the firm, adequately documented, communicated to professional personnel, and (was) being complied with during the period to provide the firm reasonable assurance of conforming with the standards of the profession for firms participating in the voluntary quality control review program for CPA firms of the American Institute of Certified Public Accountants."

The reviewed firm under the voluntary program, at its option, could submit the short-form report to the AICPA, in which case a copy would be maintained in a public file. The failure of a firm to submit a report within a three year period would cause the firm to be dropped as a participant in the program.

The voluntary program continues to be available to all members of the Institute, but is not in general use. This program has provided very significant resource material to succeeding peer review groups in the development of standards for performing and reporting reviews under the programs available to members of the Division for CPA Firms of the AICPA.

GUIDELINES FOR QUALITY CONTROL
POLICIES AND PROCEDURES

Early in the development of voluntary review programs, a high priority was set on establishing criteria against which reviewers could evaluate a firm's quality control policies and procedures. The voluntary quality control review committee concluded that it was essential that criteria be established in a more definitive fashion than was available from existing literature. Accordingly, a special committee (the Burmester Committee) was appointed to develop guidance for the establishment of quality control policies and procedures by a CPA firm intending to participate in the voluntary quality control review program for CPA firms. That committee published such a guide in 1977.

The guide published by the Burmester Committee neither interpreted nor modified the Statement on Auditing Standards No. 4, Quality Control Considerations for a Firm of Independent Auditors. Rather it provided guidelines for quality control policies and procedures which could be used as requirements to be met in connection with AICPA quality control compliance reviews conducted under other AICPA peer review programs. Evidence of the sensitivity of the extent of authority of this committee to a limited segment of practice was exemplified in the role given by council to the Auditing Standards Executive Committee in relation to pronouncements of the special committee. The document published by the Burmester Committee was subject to pre-release review and approval by the Auditing Standards Executive Committee. While the guidance to be developed by this special committee was considered essential in relation to participation in the voluntary review program, the extension of such policies beyond the participants of the voluntary program was carefully guarded.

The document published by the Burmester Committee provided suggested policies and procedures for each of the quality control elements. Use of the document was intended to provide guidance to a firm in establishing its own policies and procedures that would accomplish the objectives described in the guide. In each instance, the user was reminded that *consideration* should be given by a firm to establishing policies to accomplish the objectives described to the extent such objectives are applicable to its practice. The described policies and procedures were to be considered examples which would not necessarily include all examples appropriate in the circumstances or be limited to those illustrated. The document also addressed the responsibility of a U.S. firm to establish controls to assure that segments of its engagements performed outside the United States are performed in accordance with U.S. generally accepted auditing standards.

The development of the guide to implement the voluntary quality control review program for CPA firms extended over a considerable period of time. Painstaking efforts were taken to make this guidance relevant to a broad scope of practitioners within a framework that would not mandate practice standards to nonparticipating firms.

PEER REVIEW MOVES INTO ACTION

Restiveness of firms with SEC practice spurred by SEC actions and public utterances and broad support for the conclusion that failure to provide effective self-regulation could shortly result in more direct involvement of the government, groups within the AICPA moved to accelerate peer review activity. In 1974, a committee on self-regulation was appointed and within a period of only several months proposed an organization structure that recognized firms apart from individual membership in the AICPA.

While these recommendations were not immediately adopted, there was effort to recognize the differing needs and concerns of practice units and firms depending upon the nature and size of their practices. In 1975, Advisory Committees were formed which were composed of representatives of firms or practice units based on size characteristics. Firms were grouped into three size groups, called A, B and C. Group C was made up of the larger firms with extensive SEC practices and numbered 15 members. Group B represented firms with over 50 members of the Institute but fewer than the 15 largest firms. Group A was made up of firms with fewer than 50 members of the Institute and represented about 17,000 practice units. The Advisory Committees of the groups were generally made up of the managing partners of the firms. In the case of Group C where there were 15 firms, all were represented on the Advisory Committee. In addition, there was a group and advisory committee representing educators.

Each of the Advisory Committees was charged with advising the Board of Directors on matters of concern to them. Through this vehicle the largest 15 firms, all of which had significant SEC practices, were able to communicate and focus on the then very serious threat of government regulation of the accounting profession.

During the 1975-76 period there were repeated public criticisms of the profession made primarily by the SEC. Both the U.S. Senate and the House of Representatives had committees which announced that they would investigate whether legislation was necessary to regulate or control the profession.

It became abundantly clear to the leadership of the profession that unless significant, substantive steps were taken quickly by the profession to regulate itself, steps would be taken by the government. The profession's credibility had suffered and its future as a self-regulating body was in jeopardy.

On December 7, 1976, the late Senator Lee Metcalf published a staff study entitled, "The Accounting Establishment" prepared by the "Subcommittee on Reports, Accounting and Management" (Lee Metcalf, Chairman) of the United States Senate "Committee on Government Operations" (Abraham Ribicoff, Chairman). Simply characterized, the study was highly critical. It recommended that government take over the role of standards setting in both accounting and auditing matters. Its biases were challenged as were many of its factual references. Nevertheless, it became a widely quoted source of comment in the media and was probably quite influential on public opinion about the profession. One of its many recommendations was number 7 that:

> The Federal Government should itself periodically inspect the work of independent auditors for publicly-owned corporations. Such a mandatory inspection program should be designed to provide assurance to the public and Congress that independent auditors are performing their responsibilities competently in accordance with proper standards of conduct. Periodic quality reviews could be conducted by the General Accounting Office, the SEC, or a special audit inspection agency.

The staff study contained a long list of measures the staff of the subcommittee deemed necessary. Public hearings held by the Metcalf Committee were scheduled for the spring of 1977. At the same time the profession was getting attention from the House of Representatives and a subcommittee, chaired by Congressman John Moss from California. That subcommittee, the Subcommittee on Oversight and Investigations of the House Committee on Interstate and Foreign Commerce, commenced its examination of the nature and structure of the accounting profession in 1976. The Moss Subcommittee held public hearings in February and March of 1978.

The Metcalf Subcommittee held its public hearings in April, May and June of 1977. Some 39 witnesses testified representing a broad spectrum of interests and opinions. Managing partners of Big Eight firms, as well as other leaders of the profession, testified and suggested steps toward reform, generally through self-regulation. The SEC and critics of the profession, likewise, presented testimony some of whom called for government action. The threat of legislation and government regulation was clear. But the profession's pleading for time to demonstrate its ability to self-regulate was also heard. The Subcommittee concluded that the private sector initiatives pledged by the profession were preferable to government mandated actions and deferred taking any steps toward legislation.

Before the Metcalf Subcommittee issued its report in November 1977, the profession had already developed and voted into being its Division for CPA Firms and a series of membership requirements. Many of the Subcommittee's anticipated concerns and likely recommendations had been met with private sector initiatives sufficient to cause all to take a "wait and see" posture on the workings of self-regulation.

The threat of government regulation continued to loom over the profession as the SEC was charged with reporting annually to Congress on the profession and the sufficiency and effectiveness of its efforts at self-regulation. The SEC's first report to Congress was as of July 1, 1978. That report endorsed the concept that self-regulation by the profession was preferred and recommended that the profession be allowed time to demonstrate its ability to self-regulate. The report also clearly set forth the SEC's expectations and desires as to the form and nature of the profession's self-regulatory efforts. Its endorsement of the profession's efforts was clearly conditional on continued progress toward SEC expectations and future judgments as to effectiveness of those efforts.

THE AICPA DIVISION FOR CPA FIRMS

The AICPA Division for CPA Firms was officially in place following the adoption of a resolution of the Council of the AICPA at its meeting in September 17, 1977. The Division was made up of two sections—the SEC Practice Section and the Private Companies Practice Section. The activities of each section are governed by an executive committee having senior status within the AICPA with authority to carry out the activities of the section: membership was, and remains, voluntary.

It was clear that the threat of government regulation ran primarily to the firms auditing public companies and the specter of SEC practice. Accordingly, the SEC Practice Section membership requirements and other provisions were understandably more onerous and also more in line with the recommendations of the profession's critics.

Because this article is concerned with peer review rather than all aspects of the profession's self-regulatory efforts, only those matters which relate to peer review will be discussed.

The objectives of the SEC Practice Section were to:

1. Improve the quality of practice by CPA firms before the Securities and Exchange Commission through the establishment of practice requirements for member firms.
2. Establish and maintain an effective system of self-regulation of member firms by means of mandatory peer reviews, required maintenance of appropriate quality controls, and the imposition of sanctions for failure to meet membership requirements.
3. Enhance the effectiveness of the section's regulatory system through the monitoring and evaluation activities by an independent oversight board composed of public members.
4. Provide a forum for development of technical information relating to SEC practice.

Number 2 clearly establishes the requirements for peer review. The membership requirements obligate members to:

> 1) Adhere to quality control standards established by the AICPA Quality Control Standards Committee.

> 2) Submit to peer reviews of the firm's accounting and audit practice every three years or at such additional times as designated by the executive committee, the reviews to be conducted in accordance with review standards established by the section's peer review committee.

There are numerous other membership requirements but they are generally sufficiently unrelated to peer review itself to not merit separate discussion here.

The SEC Practice Section also has as a part of its governance a Public Oversight Board which is charged with overseeing all of its activities and reporting on them to the public. The Public Oversight Board has a distinct and active role in the peer review process as its representatives review all of the section's peer review reports and, for a significant number, further participate by reviewing peer review working papers or, in addition, by observing and actively involving themselves in oversight as peer reviews are in process.

The administration of the peer review process is under the direction of the section's peer review committee.

The private companies practice section also has as one of its membership requirements triennial peer review. Although not subject to Public Oversight Board involvement or SEC review of reports, the programs for peer review are quite similar.

Peer Review Committees

The two sections under the division for firms each established their own peer review committees. Each was charged with developing standards for performing and reporting on quality control compliance reviews and for administering a review program for its section. The implementation time for the SECPS appeared to be more time-critical than was considered practicable for the PCPS. This, however, did avoid much duplication of effort since the PCPS was able to use the material developed by the SECPS with relatively minor modification to meet its own needs. Both programs provide for triennial reviews and public reporting of results of the reviews.

SEC Practice Section Peer Review

In order to set in place an orderly, functioning program leading to peer reviews which are common in scope, approach and manner of reporting, much in the way of guidance material had to be developed. The peer review committees had available to them the materials which resulted from the substantial efforts which had preceded. Nevertheless, there were numerous policy and procedural matters which had to be addressed. The SECPS peer review committee developed and issued a comprehensive statement entitled "Standards for Performing and Reporting on Quality Control Compliance Reviews." It covers a far reaching range of matters including objectives, performance of reviews, qualifications of reviewers, scope of reviews, working papers, reporting on review results and certain procedural matters.

The original members of the peer review committee supported by AICPA staff worked long and hard to develop the section's peer review manual.

Provisions were made for the reviews, as required by the membership requirements, to be performed in any one of three ways. First is a program for reviews to be performed by teams of reviewers appointed by the Committee from among the membership of the AICPA and the sections. They are referred to as CART's (committee appointed review teams) and are administered by the committee assisted by AICPA staff. The second approach is a firm review wherein one firm engages another to perform a review. The third approach involves members of associations of CPA firms being reviewed by teams made up of association members from other firms.

Generally the CART reviews have been of firms smaller than the largest 15 or 20. Reviews of the largest firms have been performed by other firms. This is precipitated by the substantial logistical and management problems posed in reviewing a large multi-office firm with individuals from several different firms with diverse backgrounds and little prior familiarity with each other. Despite the apparent advantages and efficiencies provided by firm on firm reviews, particularly in the case of the very large firms, suspicions exist in the minds of the SEC and some others that there would be a coziness and "backscratching" approach taken by larger firms in reviewing each other. To offset this SEC concern, a program of review by appointed panels of one or three (depending on size of the reviewed firm) individuals who are independent of both the reviewing and reviewed firms was developed. The peer review committee issued a statement on Standards for Quality Control Review Panels which describes the purpose, composition, functions and report of a quality control review panel.

The need for panels remains a controversy. They were agreed to as a compromise to gain SEC concurrence with firm on firm reviews. Those involved in the reviews of the larger firms generally believe that the only practical way to accomplish an effective review of a large, multi-office firm is through the firm on firm approach. Nevertheless, suspicions exist that this approach will be less effective in finding and reporting deficiencies than a CART. The panels of practitioners from usually 3 other firms are viewed as the preservers of integrity to the process, at least by the SEC. Many practitioners view the panel as an unnecessary extra layer of oversight and expense as the POB representatives are involved in similar pursuits.

Associations face similar questions as to independence and objectivity of its reviewers. The peer review committee has established a number of conditions an association must meet in order to qualify to perform and administer review programs of its members. These involve the relationships that exist among the various firms in an association and the manner in which the association operates. The principal concerns run to insuring that reviewers are independent of the firms they review. Association reviews are also subject to oversight by quality control review panels.

There are substantial administrative considerations in conducting a program involving the peer reviews of some 500 firms every 3 years. The committee, with the aid of a number of AICPA staff personnel, is involved in a process which includes monitoring or scheduling the required reviews of each member firm. The committee, which has been meeting one to two days a month, reviews each peer review report and letter of comments. This is after a review of underlying peer review working papers by the staff and an indication from the POB representatives that they have completed their oversight role. A formal vote is taken on the acceptance of each report by the committee.

The peer review committee also becomes involved in resolving any disputes which may arise between the judgments of reviewers and reviewees, handling requests for extensions or other relief from prescribed requirements, providing direct oversight to certain CART reviews and generally seeing to it that the peer review process is functioning as contemplated.

PCPS Section Peer Review

In most respects the review program of the PCPS is similar. There are, however, a number of important distinctions. Perhaps foremost among those distinctions is the absence of Public Oversight Board involvement in the private company peer review process. Also the PCPS is not required to have review panels. Under both peer review programs, the review team issues a letter of comment on matters that may require corrective action or which may result in significant improvements in the practice of the reviewed firm. In the case of the SECPS peer review those letters along with a response by the reviewed firm become a part of the public file and therefore are a more sensitive communication. Under the PCPS letters of comment are private communications between the review team and the reviewed firm.

The SECPS made peer review a requirement within three years of joining the section. Those joining in 1978 were required to have reviews by the end of 1980, although some were granted extensions to 1981 to equalize the workload between 1980 and 1981 as most were waiting until the third year to have reviews. The PCPS made the requirement for peer reviews to be within three years of July 1, 1979. Thus, a PCPS member joining in 1978 need not have a review until 1982.

Peer Review Progress to Date

The first triennium of the SECPS peer review program got off to a humble start in terms of number of reviews taking place prior to the required third year. Only 11 firms completed peer reviews under the program in 1978. In 1979, 40 reviews were completed. It is anticipated that in 1980 about 150 reviews will be made. Certain firms with fewer than 4 SEC clients were given until 1981 to have reviews by the peer review committee in an attempt to equalize the workload as the build up in the third year posed administrative problems. Considering the start up difficulties of the program of this magnitude it is understandable that many firms would adopt a "wait and see" attitude in regard to their involvement in the review process. All firms that are members in the SECPS will have completed reviews by 1981, and it is anticipated that in years following the initial cycle the number of reviews performed in each year will be more nearly in balance than was experienced in the first triennium.

KEY ISSUES ADDRESSED BY THE
SECPS PEER REVIEW COMMITTEE

As was previously mentioned, the SEC became involved in reporting annually to Congress on the accounting profession and its self-regulatory efforts. In its report to Congress in 1979, it criticized the profession's peer review process for the failure to include in the peer reviews work performed outside the U.S. and the failure to provide SEC access to peer review working papers.

The question of including the work performed by offices outside the U.S. in the scope of U.S. peer reviews became one that pitted U.S. based SEC concerns against the professional accounting bodies of various foreign countries. The objections expressed by such groups were widespread and strongly felt. Legislation to prohibit access to working papers by outsiders was threatened in some countries if such efforts continued.

A compromise was reached which, at least for the present, is considered a reasonable solution to the problem of subjecting work performed outside the U.S. to scrutiny by U.S. reviewers. Under the compromise, the U.S. firms performing work outside the U.S. are charged with a distinct responsibility to demonstrate that they have appropriately supervised and controlled such work. The Peer Review Manual was amended to include a set of specific requirements for foreign work performed on behalf of U.S. firms.

Another key issue was that of whether the SEC needed or should have access to working papers supporting the peer reviews performed within the SECPS. The SEC contended that it could not perform its oversight function and properly report to Congress on the effectiveness of the profession's self-regulation unless it had access to underlying peer review working papers. This argument was presented despite the fact that the SEC had access to and has been reviewing the working papers of the POB. The POB in its role has access to peer review working papers and is directly involved in peer reviews to the extent it deems appropriate.

The concerns with SEC access, in addition to the general negative reaction to expanding the role of government in this self-regulatory process, was a very real concern as to breaches of confidentiality. The peer review process and the profession itself through its Code of Ethics is well attuned to the sacredness of confidentiality as it relates to client affairs. No one seemed prepared to believe the SEC would not use such access to somehow identify registrants from peer review working papers as a means of extending its review of the work of accounting firms to investigations of their client registrants.

A compromise was reached in the summer of 1980 which granted limited access to peer review working papers by the SEC via the POB. It is at this time an untested arrangement. The SEC's involvement will likely cause some sterilization of the process and thus diminish the constructive benefits of peer review realized thus far. In the three years of the SECPS peer review program the findings and recommendations show that reviewers have emphasized constructive suggestions for improvement rather than merely trying to penalize the reviewed firms through overly critical reports. The state of the art has thus improved in an environment of free and open communication that nevertheless fully preserved client confidentiality. The involvement of one not enjoying the confidence of the others involved in the process cannot help but lead to a defensive and careful use of words to avoid precipitating the feared over-reaction by the powerful, but not necessarily understanding, government agency. Hopefully, the impact of the agreed upon access by the SEC will not be as adverse as many fear.

The POB raised for consideration the issue of what should be done when a peer review uncovers a situation where the reviewer concludes that because of a significant failure in the application of generally accepted auditing standards (GAAS) the firm lacks a reasonable basis for the opinion expressed. Existing auditing literature gives guidance to auditors on what to do when subsequent discovery of material departures from generally accepted accounting principles are uncovered. The literature has not addressed failures in applying auditing standards. There is a significant difference, in that the effect of an identified departure from generally accepted accounting principles can be quantified and it is ultimately the responsibility of management to issue financial statements which comply with generally accepted accounting principles in all material respects. When there is an identified failure on the part of the auditor to properly apply GAAS, the client may be an innocent victim and there is frequently no indication that financial statements are not presented in accordance with generally accepted accounting principles. The potential for damage to innocent shareholders and others by discrediting such financial statements is great. The basis for doing so is weak.

Yet it is clear that blatant failures to apply GAAS, if uncovered, cannot be ignored. The peer review committee concluded that such situations should be reported to it promptly by reviewers when, and if, uncovered. The committee will then deal with the instances reported on a case by case basis. The action should be more timely and the result more appropriately directed toward sanctions of the firms or other corrective measures appropriate in the circumstances.

A LOOK TO THE FUTURE

Peer review is here to stay; it won't go away should anyone still be expecting or hoping for that result. The positive results in terms of a higher order of concern for ensuring that quality considerations are effectively present in all professional work on audits have been clearly demonstrated. Just as required audits of public companies have little prospect of relaxation, peer review is likely to continue to be refined and more finely tuned to needs and circumstances as they evolve.

The challenge today is to maintain and improve the effectiveness of peer review while controlling and, if possible, reducing its cost to all concerned.

The day will likely come, although not necessarily soon, that the foreign accounting bodies will acknowledge the benefits to be gained from peer review. They may continue to resist admission of U.S. personnel to their domains but they may agree to coordinate reviews conducted in their own jurisdictions with review of U.S. firms with international practices.

As the profession, both in the United States and internationally, gains experience in the peer review process, the effectiveness of peer review should be enhanced. While the initial cost of this program may seem high, the value to the public in improved reliability of financial reporting and to the profession in retained independence is also great.

MANAGEMENT REPORTS IN THE ERA

OF VOLUNTARY REPORTING ON

INTERNAL ACCOUNTING CONTROLS

John M. Guinan

Peat, Marwick, Mitchell & Co., New York

CONTENTS

ABSTRACT

Mr. Guinan reviews the issues related to the issuance of management reports as a part of companies' annual reports to stockholders, including the relationship of reporting on systems of internal accounting controls. The article reviews the early developments in the area, including reference to the Cohen Commission's recommendations, summarizes actions that have been taken by the SEC and discusses the major considerations in developing comments on internal accounting controls for management reports. In addition, the article includes a survey of the annual reports of 400 companies as to the extent of inclusion of management reports therein and, in an appendix, presents examples of portions of management reports which have been included in annual reports to stockholders.

INTRODUCTION

The movement to present management reports, which originated in 1978, has been transformed dramatically by the Securities and Exchange Commission's decision to withdraw a proposed rule that would have mandated reports on systems of internal accounting controls. In announcing the withdrawal of the proposed rule, the SEC said that it will monitor private-sector initiatives in reporting on the quality of internal accounting controls and will reconsider the need for a requirement at the end of the monitoring period. Because management reports typically contain statements on internal accounting controls, they are the principal vehicle the SEC intends to monitor. Moreover, the SEC has made clear that it intends to monitor all aspects of management reports—not just the passages on internal accounting controls.

The SEC's decision raises a number of questions about the future form and content of management reports. Will the treatment of internal accounting controls be changed by the awareness that the SEC is stressing that aspect of the reports? How will the treatment of other elements now common in the reports be affected? Will either or both expand as a result of attempts to comply with the SEC's desires? The answers to those questions depend on both future SEC action and voluntary initiatives by the private sector.

It seems an appropriate time to take stock of the issue of management reports. This article summarizes the relevant SEC release, discusses the early developments of management reports, and presents the results of a survey of management reports in 1979 annual reports to shareholders.

EARLY DEVELOPMENTS

Voluntary management reports were not first conceived solely, or even primarily, as vehicles for statements on internal accounting controls. The Commission on Auditors' Responsibilities (Cohen Commission) recommended such reports in 1978 as a remedy for the public misconception that auditors, rather than management, were responsible for the representations in the financial statements. The Cohen Commission's proposal was above all an attempt to rectify this problem by having management publicly report that it is responsible for the financial statements. The Cohen Commission also recommended that the reports include several other broad disclosures, including an assessment of the company's accounting system and controls over it, the role of the board of directors and/or audit committee, and the role of the independent accountant.

The Cohen Commission's recommendations prompted the Financial Executives Institute (FEI) and the American Institute of Certified Public Accountants (AICPA) to act. *The FEI in June 1978 endorsed the Cohen Commission's recommendation that financial statements in annual reports to shareholders be accompanied by a management report.* The FEI urged its members in June 1978 and again in December 1979 to include such a report in their annual report to shareholders.

The FEI issued in June 1978 "Guidelines for Preparation of a Statement of Management Responsibility for Financial Statements" (Guidelines). The Guidelines, which substantially coincide with the specific recommendations of the Cohen Commission, indicate that the FEI believes the public's understanding of the role of management and the independent accountant will be improved by management reports. It also believes that management reports should be presented in close proximity to the basic financial statements, possibly in conjunction with the accountants' report or in the financial review or management discussion and analysis section.

The FEI guidelines suggested that companies consider a number of subjects when preparing a management report, including the following:

- Management's responsibility for (a) preparing and presenting the financial statements in conformity with generally accepted accounting principles, (b) other financial information in the annual report, (c) the quality of data in the statements, and (d) accounting estimates and judgments.
- Management's responsibility for maintaining a system of internal accounting controls that provides reasonable assurance as to the integrity of the financial records and the protection of assets.
- Management's assessment of the effectiveness of internal accounting controls.
- The independent public accountant's responsibility for an examination and the expression of an opinion.
- The responsibilities of the board of directors and its audit committee.
- Ethical and legal policies for domestic and international business activities and the significance of any uncertainties that affect the financial statements.

A few months before the FEI endorsed the Cohen Commission's recommendations on management reports, the AICPA formed the "Special Advisory Committee on Reports by Management" (AICPA Special Committee) to consider the recommendations of the Cohen Commission. It was comprised primarily of financial executives and lawyers. In its report the AICPA Special Committee recommended that companies include in the annual report a report by management on the financial statements. The specific subject matter recommended for inclusion in the management report was substantially the same as what the Cohen Commission and FEI had recommended.

The purpose of all three groups' recommendations was to provide the users of the financial statements with a clear indication of management's responsibility for those statements and the means by which it fulfills that responsibility. All three favored voluntary initatives in management reporting. None favored mandatory inclusion of management reports in shareholder reports.

SEC ACTIONS

The SEC's decision to withdraw its April 1979 release proposing a requirement for a management statement on internal accounting controls has changed the circumstances under which voluntary management reports will be presented. The SEC intends to monitor voluntary management reports to determine whether they satisfy its purposes in proposing the requirement. *To date management reports have been flexible instruments and have not focused solely on internal accounting controls. But the prospect that the SEC will be evaluating the reports could change their nature.*

The withdrawn proposal was quite controversial. It prompted over 900 letters of comment, most of which were highly critical. The rule proposal contained no materiality guideline and would have required that the management statement on internal accounting controls be examined and reported on by independent public accountants. There was no empirical analysis of the costs and benefits of this requirement.

The SEC believes that proposing the rule to establish reporting on internal accounting controls was part of its responsibility to administer the accounting provisions of the Foreign Corrupt Practices Act of 1977 (FCPA), which are part of the federal securities laws. The FCPA's accounting provisions require public companies to devise and maintain a system of internal accounting controls sufficient to provide reasonable assurance that four basic objectives of internal accounting controls are met. These basic objectives are that transactions be properly authorized and recorded as necessary to permit preparation of financial statements in accordance with generally accepted accounting principles, that asset accountability be maintained, that assets be properly safeguarded from unauthorized use, and that assets on hand be compared with existing records at reasonable intervals and appropriate action taken with respect to any differences.

The Conditions of Withdrawal

Because voluntary management reports will be monitored by the SEC, companies that issue management reports or consider doing so should understand the terms under which the SEC intends to monitor them. The source for such an understanding is Accounting Series Release (ASR) No. 278 which, in June 1980, announced the withdrawal of the proposal for mandatory reporting on controls.

In ASR No. 278, the SEC reaffirmed its belief that it is important for companies to maintain effective systems of internal accounting controls because it is a requirement under the Foreign Corrupt Practices Act. The release also expressed the SEC's continuing belief that it is important to have management report on the effectiveness of internal accounting controls and to have independent accountants examine and report on such controls.

The SEC stated that it will reconsider the necessity and desirability of mandatory reporting after it has completed a period of monitoring that will extend through the spring of 1982. At that time the Commission may consider establishing requirements in three areas:

1. Management statements on internal accounting controls,
2. Public reporting by independent accountants on internal accounting controls, and
3. Comprehensive management reports in general.

The Commission's evaluation of management reporting in the next two years could lead to requirements in any or all of these areas.

The release sets out general criteria that will guide the SEC's decisions. They will be based on the extent of voluntary reports and management statements on internal accounting controls, on the usefulness of their disclosures, and on the procedures used to develop the reports. Although the release expresses the SEC's determination to take whatever action it considers appropriate as a result of the findings of its monitoring effort, it believes that the development of voluntary reporting on the effectiveness of internal accounting controls would be preferable to a SEC requirement.

Guidance on Content of Reports and Documentation

ASR No. 278 contains the SEC's views on assessing, documenting, and reporting on controls, compliance with the Foreign Corrupt Practices Act, other information that might be included in management reports, and auditor involvement with reporting on controls. The release refers to these views as guidance. As management reports come under closer scrutiny, many companies probably will wish to be aware of these elements of ASR No. 278. For this reason, several key points are summarized below.

Representation on Controls. The release distinguishes between management reports on internal accounting control systems that provide an explicit assessment of the effectiveness of the system and those that do not. The distinction the SEC is drawing here is the difference between reporting on the design and functioning of the system and reporting on the design alone. The management report which addresses functioning of the system would be based on some form of testing and monitoring. The SEC prefers a report that comments upon both design and functioning.

Objective of Control. The SEC believes that the users of the financial statements should be informed in the management report of the four objectives of internal accounting controls contained in the Foreign Corrupt Practices Act. The objectives can be paraphrased as long as the presentation is informative and addresses each of the objectives. One possible approach is to state that the objectives of control are to provide reasonable assurance that transactions are authorized, assets are safeguarded, and reliable financial statements are prepared.

The concept of reasonable assurance has been interpreted to mean that the benefit of a control should be matched with its cost. In making cost-benefit determinations management should recognize that the effectiveness of control systems is inherently limited by the risk of human error. At any time, carelessness, fatigue, or misunderstanding can undermine the achievement of a control objective.

Materiality. The lack of a materiality guideline was one of the most criticized elements in the SEC's proposed rule. In ASR No. 278 the SEC reemphasized its views that the internal accounting control provisions of the Foreign Corrupt Practices Act are not limited by financial statement materiality. It did recognize, however, that certain weaknesses in controls are more significant than others. For disclosure purposes the SEC believes that the management report should encompass the effectiveness of controls over those matters about which the shareholder reasonably should be informed. This implies some standard of materiality is applicable, even if none has been specified.

Period Covered by the Representation. The Foreign Corrupt Practices Act requires a company to devise and maintain a system of internal accounting controls. This is an ongoing requirement. For this reason, the SEC's proposed rule would have required an assessment of controls for the entire period covered by the financial statements. Thus the representation would have to be based on an evaluation of the condition of the system throughout the year. The SEC still believes in the approach, but it also now believes that there is value, for disclosure purposes, in management reports that address the effectiveness of the system at a point in time (e.g., the end of the fiscal year).

Testing. The SEC believes that an evaluation of controls includes some form of monitoring of controls. Monitoring includes testing control procedures and observation and supervision of day-to-day activities. The SEC believes that monitoring compliance with control procedures is not only necessary to evaluate the system but is also an integral part of a system and therefore should be ongoing. However, ASR No. 278 noted that the extent of testing is one of the cost-benefit judgments management must make.

Documentation. The SEC considers documentation of controls and of reviews of controls to be an important feature of evaluations of the system of internal accounting controls. However, it noted that a minimum level of documentation for all companies cannot be established because the appropriateness of the level of documentation should be determined in the context of the circumstances of each company. It also noted that cost-benefit decisions play a part in determining an appropriate level of documentation. The SEC warns, however, that in cases where systems subsequently fail or are circumvented, management's judgments would stand a better chance of being considered reasonable if its decisions were backed up by complete information not only on the system of control, but also on management's ongoing monitoring of it. In other words, the level of documentation may be questioned when a control problem arises.

Other Matters for the Report. The SEC is going to monitor the entire content of the management report and encourage companies to disclose whatever information management believes will make the assessment of the effectiveness of controls most informative. Among the items suggested for inclusion by the SEC are:

- Description of management's responsibility for preparation of financial statements and other financial information.
- Description of the work of the audit committee.
- Description of the work of internal auditors.
- Description of codes of conduct and an assessment of compliance.
- Discussion of the importance of the elements of the control environment that may include:
  - organizational structure,
  - communication of policies and procedures,
  - competence and training of personnel, and
  - accountability for performance and compliance with established policies and procedures.
- Description of the general approach used in reviewing and evaluating controls.
- Description of the extent to which control review and monitoring procedures are performed.

The above elements are essentially the same as the specific recommendations of the Cohen Commission, the FEI, and the AICPA Special Committee. In addition to those elements, the SEC encourages companies to explain the respective responsibilities of management and the independent accountant in the assessment of the control system.

Independent Accountants' Involvement. The SEC intends to monitor management's voluntary retention of independent accountants to assist them in assessing the effectiveness of internal accounting controls. The withdrawn proposal would have required a report by independent accountants on management's assessment of controls. This aspect of the proposed rule was criticized heavily because of its probable costs. The SEC maintained in the proposed rule that it believed these costs would be outweighed by the benefits. Nevertheless, during the monitoring period the SEC indicated that it will be collecting empirical data to determine whether the cost of independent accountants' involvement outweighs the perceived benefit. The extent of their involvement is something that will have to be decided on a company-by-company basis. The type of independent accountant involvement contemplated by the SEC is discussed under "Basis for Reporting on Controls."

★ ★ ★ ★

It is not anticipated that the SEC will take any specific action to reconsider a requirement for mandatory reporting on internal accounting controls until it has completed its monitoring period. During that period, however, the private sector will have to make decisions on management reporting fully aware that the beliefs and perspectives that led the SEC to propose mandatory reporting will continue to affect its judgments. As the SEC stated in ASR No. 278, the withdrawal of the proposals should not be interpreted as a change in its views concerning management's explicit assessment of controls and auditor examination of such controls.

BASIS FOR REPORTING
ON CONTROLS

There are two major considerations in developing comments on internal accounting controls for management reports. They are what to say and the basis for whatever is said. The Cohen Commission, the FEI, and the AICPA Special Committee provided some guidance on appropriate comments. The SEC also endorsed similar elements in ASR No. 278. The guidance and recommendations of these groups have already been described. Representations that have been made in published management reports are reviewed below (see "Survey of Management Reports"). This section focuses on the basis for the representation.

*The basis for an assessment of the effectiveness of controls is an ongoing evaluation of the design and functioning of the system of internal account-*ing controls. SEC Chairman Williams said at the time the proposal for mandatory reporting was withdrawn that compliance with the accounting provisions of the Foreign Corrupt Practices Act and the essence of a management reporting process on controls can be summed up by three steps—"a review and strengthening of controls, the fostering of a positive control environment, and system documentation." An ongoing review and evaluation would indicate whether the accounting controls, control environment, or system documentation need to be strengthened in order to assess the effectiveness of controls in the management report. (For a discussion of evaluating the system of controls, see "Reporting on Internal Accounting Control," K.W. Stringer and G.L. Holstrum, in *Annual Account-ing Review,* vol. 2, edited by S. Weinstein and M. Walker (Harwood Academic Publishers, Chur, Switzerland, 1980), pp. 143–156.)

Internal Audit Assistance

A good source for management to draw upon for assistance in evaluating controls is the internal audit department. It can help in the following ways:

- Assist in developing corporate procedures and guidelines,
- Evaluate the adequacy of changes in procedures prompted by identified deficiencies, and
- Test the functioning of procedures.

The internal audit department can also serve as an interface with the independent accountants if management determines there is a need for their involvement.

Independent Accountants' Involvement

The independent accountant can perform several types of services in connection with a management report, including a separate accountants' report on the system of internal accounting controls. The type of service is dictated by the needs of management and the type of report desired. The guidelines for reporting are contained in *Statement on Auditing Standards No. 30,* "Reporting on Internal Accounting Controls" (SAS 30).

SAS 30. There are several different types of accountants' reports that can be issued in accordance with the guidelines in SAS 30. Accountants can be retained to express an opinion on the entire system of controls based on a full-scale comprehensive review of controls or requested to express some limited assurance about controls based solely on a study and evaluation made as part of an audit. In addition, accountants can be engaged to issue reports to management that have a special purpose—for example, to provide an opinion on the design of controls but not on how they are functioning.

Comprehensive reviews of the system. Accountants can issue an opinion on the entire system of internal accounting controls only if they perform a comprehensive review of the system. Under SAS 30 a comprehensive review consists of four steps: plan the scope of the engagement, review the design of the system, test compliance with prescribed procedures, and evaluate the results of the review and tests. SAS 30 does not restrict the distribution of the accountants' report on the system based a comprehensive review of controls. The report could accompany management's assessment of the effectiveness of controls in the annual report to shareholders.

Limited reviews of controls. Limited assurance reports which are intended solely for use by management and boards of directors can be issued in connection with audits. The report discloses whether material weaknesses in controls were uncovered during the audit. It can provide some support for management's assessment of the effectiveness of controls. Such reports must specify the limited purpose of the study and evaluation of controls in connection with an audit and must contain a disclaimer of an opinion on the entire system of internal accounting controls.

Other Services. Independent accountants can provide other services with regard to the company's system of internal accounting controls. For example, accountants may be engaged to work with the internal audit department to develop monitoring techniques. In these circumstances the accountant may communicate the results of his work by letter, memorandum, or other less formal means.

★ ★ ★ ★

As stated above, the basis for a representation on controls is an ongoing review and evaluation. This includes determining whether the controls, control environment, and system documentation needs strengthening. Although the internal audit department and the independent accountants can assist management in making this determination, in the final analysis management alone must decide whether the basis for its representation is sufficient.

SURVEY OF MANAGEMENT REPORTS

Now that the conditions in which management reports will be presented have changed, companies will be determining whether to issue reports for the first time or whether to revise the presentations they have already developed. In order to provide some perspective for such decisions, the author surveyed the form and content of management reports issued by a sample of public companies in 1979. *Of the 400 annual reports surveyed, 168 (42%) contained a report by management. The same group issued only 75 (19%) management reports in the previous year.*

Extent of the Survey

The 400 annual reports were selected at random from reports of public companies. The companies covered a wide range of industries, including the manufacturing, financial, extractive, service and utility industries. Table I summarizes the industry classifications of the surveyed companies. Table II categorizes the surveyed companies by annual sales volume. Two hundred twenty-one of the 400 enterprises are included in the *Fortune* 500 industrial companies, and 108 of those contained a report by management.

Content of Management Reports

The content of the management reports in the survey was analyzed by using four broad topics: (1) management's responsibility for financial statements, (2) role of the audit committee, (3) role of independent accountants, and (4) system of internal accounting controls. The four topics include the subjects recommended by the Cohen Commission, the FEI, and the AICPA Special Committee. They are also the broad areas the SEC plans to monitor. Most of the management reports addressed all four broad areas. Examples of the specific representations made by the selected companies appear in the Appendix.

Management's Responsibility for Financial Statements. One hundred sixty-six (99%) of the reports in the survey addressed management's responsibility for financial statements. Several of those reports also ad-

TABLE I

Industry Classifications
of Surveyed Companies

Industry	Number of companies in survey	Number of companies presenting management reports	Percentage of companies presenting reports
Manufacturing	209	93	44%
Financial Institutions	55	22	40%
Extractive	41	17	41%
Service	21	6	29%
Utilities	36	19	53%
Other	38	11	29%
	400	168	42%

TABLE II

Sales Volume of
Surveyed Companies

Annual Sales ($000,000)	Number of companies in survey	Number of companies presenting management reports	Percentage of companies presenting reports
$ 100 – 999	142	32	23%
$1,000 – 1,999	99	39	39%
$2,000 – 2,999	64	31	48%
$3,000 – 3,999	31	21	68%
$4,000 – 4,999	16	8	50%
more than $4,999	48	37	77%
	400	168	42%

dressed management's responsibility for all information presented in the annual report, and 132 (79%) of the reports stated that the preparation of financial statements necessarily includes amounts determined by management's best judgment and estimates. One hundred fifty-nine (95%) of the management reports included a specific representation of the conformity of the financial statements with generally accepted accounting principles or other applicable standards.

The FEI Guidelines and the Cohen Commission recommended that the management report be signed by the chief financial officer and/or the chief executive officer. Eighty-two (49%) of the reports examined were signed by one or more company officers. Table III summarizes the positions of those who signed the reports.

Role of the Audit Committee. One hundred sixty-five (98%) of the surveyed reports discussed the role of the audit committee. Several noted that the audit committee meets regularly with the independent and internal auditors to discuss the results of their audits and their opinions on the adequacy of controls. Many of the reports also stated that the board members serving on the audit committee were independent.

Role of Independent Accountants. One hundred forty-seven (88%) of the management reports in the survey either discussed the role of the independent accountants or made reference to their opinion on the financial statements. Almost all of the remaining management reports were presented on the same page of the annual report that contained the accountants' report.

One hundred thirty (77%) of the surveyed reports discussed the independent accountants' work in connection with internal accounting controls. Some referred to the review of controls performed during an audit; others noted that the independent accountants discussed the findings of their review with the audit committee.

System of Internal Accounting Controls. One hundred sixty-four (98%) of the management reports contained representations on the company's system of internal accounting controls. The types of disclosures included:

- objectives of controls,
- monitoring the system,
- role of internal audit department, and
- control environment.

TABLE III

Signatories of Surveyed
Management Reports

Single Signature	Number of Management Reports
Chief executive officer	3
Chief financial officer	15
Controller	5
Other	1
	24

Two Signatures	
Chairman and president	2
Chief executive officer and chief financial officer	45
Chief financial officer and controller	10
	57

Three Signatures	
Chief executive officer, chief financial officer, and chief accounting officer	1
	82

Objectives of controls. One hundred fifty-five (90%) of the management reports discussed the objectives of internal accounting controls. The form of this discussion varied, ranging from a complete recitation of the four objectives of control to a paraphrase of them. In assessing the achievement of the objectives, a majority of the surveyed reports discussed the relationship between the costs of controls and their benefits and/or the inherent limitations of control.

Monitoring the system. One hundred fifty-six (93%) of the reports discussed how management monitors the system of control. Sixty-one

(36%) reports contained an explicit representation on the functioning of controls.

Role of internal audit department. One hundred sixty-two (96%) of the reports discussed the role of the internal audit department. Most of the disclosures described the role the department played in monitoring the control system.

Control environment. The control environment includes procedures to communicate established policies and procedures, methods to select and train qualified personnel, organizational arrangements to delegate authority and segregate responsibilities, the program of internal audits, and procedures for follow-up by management. Ninety-four (56%) of the reports in the survey discussed aspects of the control environment other than the role of the internal audit department. Fifty-eight (35%) specifically commented on documentation of control procedures. Thirty-four (20%) of the reports specifically addressed codes of conduct or ethical behavior and/or compliance with them.

CONCLUSION

The management report has been a private-sector initiative since its inception. It is a very useful means of informing financial statement users of the individual roles that management, the board of directors, and the independent accountants have in the process of presenting financial statements. Its rapid development in the past few years demonstrated the vigor of private-sector initiatives and the depth of the commitment to management reports. In my opinion, there is good reason to believe that the management report will continue to develop in response to the needs of investors without regulatory intervention.

APPENDIX

MANAGEMENT REPORT REPRESENTATIONS

Management's Responsibility for Financial Statements

The consolidated financial statements . . . , as well as other information contained in this report, were prepared by management which is responsible for their integrity and objectivity. (*The Southland Corporation*)

It is management's responsibility to see that such financial statements accurately reflect the financial position of the Company and its operating results. (*Campbell Taggart, Inc.*)

Management is responsible for the content of the financial statements included in this annual report and the information contained in other sections of this annual report, which information is believed to be consistent with the content of the financial statements. Management believes that the financial statements have been prepared in conformity with generally accepted principles appropriate in the circumstances to reflect, in all material respects, the substance of events and transactions that should be included. The financial statements of necessity reflect Management's judgments and estimates as to the effects of events and transactions that are accounted for or disclosed. (*The Chase Manhattan Corporation*)

The company has prepared the consolidated financial statements, including notes, in accordance with generally accepted accounting principles consistently applied. Financial information included elsewhere in this annual report is consistent with the data included in the financial statements. (*Moore McCormack Resources, Inc.*)

We have prepared the accompanying statement of financial position of [the Company] and consolidated affiliates as of December 31, 1979 and 1978, and related statements of earnings, changes in financial position and changes in share owners' equity for the years then ended, including the notes, industry and geographic segment information, and supplementary information on the effect of changing prices. The statements have been prepared in conformity with generally accepted accounting principles appropriate in the circumstances, and include amounts that are based on our best estimates and judgments. Financial information elsewhere in this Annual Report is consistent with that in the financial statements. (*General Electric Company*)

Role of the Audit Committee

The Audit Committee of the Board of Directors, composed solely of outside directors, meets periodically with the Company's management, internal auditors and independent certified public accountants to review matters relating to the quality of financial reporting and internal accounting control and the nature, extent and results of the audit efforts. The independent certified public accountants have free access to the Audit Committee. (*Xerox Corporation*)

The Board of Directors elects an Audit Committee from among its members who are neither officers nor employed of the Company. Acting on behalf of the Board, the Committee approves major accounting policies and periodically reviews principal internal controls to assure their adequacy. The Committee recommends to the Board of Directors, for approval by the stockholders, the appointment of the independent auditors who conduct the annual examination of the Company's financial statements. The Committee also provides a channel of communications between the Board of Directors and accounting personnel, internal auditors and independent auditors; reviews the scope of the annual examination of accounts; reviews and approves the other services performed by the independent auditors; and reviews the division of responsibility between the internal and independent auditors as well as their findings and recommendations. (*Conoco Inc.*)

The Board of Directors, through its Operating and Audit Committees, monitors the financial and accounting administration of the Company, including the review of the activities of both the internal auditors and the independent public accountants, the review and discussion of periodic financial statements, and the evaluation and adoption of budgets.... The auditors met with members of the Audit Committee to discuss the results of their examination, and were afforded an opportunity to present their opinions in the absence of management personnel with respect to various financial matters. (*Stauffer Chemical Company*)

The Board of Directors pursues its oversight role for the financial statements through its Audit Committee composed of three non-management directors. The Audit Committee meets at least three times a year with management, the internal auditors, and the independent auditors. The independent auditors and internal auditors have access to the Audit Committee to discuss internal accounting controls, auditing, and financial reporting matters. (*Nalco Chemical Company*)

The Company has had an Audit Committee of the Board of Directors for more than ten years. The Committee currently consists exclusively of directors who are not employees of the Company, and meets as required but at a minimum of three times a year. The Committee has been established for the general purpose of satisfying itself as to the integrity of the Company's accounting and financial reporting, maintaining external and internal audit functions, and continuously emphasizing the need for internal financial controls. Annually the Committee also approves the extent of non-audit services provided by the independent accountants, giving due consideration to the impact of such services on auditor independence. The independent accountants and the internal auditors have full and free access to the Audit Committee and meet with it, with and without management being present, to discuss all appropriate matters. (*Atlantic Richfield Company*)

Role of Independent Accountants

The accountants' report expresses an informed judgment as to whether the financial statements, considered in their entirety, present the Company's financial position and results of operations in conformity with generally accepted accounting principles. Their procedures include obtaining an understanding of the Company's systems and procedures and performing tests and other procedures as they deem necessary to provide reasonable assurance, giving due consideration to materiality, that the financial statements contain neither misleading nor erroneous data. While the independent accountants make tests of Company procedures, it is neither practical nor necessary for them to examine all of the Company's transactions. (*Crum and Foster*)

The independent auditors are engaged to express an opinion on our financial statements. Their opinion is based on procedures believed by them to be sufficient to provide reasonable assurance that the financial statements are not materially misleading and do not contain material errors. (*First International Bancshares Inc.*)

Their examination [the independent accountants] was conducted in accordance with generally accepted auditing standards. Such standards require a review of internal controls, examination of selected transactions and other procedures sufficient to provide reasonable assurance that the financial statements are neither misleading nor contain material errors. The Auditor's Report ... does not limit the responsibility of management for information contained in the financial statements and elsewhere in the Annual Report. (*Central and South West Corporation*)

The financial statements have been examined by independent auditors.... Their role is to render an independent professional opinion on management's financial statements based upon performance of procedures they deem appropriate under generally accepted auditing standards. (*Manufacturers National Corporation*)

The consolidated financial statements have been examined by our independent certified public accountants.... Their examination was conducted in accordance with generally accepted auditing standards and included a review of the system of internal accounting controls to the extent necessary to support their report ... as to the fair presentation, in the consolidated financial statements, of the company's financial position, results of operations, and changes in financial position. (*American Cyanamid Company*)

Effectiveness of Internal Accounting Controls

[The Company's] system of internal controls is designed to provide reasonable assurance that the financial records are accurate, the Company's assets are protected and financial statements present fairly the financial position and the results of operations. The system's adequacy and effectiveness is monitored by [the Company's] internal audit staff. (*Hospital Corporation of America*)

[The Company] maintains a highly developed system of internal accounting control. It consists, in part, of organizational arrangements with clearly defined lines of responsibility and delegation of authority. We believe this system provides reasonable assurance that transactions are executed in accordance with management authorization, and that they are appropriately recorded, in order to permit preparation of financial statements in conformity with generally accepted accounting principles and to adequately safeguard, verify and maintain accountability of assets. An important element of the system is a continuing and extensive internal audit program. (*International Business Machines Corporation*)

The integrity of the Company's financial records, from which the financial statements are prepared, is largely dependent on the Company's system of internal accounting controls. The purpose of the system is to provide reasonable assurance that: Transactions are executed in accordance with management's authorization; transactions are appropriately recorded in order to permit preparation of financial statements which, in all material respects, are presented in conformity with generally accepted accounting principles consistently applied; and assets are properly accounted for and safeguarded against loss from unauthorized use. Underlying this concept of reasonable assurance is the fact that limitations exist in any system of internal accounting based on the premise that the cost of such controls should not exceed the benefits derived therefrom.

To enhance the effective achievement of internal accounting controls, the Company carefully selects and trains its employees, gives due emphasis to appropriate division of clearly defined lines of responsibility and develops and communicates written policies and procedures. Based on a review and monitoring of internal accounting controls, augmented by an internal auditing function and the oversight responsibilities of the outside directors comprising the Audit Committee of the Company's Board of Directors, management believes that the Company's internal accounting controls are adequate, appropriately balancing the cost/benefit relationship. (*UAL Inc.*)

The company maintains systems of internal controls, policies and procedures which it believes will ensure that its accounting, administrative procedures and reporting practices are of the highest quality and integrity. The company also maintains an internal auditing function which constantly evaluates the adequacy and effectiveness of such internal controls, policies and procedures. The company's business ethics policy, which is regularly communicated to all levels of the organization, requires employees to maintain high ethical standards in their conduct of company affairs. (*Kraft Inc.*)

The company maintains accounting and reporting systems, supported by an internal accounting control system, which management believes are adequate to provide reasonable assurances that assets are safeguarded against loss from unauthorized use or disposition and financial records are reliable for preparing financial statements. During 1979, the company in conjunction with ... its independent accountants, performed a comprehensive review of the adequacy of the company's internal accounting control systems. Based on this review, it is management's opinion that the company has an effective system of internal accounting control. (*Anheuser-Busch Companies, Inc.*)

In meeting its responsibility for preparing reliable financial statements, management maintains and depends upon a system of internal accounting controls which is designed to provide reasonable assurance that assets are safeguarded, and that transactions are executed in accordance with management's authorization and properly recorded to permit the preparation of financial statements in accordance with generally accepted accounting principles. The concept of reasonable assurance is based on the recognition that judgments are required to assess and balance the cost and expected benefits of a system of internal accounting controls. Written internal accounting control and other operating policies and procedures supporting this system are communicated throughout the Company. Adherence to these policies and procedures is continuously reviewed through a coordinated audit effort of the Company's internal audit staff and independent certified public accountants. (*The Singer Company*)

The Corporation maintains a system of internal accounting controls, supported by documentation, to provide reasonable assurance that assets are safeguarded and that the books and records reflect the authorized transactions of the Corporation. Limitations exist in any system of internal accounting controls based upon the recognition that the cost of the system should not exceed the benefits derived. [The Corporation] believes its system of internal accounting controls, augmented by its internal auditing function, appropriately balances the cost/benefit relationship. (*Westinghouse Electric Corporation*)

Management depends on the company's system of internal accounting controls to assure itself of the reliability of the financial statements. The internal control system is designed to provide reasonable assurance that assets are safeguarded and transactions are executed in accordance with management's authorization and recorded properly to permit the preparation of financial statements in accordance with generally accepted accounting principles. Despite the exercise of care in designing control procedures, management recognizes that errors or irregularities may nevertheless occur. Periodic reviews are made of internal controls by the company's staff of internal auditors and corrective action taken if needed. Management believes that the company's accounting controls provide reasonable assurance that errors or irregularities that could be material to the financial statements are prevented or would be detected within a timely period by employees in the normal course of performing their assigned functions. (*Kerr-McGee Corporation*)

The accounting system and related internal accounting controls...are designed to provide reasonable assurance that the financial records are reliable for preparing financial statements and maintaining accountability for assets and that assets are safeguarded against loss from unauthorized use or disposition. The system in use ... provides such reasonable assurance, supported by the careful selection and training of staff, the establishment of organizational structures providing an appropriate and well-defined division of responsibilities and the communication of policies and standards of business conduct throughout the institution. (Citicorp)

The management of the Company maintains systems of internal accounting controls and procedures to provide reasonable assurance that its assets are safeguarded against loss from unauthorized use or disposition, and that the financial records provide a reliable basis for the preparation of financial statements and other data, as well as maintaining accountability for corporate assets. Internal accounting control is maintained by: 1) the selection and proper training of qualified personnel; 2) an appropriate separation of duties in organizational arrangements; 3) the establishment and communication of accounting and business policies together with detailed procedures for their implementation; 4) an extensive program of internal auditing, with prompt follow-up, if necessary, at appropriate levels of management; and 5) a detailed budgeting system which assures that expenditures are charged to the appropriate budget center or capital appropriation.

During 1979 the Company appointed a special committee of corporate officers which carried out a detailed review of accounting control systems throughout the corporation. The review confirmed management's belief that [the Company's] internal controls have in the past, and continue to accomplish their intended objectives. (*Inland Steel Company*)

STATUS OF REQUIRED
CONTINUING EDUCATION FOR
CERTIFIED PUBLIC ACCOUNTANTS

Robert L. Gray

Executive Director,
The New York State Society of
Certified Public Accountants

CONTENTS

ABSTRACT

Mr. Gray presents a detailed analysis of the history and current developments related to required continuing education for certified public accountants. He reviews the initial efforts that were made in this area and indicates where the profession stands currently, both on an overall basis and in individual states where requirements have been adopted or proposed. He covers such specific areas as types of courses, organizations which are capable of providing such programs, the national standards that have been developed for measuring the adequacy of programs and discusses the problems of accreditation of specific courses. This article provides an excellent summary of the subject and will serve as a basis for study of the subject by individuals who wish to pursue it further.

OVERVIEW

Prior to the end of World War II, there were generally no significant on-going, professionally-oriented educational programs available to CPAs. The need to update the numerous returning servicemen on new developments in the public accounting profession inspired state societies to begin playing a role in continuing education.

Approximately ten years after the start of this trend in 1945, the American Institute of Certified Public Accountants (AICPA), the national organization of the profession, began making available educational programs for their members. Today, this activity remains one of the most important roles of the AICPA.

Beginning in the 1970's, required continuing education became a major factor, either as an actuality or as a potential factor, in the future of all practicing CPAs. As a result, accounting firms and state societies greatly expanded their educational activities.

In-house training programs, long an exclusive activity of the "Big Eight" accounting firms, are now conducted by all of the largest twenty firms while numerous state societies, including California, New York, Illinois and Texas, have established foundations specializing in education for practicing CPAs.

As the profession faces the 1980's, two major forces impact the CPA: the tremendous volume of new technical information needed by the professional and the concurrent "fallout" of information that is no longer valid or pertinent. This rapidity of change, both in acquiring the new knowledge and discarding the obsolete, is the dual challenge in training currently facing the profession.

HISTORY OF REQUIRED CONTINUING EDUCATION

Marvin Stone, President of the American Institute of Certified Public Accountants, formally introduced the idea of required continuing education for CPAs in 1967. His remarks were directed to a conference on ethics which was grappling with the problem of substandard accounting work.

Stone was convinced that "most substandard work is the result of ignorance rather than willfullness" and suggested that the problem be attacked by attempting to dispel ignorance through a program of required continuing education.[1]

The only reason CPAs are licensed, Stone asserted, is to protect the public. As such, the public is entitled to some assurance that, in an age of exploding information and knowledge, the CPA possesses enough current knowledge to prevent obsolescence. Through required continuing education, a good beginning step toward providing that degree of assurance could be achieved, concluded Stone.[2]

In 1971, following two years of intensive study, a special ad hoc committee on continuing education chaired by Elmer G. Beamer, presented a resolution to the AICPA's governing council recommending required continuing education. It was the committee's conviction that the great majority of the profession favored such a requirement.

Some of the Beamer Committee's key points focused on the following:

Definition of Continuing Education. The concept was defined as "formal programs of learning which contribute directly to the professional competence of an individual after he has become a CPA."

The Need for Continuing Education. The dramatic explosion of knowledge was cited as making continuing education the alternative to obsolescence.

Why Continuing Education Should Be Required. Available evidence indicated that only 14% of all CPAs were voluntarily continuing their education.

What Kind of Continuing Education Is Needed? It was determined that, because the accounting field was so broad, there was no single pattern of continuing education appropriate for all CPAs. Therefore, it was left to the judgment of the individual CPA to determine for himself the subject matter appropriate to his needs.

At the spring 1971 AICPA Council meeting, the Beamer committee's recommendation was adopted. The states were urged to require that all CPAs demonstrate they are continuing their professional education on the basis that:

> ...the explosion of knowledge and the increasing complexity of practice make it essential that certified public accountants continue to develop their competence, and

> ...the public interest requires that certified public accountants provide competent service in all areas of their practice, and

> ...formal programs of continuing education provide certified public accountants with the opportunity to maintain and improve their competence...[3]

The AICPA's Council also requested that the National Association of State Boards of Accountancy (NASBA) support actions by the states to require continuing education as a condition by which CPAs could renew their permits to practice. In 1972, NASBA did so by urging states and jurisdictions to adopt such guidelines, by statute or regulations.

Since the approval of the AICPA Council resolution in 1971, required continuing education for CPAs has experienced rapid growth. The number of CPAs who are required to continue their professional education is estimated at 64%, or 54,000 CPAs of the 84,000 CPAs practicing public accounting in 1979.

Strong support from practicing CPAs and state legislatures alike has been evident. Proponents of required continuing education believe it is necessary to promote the learning and application of new knowledge among CPAs. With the CPA's services affecting clients, third parties and the public, proponents feel these entities are entitled to some assurance that the CPA possesses sufficient current knowledge to avoid engaging in substandard work through ignorance.

Opponents, on the other hand, do not argue against the value of continuing education but see competence as the real issue. A required program of continuing education, this group believes, will not necessarily produce competence but results in additional burdens for the practitioner.

Although proponents agree that required continuing education is not the only remedy for poor performance, they strongly believe in the concept as a significant step toward the goal of providing our society with reliable, independent, consumer-oriented, quality accounting and related services.

THE NEED FOR REQUIRED CONTINUING EDUCATION

It is the consensus of the leaders of the profession, government and other interested groups, that participation in formal career-long education plays a significant role in maintaining and improving the quality of professional practice. The following points are cited in support of this premise:

1. In response to a concern regarding the quality of professional practice around the nation, the National Association of State Boards of Accountancy, at its annual meeting on September 29, 1972, adopted a resolution stating in part: "Whereas, formal programs of continuing education provide certified public accountants ... with the opportunity to maintain and improve their competence ... (the association) urges each of the several states to institute ... a requirement, by legislation or regulation, that certified public accountants ... demonstrate that they are continuing their professional education."[4]

The National Association of State Boards of Accountancy, a national professional association of the regulatory boards and agencies in the 50 states, further stated that a minimum requirement of 120 hours of formal education (over a three year period) become a "condition precedent to the re-registration, renewal of permit to practice, or other validation of their professional designation."[5]

2. The Securities Exchange Commission has imposed sanctions,[6] instituted litigation and formalized criticism of the professions.[7] In response to these actions, one of the most visual changes made by the accounting profession was the creation by the AICPA, in 1977, of the Division for CPA Firms, and, within that division, the SEC Practice Section which mandates extensive training programs. In every member firm, each member of the professional staff is required to complete at least 120 hours of classes over a three year period to help the practitioner sustain his professional competence.[8]

The Special Investigations Committee of the SEC Practice Section monitors alleged or possible audit failures and recommends the imposition of sanctions to the SEC Practice Section's Executive Committee. Prominently featured in the list of types of sanctions which may be imposed is "additional requirements for continuing professional education."[9]

3. The U.S. Congress has shown major concern and expressed strong criticism of the conduct of professional practice.[10] Congress formed a special investigative committee which issued a critical

report, indicating, among others, a need for continuing professional education.[11]

4. Various private studies also confirmed this need for continuing professional education. One such study revealed that 31% of a 20,000 member professional group devoted no time to formal educational programs and that 11% of those who did participate, were spending less time in the current year than in the prior year.[12]

5. Leading insurance underwriters, concerned about an unacceptable level of quality of practice, are now providing credits against premiums for those practitioners and firms actively participating in formal career-long learning.[13] Despite the discounts offered, only a small number of firms has taken advantage of this program.

6. Many practicing professionals themselves have publicly expressed concern about the declining quality of work they have observed occurring within their profession by those who no longer have current and valid knowledge, and who are also uneducated as to their social and ethical responsibilities.[14]

In conclusion, practicing professionals recognize that there is a constantly changing body of knowledge, and in order to enable them to discharge their public responsibilities, both economic and social, they recognize that they:

1. Must reacquaint themselves with the topic areas of previously acquired knowledge; and
2. Must selectively reinforce the subject matter of previously acquired knowledge; and
3. Must learn in greater depth, for application purposes, previously acquired knowledge; and
4. Must unlearn that which is obsolete in their previously acquired knowledge; and
5. Must master the subject matter of newly emerging knowledge.[15]

REQUIRED CONTINUING EDUCATION STATES

As of September 1980, 36 states and the District of Columbia, had enacted statutes or State Board regulations, requiring continuing professional education for CPAs as a prerequisite for renewal of their license to practice. These states are shown in Table 1.

TABLE 1

State	Legislation Enacted	State	Legislation Enacted
Alabama	1973	Minnesota	1976
Alaska	1976	Montana	1979
Arizona	1979	Nebraska	1971
Arkansas	1979	Nevada	1973
California	1972	New Mexico	1977
Colorado	1973	North Carolina	1979
Connecticut	1978	North Dakota	1975
District of Columbia	1978	Ohio	1974
Florida	1973	Oklahoma	1980
Georgia	1977	Oregon	1975
Hawaii	1973	Pennsylvania	1976
Indiana	1979	Rhode Island*	1979
Iowa	1974	South Carolina	1974
Kansas	1973	South Dakota	1973
Louisiana	1979	Tennessee	1980
Maine	1979	Vermont	1975
Maryland	1976	Washington	1973
Massachusetts*	1978	Wyoming	1975
Michigan	1976		

*Legislation requiring continuing education was not enacted. The Rhode Island and Massachusetts Boards of Public Accountancy adopted, through regulatory means, mandatory CPE.

EFFECTIVENESS OF REQUIRED CONTINUING EDUCATION

A survey was made of the Immediate Past-Presidents of State CPA Societies where required continuing education has been in effect for at least the previous two years.

Immediate Past-Presidents were selected since they have most recently completed an intense period of responsible professional leadership working closely with hundreds of rank and file practicing CPAs.

The group surveyed, a total of twenty-four individuals, was asked to respond confidentially to a total of six questions. With a unanimous (100%) response rate, this group provides much insight into how the effectiveness of continuing education is viewed by those CPAs who are required to participate.

The subjective nature of the questions produced several distinct trends, especially a most positive tone in areas concerning the effectiveness of required continuing education in raising a CPA's technical competence and whether the public's best interests were being served by required continuing education.

A large majority (84%) of the respondents found that there was an increase in awareness of technical standards among members. While there were no negative responses, 16% were unsure. Again, when asked if there was an increase in technical competence, a majority (76%) believed there was. Four percent (4%) did not think so while 20% were unsure.

The number of respondents agreeing that required continuing education significantly reduces substandard work was also high with sixty-three percent (63%) replying affirmatively. Thirty-three percent (33%) were not sure and one respondent disagreed. The general consensus seems to be that substandard work is reduced, but over a period of time, not overnight.

It was the overwhelming opinion of the respondents (100%) that required continuing education is worth both the time and cost involved for the membership. There was also total affirmative agreement among the twenty-four (24) respondents that the public's best interests are being served.

The belief that the majority of members approach required continuing education seriously was reinforced by the overwhelming majority of respondents, eighty-three percent (83%) of whom believe that less than 10% of their members are "just putting in time." All respondents feel that less than 10% of their members leave early when attending educational programs while no one believes that members have other people attend for them.

All twenty-four (24) respondents agree that members participate in continuing education courses that are relevant to their areas of practice. The general consensus was that the time involved, as well as the cost, makes it inadvisable for a CPA to take courses that are irrelevant.

As further evidence of the value placed on the effectiveness of continuing education, the AICPA in 1977 created the Division for CPA Firms comprised of the Private Companies Practice Section and SEC Companies Practice Section. All professionals in member firms are required to participate in at least one hundred twenty hours of qualifying continuing education every three years.

One of the nation's leading underwriters of professional liability insurance also recognizes the importance of continuing education in reducing the incidence of substandard performance by offering discounts to professionals who participate in educational activities.

Furthermore, sanctions against CPA firms imposed by the Securities and Exchange Commission have included a study of the firm's continuing professional education training programs for its staff members as part of the review of the firm's procedures and quality control of handling engagements. In addition to reviewing the adequacy of the educational programs and the degree of participation of staff members, the reviewers have frequently suggested improvements in the quality, quantity and requirement for attendance in firm continuing professional education. It is clear that in the SEC's review of the work done by professionals, there exists a belief that a lack of current technical knowledge is contributing to unacceptable performance.

TRENDS IN NON-REQUIRED
CONTINUING EDUCATION STATES

This survey was conducted to obtain valuable input from the Executive Directors of those State CPA Societies that do not have continuing education requirements. Since thirty-four states at the time of this study had requirements in effect, questionnaires were mailed to the thirteen states having no requirements.

Of the thirteen (13) questionnaires mailed, eleven (11) responses were received, providing for a very high response rate of 85%.

Trends also became evident within this group with 82% of responding states either planning to sponsor required continuing education legislation or expecting their State Board to adopt requirements.

As reflected in Table 2 on the following page, nine (9) of the eleven (11) respondents indicated that they were either planning to sponsor required continuing education legislation or were expecting requirements to be adopted by their State Board. The initiative in sponsoring required continuing education is being taken by seven (7) of the eleven (11) state CPA Societies.

In the majority of cases, the average number of hours per year is forty (40) which is in line with what has obviously become a national standard with only a few exceptions.

TABLE 2

State	Planning to Sponsor Legislation	Hourly Requirements of Sponsored Legislation	Date of Effective Passage	Effective Date
Idaho	no plans	—	—	—
Mississippi	yes	40 hrs/yr. average	in year presented	January following year presented
Missouri	yes	40 hrs/yr. average	1980	—
New Jersey	yes	no decision yet	do not know	—
New York	yes	no decision yet	do not know	—
Puerto Rico	yes	30 hrs/yr. average	1979-80	3 years after approval
Rhode Island	*	40 hrs/yr. average	—	—
Tennessee	yes**	40 hrs/yr. average	January-May 1980	when Governor signs
Utah	yes	40 hrs/yr. average	January 1981	January 1982
West Virginia	no plans	—	—	—
Wisconsin	***	40 hrs/yr. average	1979-80 or 1981-82	date set by Accounting Examining Board

*adopted by regulation in 1979
**legislation enacted in 1980
***to be adopted by regulation

PROBABLE CHANGES IN REQUIRED
CONTINUING EDUCATION PROGRAMS

This survey was designed to elicit responses from the Executive Directors of State CPA Societies where some form of continuing education requirements exist.

Thirty-four (34) questionnaires were mailed and thirty-two (32) responses were received, which provides for a 94% response rate.

It must be kept in mind that the total population of thirty-four (34) states represents both those states that have required continuing education programs actively under way and those where enabling legislation has been passed but the effective dates for implementation have not yet arrived.

In light of the exceptionally high rate of response, it is easy to view the emergence of certain trends. For example, almost 75% of the respondents stated that there had been no changes in their state's required continuing education program.

Most states require the national standard of 40 hours of continuing education per year. Of those states replying that there were changes in their program, a trend toward the national standard of 40 hours can be discerned.

As reflected in Table 3 on the following page, nine (9) of the thirty-two (32) respondents indicated that there had been changes in their state's program. When asked if they personally saw any areas in their state's program that needed modification, five (5) respondents offered recommendations while twenty-four (24) respondents indicated no modification was necessary. These responses are detailed in Table 4.

MAJOR CATEGORIES OF
TYPES OF COURSES TAKEN

The topics needed and available to the practicing CPA are divisible into two main groups: technical and CPA skill-related non-technical. In both these areas there exists an ample selection of topics which is continually expanding.

The technical grouping consists of the two generalized areas of taxation and accounting and auditing. Within these areas exist specific categories such as: industry, government, education; international, municipal and statistics; advanced, intermediate and beginning; large, medium sized and small firms; pronouncements, rulings and laws; past, existing and pending developments; public, private and non-profit; computerized, machine and

TABLE 3

States Indicating Changes in Their
Required Continuing Education Program

State	Nature of Change
Alabama	Change from ninety-six (96) hours over three (3) years to forty (40) hours per year
Florida	Specific change not provided
Louisiana	Specific change not provided
Maine	Bill passed requiring ten (10) hours of CPE for licensing
Montana	Required continuing education enacted as an amendment to existing law
Nebraska	Forty percent (40%) of CPE must be in areas of accounting and auditing
Oregon	Stricter enforcement
Pennsylvania	Effective date delay
Washington	Reporting date

TABLE 4

Personal Recommendations by Respondents

State	Recommendations
Hawaii	State is too lenient in granting CPE accreditation
New Mexico	Guidelines for a "qualified" program must be made very clear
Maine	The ten (10) hour requirement should be expanded
South Carolina	The hours required do need to double from the current forty (40) every two years
Oregon	Tighten rules pertaining to sponsorship agreements

manual; cost, management and internal systems; financial, treasury and accounting controls; insurance, pensions and benefits. The list is long and the probability for a CPA to find the precise course needed is excellent.

The CPA skill-related non-technical group consists of the following generalized categories: communications, supervisory and systems. The overall term of "management" is often applied to them. Within these exist specific categories such as: written and oral communications; inter-personal techniques; motivation; organization, data processing; human resources; etc.

Although information is not available on the mix of courses conducted in-house by the larger firms, data available from the AICPA provides some insight into the types of courses taken by participants in 1979-80 is shown in Table 5.

PROVIDERS OF CONTINUING EDUCATION

As more and more states adopted required continuing education for CPAs, numerous organizations entered the field as suppliers of educational programs. Others, already engaged in educational activities, intensified their efforts.

For purposes of describing the providers of CPE, they have been classified into two major groups:

Within the Profession

1. Professional State Societies of CPAs
2. AICPA
3. Accounting Firms
4. CPA Consultants
5. Universities & Colleges with professional accounting degree programs
6. Associations of Accounting Firms

Outside the Profession

1. Private Seminar Organizations
2. Professional Seminar Organizations
3. Consultants
4. Universities & Colleges

TABLE 5

Percentage of Participant Attendance
By Course Category

Taxation	42%
Accounting & Auditing	32%
Industry	8%
Management Advisory Services	7%
Practice Management	5%
Government	4%
General Professional	2%
	100%

Within the Profession

Professional State Societies. Over 80% of the nation's CPAs are practicing in the following eight states: New York, California, Illinois, Texas, Pennsylvania, Massachusetts, Florida and Ohio. Each state offers an extensive program of technical seminars and educational events. In addition, neighboring smaller states offer modest but more than adequate similar programs.

AICPA. The national professional Institute offers a wide range of educational materials in the areas of group study, self-study and video. The AICPA is one of the leading suppliers of courses to the states societies who sponsor programs and to firms.

Accounting Firms. The large accounting firms have now made many of their internally developed training programs available to smaller firms and industry at large. Over the last several years their commitments—both in dollars and hours invested—have increased severalfold.

The larger firms now have extensive educational capabilities and resources which assure that their employees, professional staff and partners can satisfy even the stiffest continuing education requirements. Their formal curriculum covers the entry level accountant right up to the senior partners and make use of self-study training, on the job training and professionally run courses on both the local office level as well as on a national basis.

CPA Consultants. Numerous consulting firms have been formed by CPAs who have held positions within the profession and have acquired expertise in training. These former positions were usually within the internal training department of a firm or within the CPE Division of a professional state society. CPA consultants, in addition to offering a variety of courses, advise accounting firms on their overall internal training program.

Universities and Colleges with Professional Accounting Degree Programs. Many of our leading institutions of higher learning, which maintain accounting degree programs taught by CPAs, are offering their courses to the practicing CPA both within and outside the degree program format. Many of these courses are scheduled at night and on weekends to fit into the working accountant's busy time schedule. These courses are of a basic nature and are not of much use to the experienced practitioner. Their strongest appeal is in the area of the theoretical rather than the practical or technical.

Association of Accounting Firms. There has been a widespread growth in national associations of accounting firms which pool their resources to better serve their clients. One major shared activity is the mounting of an impressive continuing education program. This program allows all participating firms to obtain better cost benefits from their considerable investment in training.

Outside the Profession

Private Seminar Organizations. Private seminar groups have either added to their existing product line or redesigned their accounting and taxation programs to order to make them more attractive to the licensed CPA. These groups normally advertise heavily and schedule their public meetings in leading hotels. Meetings are held in large metropolitan centers but they are attended by CPAs from both rural and metropolitan areas.

Professional Seminar Organizations. These entities are very similar to their private counterparts except that they maintain a close relationship with an organized profession yet remain independent. The better known of these groups are: The Practicing Law Institute (PLI); The National Association of Accountants (NAA); and The Institute of Internal Auditors (IIA).

Consultants. Numerous non-CPA consultants exist in the field usually offering courses in such areas as report writing, managerial skills, etc.

Universities and Colleges. Numerous institutions of higher learning have entered the adult education field and are offering accounting and financial courses throughout the nation. Not only do these schools hold these courses on their main campuses, but they are also scheduled in satellite campuses. These "off-campus" satellite locations are, in many instances, innovative. Such sites as commuter trains, military academies and major industrial corporations are just a few examples.

Many of these schools have formal divisions of accounting education under whose authority the non-credit courses are held. Regular courses, falling within the normal curriculum are also available to CPAs.

NATIONAL STANDARDS FOR COURSES[16]

Current national standards for formal group and self-study program focus on (1), *Program Development*; (2), *Presentation*; (3), *Measurement* and (4), *Reporting* (i.e. Documentation).

In the area of *Program Development*, the main emphasis is on the principal that the course must contribute to the competence of a CPA on a current basis. In addition, it must be made clear, in advance, if there are certain educational and/or experience prerequisities and what level of knowledge or competence is expected from prospective attendees. The program developer and reviewer should be separate individuals who are both qualified in the subject matter and in instructional design.

The Standards for *Presentation* concentrate on the instructor, who (just as the developer and reviewer) must be qualified both with respect to course content, as well as teaching methods to be used. Attendees should have the appropriate education and/or experience required by the course and the number of participants, along with the physical facilities used by the course, should be consistent with the teaching method.

In advance of the presentation, attendees must be informed of course objectives, prerequisites, experience level, content, advance preparation, teaching method and credit hours involved. All programs must be evaluated for quality by the program's sponsor, instructor and participant.

For program *Measurement*, the 50-minute hour is the yardstick. Attendees at live presentations are granted the full fifty (50) minutes as one hour of credit whereas users of self-study material only receive one-half (½) that amount of credit. Instructors receive three (3) times that amount for first time assignments which count as preparation and presentation time. (However, required education for an instructor can never consist of less than one half (½) of his total allowed time to be other than that of a student.)

Finally, the national standards for *Reporting* insist that records be kept for five (5) years documenting the following:

	For Participant	For Sponsor
Date(s)	X	X
Location	X	X
Number of CPE hours	X	X
Title and/or Description	X	
Outline of Course		X
Sponsor	X	
Attendance List		X
Instructor(s)		X

ACCREDITATION[17]

In 1979 a special committee on CPE accreditation, appointed by the AICPA, recommended that action be taken to urge all sponsors of CPE courses for the profession to adopt the Standards. Since the recommendation of the special committee, the Standards have been recognized as national standards and have been approved by most State CPA Societies.

Consequently, accreditation of a course of study is accomplished by having the course Standards adopted by:

1. NASBA—National Association of State Boards of Accountancy;
2. Participating CPA firms in both the private companies and the SEC practice section of the AICPA;
3. CPE division of the AICPA;
4. State Societies of CPAs;
5. All other responsible developers and sponsors of CPA seminars;

When the above entities adopt the course Standards, they should notify prospective attendees with the following statement:

We have adopted and complied with the *Statement on Standards for Formal Group and Formal Self-Study Programs* published by the American Institute of Certified Public Accountants (or the NASBA equivalent). This program is designed to qualify for _____ hours of credit. (optional sentence)

Compliance with these Standards should be reviewed periodically by a competent and impartial observor.

It is further intended that these substantive national educational Standards for quality and course accreditation procedures be part of a continuing educational program consisting of 120 hours over a three (3) years period which would serve as a condition of renewal of a CPA's license to practice.

OTHER PROFESSIONS

The number of states having required continuing education for members of professions other than that of certified public accounting is also increasing.

Over a period of almost three years, from September 1977 to June 1980, and as reflected in Table 6, there has been a definite trend toward required continuing education for other professionals.

As can be seen from the table, CPAs and optometrists are in the forefront with thirty-five (35) and forty-four (44) states, respectively, requiring continuing education.

It may be noteworthy to indicate that the trend toward required continuing education over the brief period of this study is even more dramatic considering the amount of time required for the introduction and passage of legislation.

CONCLUSION

Since Marvin Stone proposed required continuing education for CPAs in 1967, thirty seven states have adopted requirements for the relicensing of CPAs. Strong support has been forthcoming from state legislatures, leaders of the accounting profession and practitioners who believe, in the words of the Beamer Committee report, that "Simply put, continuing education is the alternative to obsolescence."

The trend toward required continuing education for all CPAs is clearly on the rise as evidence indicates that required continuing education is a solid step in the direction of eliminating poor performance.

With the acceptance of the Beamer Committee report by AICPA Council in 1971, the profession acknowledged that each of its members had an obligation to continue his or her education throughout his or her

TABLE 6

Number of States Requiring Continuing Education

	Sept. 1977[a]	June 1980[b]
CPAs	23	37
Dentists	8	10 + 1 required under certain circumstances
Lawyers	7	9 + 6 required under certain circumstances
Nurses	7	13 + 6 required under certain circumstances
Optometrists	44	44
Pharmacists	14	22
Physicians	11	24 + 1 required under certain circumstances
Veterinarians	18	24

[a]"States Requiring Continuing Education for Professionals," *New York Times*, September 11, 1977.

[b]Dr. Louis E. Phillips, Director, Division of Continuing Education, Furman University.

career. In the interest of the profession—and more importantly, the public which it serves—it is essential that action be taken to require continuing education of CPAs in all fifty states.

SELECTED ARTICLES AND REPORTS

Lembke, V.C., J.H. Smith and V.H. Tidwell. "Compulsory Continuing Education for CPAs". *Journal of Accountancy*, v 129 (April, 1970) pp. 61–65.

AICPA Report of the Committee on Continuing Education. April 7, 1971, 11 pages typewritten.

Leuallen, E.E. "Continuing Education for the Professions". In *NASBA Proceedings: 1971 Annual Meeting*, pp. 27–28.

Beamer, Elmer J. "Continuing Education—A Professional Requirement". *Journal of Accountancy*, v 133 (January, 1972), pp. 33–39.

Stone, Marvin L. "The Arguments for Requiring Continuing Education by Legislation". *Journal of Accountancy*, v 133 (January, 1972), pp. 56–58.

Williamson, Harold E. "The Arguments Against Requiring Continuing Education by Legislation". *Journal of Accountancy*, v 133 (January, 1972), pp. 58-60.

Mason, Craig A. "Continuing Education: An Attack on Professional Incompetence". *Ohio CPA,* (1972), pp. 121-131.

Stavisky, Norman H. "Case for Mandatory Continuing Education". *Massachusetts CPA Review,* v 47 (March/April 1973), pp. 8-9.

Sprague, W.D. "The Case for Universal Professional Development". *The CPA Journal,* v 43 (September, 1973), pp. 747-753, 798.

Horovitz, Samuel. "Mandatory Continuing Education—Pros and Cons". *Pennsylvania CPA Spokesman,* v 44 (October, 1973), pp. 9-11.

"Required Professional Development". *The Canadian Chartered Accountant*, January, 1974), pp. 21-25.

Report on the Conference on Continuing Education Requirements, National Association of State Boards of Accountancy, (July, 1975).

Statement on Standards for Formal Group and Formal Self-Study Programs, Continuing Professional Education Division, American Institute of CPAs (1976).

White, Gary E., Thomas A. Buchman. "The Continuing Education Requirement: How Effective?" *The CPA Journal*, (December, 1977), pp. 11-15.

Phillips, Louise E. "Mandatory Continuing Education for Licensed Professionals Is HereTo Stay" *Association Management,* (April, 1978), pp. 79-86.

Report of the Special Committee on CPE Accreditation (April 4, 1979), *AICPA.*

NOTES

1. Stone, Marvin L. "The Arguments for Requiring Continuing Education by Legislation." *Journal of Accountancy*, v 133 (January, 1972), pp. 56-58.

2. Ibid.

3. "Resolution on Continuing Education," AICPA, May 12, 1971.

4. National Association of State Boards of Accountancy, *Model Provisions for Required Continuing Education*, 1972.

5. Ibid.

6. Securities and Exchange Commission, *Report to Congress on the Accounting Profession and the Commission's Oversight Rule*, 1980.

7. Harold M. Williams, Chairman—Securities Exchange Commission, *Professional Self Government: An Interim Report*—an address delivered at the AICPA Fifth Annual Conference on Current SEC Developments, January 4, 1978.

8. American Insitute of Certified Public Accountants, *What Is The Division For CPA Firms?*, 1980.

9. American Institute of Certified Public Accountants, *Organizational Structures and Functions Of The SEC Practice Section Of The AICPA Division For CPA Firms* as amended November 29, 1979.

10. Senator Lee Metcalf, Chairman, *The Accounting Establishment*, prepared by the Subcommittee On Reports, Accounting and Management of the Committee on Government Operations for 94th Congress 2nd Session, December 1976.

11. Congressman John E. Moss, Chairman, *November 1977 Staff Report*, prepared by the Subcommittee On Reports, Accounting and Management of the Senate Committee on Governmental Affairs, November 1977.

12. Roper Organization, Inc., "A Study of New York State Society of Certified Public Accountants Members' Professional Development Activities", 1976.

13. INA Underwriters Insurance Company, "Sponsorship Agreement", November 19, 1978.

14. Thomas J. Burns and Edward N. Coffman, "The Ascending Profession of Accounting". *The CPA Journal* Vol. XLVII No. 3 (March 1977), 33-34. See also Seymour Eisenman and Steven B. Lilien, "Accounting Deficiencies In Financial Statements". *The CPA Journal*, Vol. XLVIII No. 7 (July 1978): 33; Harold L. Monk, Jr., "Accounting and Auditing Deficiencies", *Florida Accountancy News* (19780; and Arnold Schneidman, "Need for Auditors' Computer Education", *The CPA Journal*, Vol. XLIX No. 5 (June 1979): 31.

15. Lundy, Todd, Chairman, *Report of the Ad Hoc Committe On-Long-Range Planning*, New York: AICPA Professional Development Division, April 1973.

16. "Statement on Standards for Formal Group and Formal Self-Study Programs", AICPA, 1976.

17. "Report of the Special Committee on CPA Accreditation" AICPA, April 4, 1979.

APPENDIX

CONTINUING EDUCATION REQUIREMENTS BY STATE

State	Law	Board Regulations	Reporting Form	Coverage	Hours	Reciprocity	Comments	State
Alabama	X	X	X	All certificate holders in practice.	96 in 3 years preceding renewal through 9/30/80, then 40 hours per year.	Must meet requirements 3 years after certification in Alabama.	Includes nonresidents 40 hours per year effective 10/1/80 for the year ended 9/30/81.	Alabama
Alaska	X	X	X	Persons licensed to practice as (holders of a permit to practice).	60 in 2 years preceding biennial renewal.			Alaska
Arizona	X	X	Not yet	All registrants in public practice; others must complete 10 hours per calendar year (may be deferred until one year prior to entry into public practice).	40 hours per calendar year. May carry over up to 40 hours to next year provided had 48 hours or more in current year.	40 hours during the one year immediately prior to initial registration.	CPA firms must obtain the Board's approval of self study programs they sponsor.	Arizona
Arkansas	X	X	Not yet	All holders of a permit to practice.	40 hours per year or 120 hours in 3 years preceding renewal.	Must complete proportionate amount of year's CPE requirement from date of application for the permit to the next succeeding June 30.	Effective 7/1/80.	Arkansas
California	X	X	X	Resident licensees in practice.	80 hours every 2 years.	40 hours within 12 months prior to filing application and practicing.	CPA firms may qualify all programs in advance.	California
Colorado	X	X	X	Resident licensees in practice.	120 hours in 3 years preceding annual renewal.	10 hours per full quarter for the first year, 40 hours during the first full calendar year; 80 hours during the first two full calendar years; thereafter, 120 hours in three preceding years.	Regulations include with some changes the "Statement on Standards for Formal Group and Formal Self-Study Programs."	Colorado
Connecticut	X		X	All licensees holding or applying for an annual registration card.	120 hours in 3 years preceding annual renewal, including at least 20 hours every year.	Prior to application for reciprocity being granted, must have taken 10 hours per full quarter year period remaining in the current registration year.	Regulations include, in substance, the development and Presentation Standards from the "Statement on Standards for Formal Group and Formal Self-Study Programs."	Connecticut
District of Columbia	X	Not yet	Not yet	All CPAs licensed to practice in D.C.				District of Columbia
Florida	X	X	X	All CPAs licensed to practice public accounting in Florida.	64 hours of continuing education, of which 16 must be in accounting and related topics, will be required in each 2-year reestablishment period.	2 year reestablishment period begins on the July 1st following the fiscal year in which the Florida certificate is issued.	See Exhibit II, Page 3 for the transition rules from the old 3-year reestablishment period to the new 2-year period.	Florida
Georgia	X	X	X	All holders of a permit to practice.	60 hours in 2 years immediately preceding the renewal date. May carry over up to 15 hours to next period.		CPA firms' courses must be approved by the state board in advance. So must self-study and correspondence courses. Effective 12/31/79. Sponsors are expected to follow the "Statement on Standards for Formal Group and Formal Self-Study Programs."	Georgia

State			Applicability	Hours Required	Initial/Prorate Provisions	Comments
Hawaii	X	X	All holders of a permit to practice.	80 hours in biennium. May carry over excess up to 80 hours. Also may make up deficiency in succeeding biennium in addition to completing that biennium's 80 hour minimum.	Must have had 40 hours in year prior to date of filing application for initial permit to practice.	Program sponsor must issue written evidence of attendance to each attendee with suggested continuing education hours shown thereon. All firms' and "other organizations'" programs (group and individual study) must be approved annually by the Board on a form prescribed by the Board.
Indiana	X	Not yet	All holders of a permit to practice.	60 hours 7/1/80 through 12/31/81; thereafter, 80 hours every 2 years.	10 hours per full calendar quarter from date of issuance of license to end of biennial period.	Programs must be given by approved sponsors. Effective 7/1/80.
Iowa	X	X	All holders of a permit to practice.	120 hours every 3 years.	No hours required for first renewal if renewal date is less than 12 months from date of application, 40 hours required in 12 months preceding 12/31 before the next renewal date, 80 hours by the following 12/31 and thereafter 120 hours in 3 preceding years.	Includes nonresident permit holders.
Kansas	X	X	All holders of a permit to practice in Kansas.	40 hours per year.	Must complete proportionate amount of year's requirement (from date of filing application for the period to the next succeeding June 30).	Credit is granted generally on a 60 minute hour basis. However, when a specific program is 50 minutes long, it may be counted as an hour.
Louisiana	X	Not yet	All licensees (whether or not residents of Louisiana).	60 hours in 3 year period 1980–82, 90 hours in 3 year period 1983–85, 120 hours every three years thereafter.	Must comply with CPE requirements on a prorate basis for compliance period.	Licensees may elect a reporting period ending on other than December 31. Regulations include, in substance, the Development and Presentation Standards from the "Statement on Standards for Formal Group and Formal Self-Study Programs." Program sponsors must maintain records demonstrating compliance with these standards. Effective 7/1/80.
Maine	X	Not yet	All holders of a permit to practice.	12 hours per year. May carry over up to 3 hours to next year.	Must comply with CPE requirements before a permit will be issued.	
Maryland	X	X	All CPA certificate holders engaged in the practice of public accountancy in the state.	40 hours per year. May carry over excess up to 2 years.		Board may offer a written examination in lieu of a program of CPE. Generally, all programs will be approved by the Board where possible through an annual written agreement with the sponsor.
Massachusetts		X	All licensees.	80 hours in 2 years preceding biennial re-registration. 40 hours for 1980 renewals.	Must comply with CPE requirement on prorate basis when license next renewed.	Effective 7/1/79.

CONTINUING EDUCATION REQUIREMENTS (cont.)

State	Law	Board Regulations	Reporting Form	Coverage	Hours	Reciprocity	Comments	State
Michigan	X	X	X	All licensees in public practice.	40 hours in years ended 6/30/79 and thereafter 20% of minimum hours must be in accounting and auditing subjects. May carry over excess hours to the next year.	Must complete 8 hours in accounting or auditing subjects within six months of licensure unless meet CPE requirements when licensed also must complete prorate amount of CPE period's requirement.	Board may offer a written examination in lieu of a program of CPE.	Michigan
Minnesota	X	X	X	All licensees engaged in the practice of public accounting in the state.	120 hours in 3 years preceding re-licensing.	Must comply with CPE requirement on a prorate basis when license next renewed.	Effective 12/31/80.	Minnesota
Montana	X	Not yet	Not yet	CPAs engaged in the practice of public accounting.			Effective 3 years after the Board's rule establishing CPE requirements becomes effective.	Montana
Nebraska	X	X	X	Everyone holding a permit to practice.	15 days in preceding 3 years, 40% must be in principles and practices of accounting and auditing.	15 days in 3 years preceding first renewal of annual permit.	Includes nonresidents (120 hours by Board policy). CPA firms may apply to the Board for designation as an approved sponsor for in-firm CPE programs.	Nebraska
Nevada	X	X	X	Resident licensees in public practice.	80 hours in each 2 year period preceding registration at least 24 hours each calendar year.	24 hours within 6 months after filing application. (May receive credit for education completed in six months prior to filing.)	CPA firms may qualify all programs in advance.	Nevada
New Mexico	X	X	X	Resident licensees in public practice.	120 hours in each 3 years preceding re-registration.	Must complete prorata amount to next renewal date.	Effective 12/31/79.	New Mexico
North Carolina	X	X	X	All North Carolina CPAs who practice in the state.	20 to 40 hours per year (State Board to decide), may carry over up to two additional years' hours.		Effective 1/1/83.	North Carolina
Ohio	X	X	X	All holders of permits to practice.	120 hours every 3 years. May carry excess up to 1/3 of the requirement for the next reporting period. Have one year to make up any deficiencies plus 1/3 of the next period's requirement.	Must complete pro rata amount to next reporting date.	Program sponsors may pre-register all programs, Board may offer an examination in lieu of a program of CPE.	Ohio
Oklahoma	X	Not yet	Not yet	All holders of permits to practice.	Not more than 24 hours per year.		Effective 7/1/80	Oklahoma
Oregon	X	X	X	All licensees engaged in the practice of public accounting in the state.	40 hours per year. May carry over excess hours for 2 years, but must have at least 20 hours each year. PAs are required to meet 24 hours of CPE per year and may carry-over excess for 2 years but must have at least 12 hours per year.	Must complete pro rata amount to next reporting date. By next reporting date, must have completed 80 hours in recently and preceding year.	CPA firms may qualify all programs in advance.	Oregon
Pennsylvania	X	X	X	All holders of permits to practice.	80 hours in 2 years immediately preceding renewal, including at least 32 hours of accounting and	Must meet the CPE requirements for past two years to obtain a certificate.	Effective for biennial permits issued 9/1/81. Regulations include, in substance, the Dev-	Pennsylvania

Jurisdiction	AICPA recommendations	NASBA recommendations	Who must comply	CPE requirement	Other provisions
Rhode Island	X	Not yet	All holders of permit to practice.	120 hours (15 days) in 3 years preceding annual registration.	...auditing subjects and 16 hours of tax subjects. May not carry over excess credits.
South Carolina	X	X	All licensees who practice public accounting in South Carolina and are not yet 72.	60 hours in 2-year period preceding July 1 of each even-numbered year. At least 8 hours must be in accounting and/or auditing subjects.	Must complete pro rata amount to next reporting date.
South Dakota	X	X	All licensees in public practice.	96 hours in 3 years preceding annual licensing.	Must complete 32 hours within one year from the June 30 after receiving South Dakota certificate. Must complete 64 hours in two following years. May receive credit for education completed prior to filing application. CPA firms may qualify all programs in advance.
Tennessee	X	Not yet	All licensees.	120 hours in 3 years preceding license renewal.	
Vermont	X	X	All holders of permits to practice.	90 hours in 2 years preceding biennial re-registration.	Effective 6/30/80.
Washington	X	X	All licensees in public practice.	120 hours (15 days) in 3 years preceding annual licensing 16 hours (2 days) in each calendar year and 48 hours (6 days) in each 3-year period must be in accounting-related or auditing-related subjects. 8 hours in these subjects in 3½ years ended 12/31/79, and 24 hours in 3 years ended 12/31/80. 48 hours every 3 years thereafter. A licensee is exempt from the accounting and auditing subject requirement for any calendar year during which he was not involved in preparing financial reports provided he does not expect to be involved in the succeeding calendar year.	Must meet requirements three years following the end of the calendar year in which the individual's first permit to practice is issued.
Wyoming	X	X	All holders of live permits to practice.	120 hours in 3 years preceding annual licensing.	120 hours in 3 years preceding first renewal of annual permit.
AICPA recommendations			All holders of permits to practice.	120 hours (15 days) in 3 years preceding registration.	Must meet requirements 3 years after initial registration.
NASBA recommendations			All residents licensed to practice as public accountants.	120 hours in 3 years preceding registration. (Period may vary, but hours should average 40 per year.)	Must comply with regulations on a pro rata basis when license next renewed.
AICPA Division for CPA Firms			All professionals in member firms, including CPAs and Non-CPAs, who are in the U.S.	120 hours every three years, including 20 hours every year.	NASBA has adopted the essence of the "Statement of Standards for Formal Group and Formal Self-Study Programs." Each firm may select its own "educational year."

Notes (continued from preceding page): ...elopment and Presentation Standards from the "Statement on Standards for Formal Group and Formal Self-Study Programs." Program sponsors may qualify programs with the Board in advance. Effective 1/1/83.

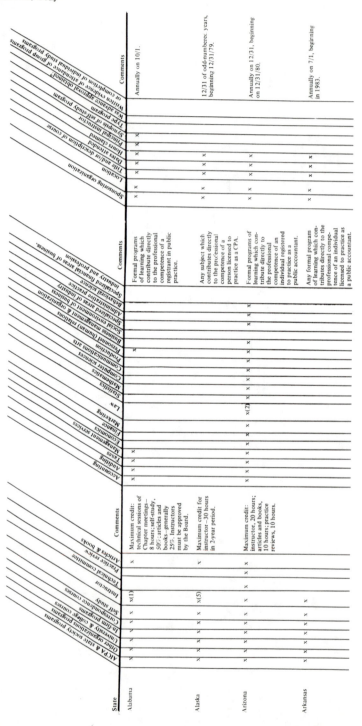

Acceptable programs and credit limitations

State	AICPA & state society programs	Other organizations programs	University & college programs	Correspondence courses	In-firm programs	Self study	Instructor	Technical committee	Practice review	Articles & books	Comments
Alabama	x	x	x	x	x	x	x(1)		x		Maximum credit: technical sessions of Chapter meetings—8 hours; self-study, 50%; articles and books—generally 25%. Instructors must be approved by the Board.
Alaska	x	x	x	x	x	x(5)					Maximum credit for instructor—30 hours in 2-year period.
Arizona	x	x	x	x	x	x	x	x	x	x	Maximum credit: instructor, 20 hours; articles and books, 10 hours; practice reviews, 10 hours.
Arkansas	x	x	x		x	x					

Acceptable subjects

State	Accounting	Auditing	Taxes	Economics	Finance	Management services	Marketing	Law	Statistics	Mathematics	Computer sciences	Communications arts	Production	Personnel (human) relations	Business management	Social environment of industry	Specialized areas of industry	Administrative areas of organization	Behavioral science	Specialized practice	Specialized financial areas of business, industry and profession	Comments
Alabama	x	x	x										x									Formal programs of learning which contribute directly to the professional competence of a registrant in public practice.
Alaska																						Any subject which contributes directly to the professional competence of a person licensed to practice as a CPA.
Arizona	x	x	x	x	x	x	x	x(2)	x	x	x	x	x	x	x	x	x	x	x			Formal programs of learning which contribute directly to the professional competence of an individual registered to practice as a public accountant.
Arkansas																						Any formal program of learning which contributes directly to the professional competence of an individual licensed to practice as a public accountant.

Records required

State	Sponsoring organization	Location	Title and/or description of course	Dates attended	Hours claimed	Principal instructor	Synopsis of self-study program	Type of program	Written evidence of attendance of individual study programs or completion of group study programs	Was advance approval obtained?	Comments
Alabama	x	x	x	x	x						Annually on 10/1.
Alaska	x	x									12/31 of odd-numbered years, beginning 12/31/79.
Arizona	x	x									Annually on 12/31, beginning on 12/31/80.
Arkansas	x	x									Annually on 7/1, beginning in 1983.

State	Maximum credit	Acceptable areas / notes	Reporting
California	Maximum credit: instructor—50% of total; articles and books—generally 25%.	For continuing education credit to be granted, each licensee shall have completed an acceptable diversification of course work.	Biennially on birth date, beginning 7/79.
Colorado	Maximum credit: self-study—generally 25%; instructor—50%; articles and books—50%.	Also other areas if they contribute to one's professional competence.	Annually on 12/31.
Connecticut	Maximum credit: instructor—20 hours per year; articles and books generally 10 hours per year; non-credit college courses 10 hours per year.	Also other areas if they contribute directly at a professional level to the professional competence of a licensee in public practice. Beginning with the 3 years ended 12/31/81, at least 40 hours must be in these areas.	Annually on 7/31, beginning in 1980.
		Formal programs of learning which contribute directly to the professional competence of an individual registered to practice public accounting. Also other areas if the applicant can demonstrate they contribute to his professional competence.	
Florida	Maximum credit: articles and books—20 hours in 2-year reestablishment period. No credit after second instruction of same course.	At least 25% of minimum must be in accounting-related and auditing-related subjects; other formal programs of learning "which contribute directly to the professional competency of an individual following licensure to practice public accounting" also count.	Must report by 7/15 prior to biennial license renewal. Hours claimed divided between (a) accounting and auditing, and (b) other.
Georgia	Maximum credit: articles and books—15 hours.	And such other subjects as deemed appropriate by the Board.	Biennially on 12/31, beginning in 1979.
Hawaii	Maximum credit: instructor—20 hours; books and articles—10 hours; practice...	Qualifying subjects include but are not limited to those shown.	Report biennially on 11/30 of every odd-numbered year.

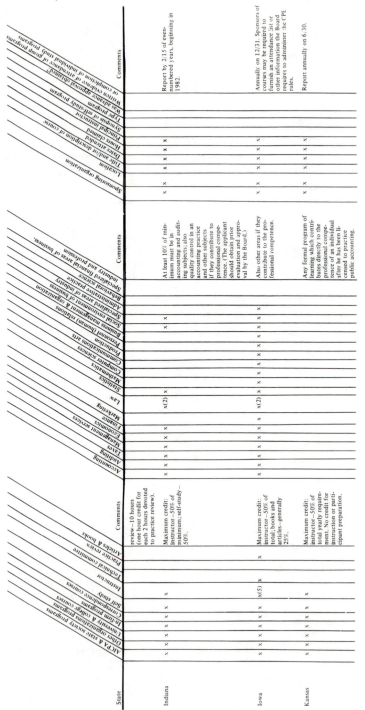

Program types

State	AICPA & state society programs	Other organizations programs	University & college programs	Correspondence courses	Curriculum & college courses	Self study	Instructor	Technical committee	Practice review	Articles & books	Comments
Indiana	x	x	x	x	x	x			x		review–10 hours (one hour credit for each 2 hours devoted to practice review).
Iowa	x	x	x	x	x	x(5)					Maximum credit: instructor–50% of minimum; self-study–50%. Maximum credit: instructor–50% of total; books and articles–generally 25%.
Kansas	x	x	x	x	x	x					Maximum credit: instructor–50% of total yearly requirement. No credit for instruction or participant preparation.

Subject areas

State	Accounting	Auditing	Taxes	Management services	Economics	Finance	Marketing	Law	Statistics	Mathematics	Computer sciences	Communications arts	Production	Personnel (human) relations	Business relations	Social environment & organization	Specialized areas of industry	Administrative practice	Behavioral science	Specialized science	Specialized financial areas of industry and profession	Comments
Indiana	x	x	x	x		x		x(2)							x	x						At least 10% of minimum must be in accounting and auditing subjects; also quality control in an accounting practice and other subjects if they contribute to professional competence. (The applicant should obtain prior evaluation and approval by the Board.)
Iowa	x	x	x	x		x		x(2)							x	x						Also other areas if they contribute to the professional competence.
Kansas	x	x	x	x		x																Any formal program of learning which contributes directly to the professional competence of an individual after he has been licensed to practice public accounting.

Documentation

State	Sponsoring organization	Location	Title and/or description of course	Dates attended	Hours claimed	Principal instructor	Synopsis of self-study program	Type program	Was advance approval obtained?	Written evidence of attendance or completion of individual or group programs	Comments
Indiana	x	x	x	x	x						Report by 2/15 of even-numbered years, beginning in 1982.
Iowa	x	x	x	x	x						Annually on 12/31. Sponsors of courses may be required to furnish an attendance list or other information the Board requires to administer the CPE rules.
Kansas	x	x	x	x	x						Report annually on 6.30.

State	Maximum credit	Description	Report
Louisiana	Maximum credit: instructor—50% of total; articles and books—25%.	Also other areas that contribute to the licensee's professional competence.	Report annually on 12/31 (or other fiscal year-end selected by the licensee). Alternatively, the licensee's firm may file a sworn statement that the members and/or employees it lists have met the CPE requirements.
Maine	Maximum credit: instructor—50% of total.	Any formal program of learning which contributes directly to the professional competence of a registrant in public practice.	Report annually on 6/30, beginning on 6/30/81.
Maryland	Maximum credit: instructor—20 hours; self-study—20 hours.	Any formal program of learning which contributes directly the professional competence of an individual after he has been enrolled to practice public accounting.	Must also submit evidence to support fulfillment of requirements if program not previously approved by Board.
Massachusetts	Maximum credit: instructor—50%; articles and books, generally 25%.	Any formal program of learning which contributes directly to the professional competence of a registrant in public practice. Also other subjects if they contribute to the registrant's professional competence.	Report biennially on 6/30, beginning in 1980.
Michigan	Maximum credit: self-study—50% of total; instructor—50%; articles and books—25%; committee meetings—25%.	At least 20% of minimum must be in accounting and auditing subjects; other subjects which "are designed to insure reasonable currency of knowledge as a basis for a high standard of practice as a CPA and which are relevant to the services rendered by the licensee also count. Also Professional Ethics for CPAs.	Report annually by 9/30. Upon the request of an attendee a sponsor must provide the person with a certificate of attendance and a comprehensive program description.
Minnesota	Maximum credit: instructor—50%; articles and books, generally 25%.	Any formal program of learning which contributes directly to the professional competence of the individual licensed to practice as a CPA.	Report annually on 12/31, beginning in 1980, or 3 years after initial registration, whichever is later.

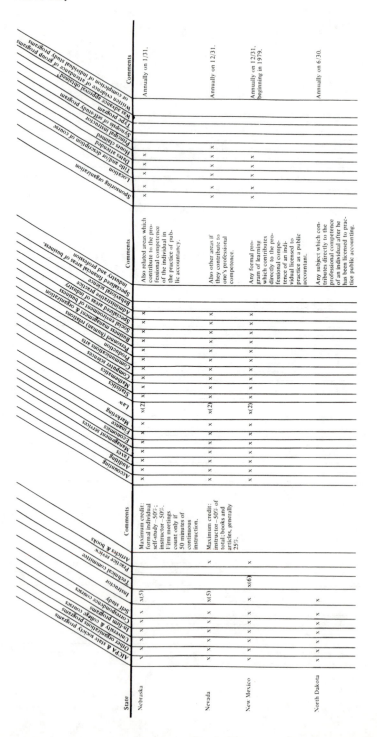

State	Reporting date	Qualifying subjects	Credit limitations
Ohio	November 15 every thid 1 year.	Any formal program of learning which contributes directly to the professional competence of an individual after he has been licensed to practice public accounting.	Maximum credit: instructor – 50% of total; articles and books – 50% (25% without submitting manuscripts).
Oregon	Annually on 7/1.	Also other subjects if the licensee can demonstrate they contribute to his professional competence.	Maximum credit: instructor – 50% of total; articles and books – generally 25%
Pennsylvania	9/1 of odd-numbered years.	Also other subjects if the permit holder can demonstrate they contribute to the maintenance of his professional competence.	Maximum credit: correspondence courses – 50% of total; self-study courses – 25%; instructor – 50%; books and articles – generally 25% and no more than 50%.
Rhode Island	Annually on 12/31.	Any formal program learning which contributes directly to the professional competence of an individual after he has been licensed to practice public accounting.	
South Carolina	7/1 of even-numbered years.	At least 20% of the hours must be in accounting and/or auditing subjects.	
South Dakota	Annually on 7/1.	Also other subjects which contribute directly to the competence of the licensee in public practice.	Instructors must be approved by Board of Accountancy Self Study; includes studying tax laws, accounting periodicals, publications and tape recordings if synopsis prepared.
Vermont	June 30 of even-numbered years, beginning in 1980. Will not have to report specific programs.	Any formal program of learning which contributes directly to the professional competence of the individual after he has been licensed to practice public accounting.	

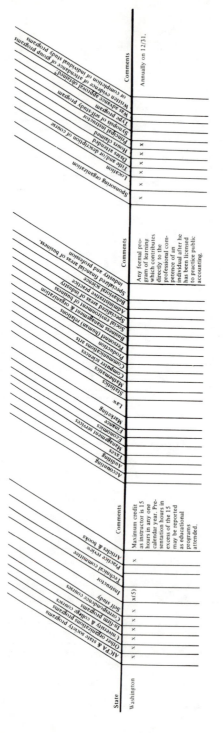

State	AICPA & state society programs	Other organizations programs	University & college programs	In-firm programs	Correspondence courses	Self study	Instructor	Technical committee	Practice review	Articles & books	Comments	Accounting	Auditing	Taxes	Management services	Economics	Finance	Marketing	Law	Statistics	Mathematics	Computer sciences	Production	Communications arts	Personnel (human) relations	Business management	Social environment of business	Specialized areas of business	Administrative practice	Behavioral science	Specialized financial areas of business	Industry and profession	Comments	Sponsoring organization	Location	Title and/or description of course	Dates attended	Hours claimed	Principal instructor	Sponsor of course	Type program	Self-study program	Was advance approval obtained?	written evidence of attendance or completion of group programs or individual study programs	Comments
Washington	x	x	x	x	x	x	x(5)			x	Maximum credit as instructor is 15 hours in any one calendar year. Presentation hours in excess of the 15 may be reported as educational programs attended.																						Any formal program of learning which contributes directly to the professional competence of an individual after he has been licensed to practice public accounting.	x	x	x	x	x					Annually on 12/31.

INFLATION ACCOUNTING

Sir Douglas Morpeth
Touche Ross & Co.

ABSTRACT

Realisation that historical cost accounting is misleading in the face of inflation has not resulted in a universal acceptance of the need to change the method of accounting. The accounting profession in many countries has been making considerable efforts to develop an acceptable system which reflects the effects of price changes, but without government support and a prolonged period of inflation this has proved difficult. The U.K. and U.S. both have accounting standards in effect, but the U.K. standard has adopted the CCA method using the physical concept of maintenance of operating capability in the measurement of profit. The stage of development of inflation accounting varies considerably and there is a need for leadership, perhaps from the International Accounting Standards Committee, so that one method becomes adopted. International business and international investors are both interested in harmonisation and comparability and the accounting profession must work to that end.

The measurement of profit on the historical cost system of accounting has been an accepted and well understood method for a very long time. The whole of the accounting profession, management, shareholders, employees and government have been accustomed throughout their careers to think of measuring profit as the surplus of sales over the cost of what is sold or consumed. This view of profit is ingrained in us. We regard it as simple and objective, something which we can understand and relate to and feel comfortable with. The auditor knows how to give a true and fair—or a fairly presented—report on accounts presented under the historical cost convention.

It comes as a shock to find that this historical cost system has a flaw in it. The unit of measurement—the currency unit—does not remain stable.

It changes in value, and in a period of inflation loses value, in terms of purchasing power. Using a currency unit which is changing in value all the time is like using a measuring rod shrinking in length to measure the length of a bridge. Decisions made on the basis of the answer could cause considerable complications and would almost certainly be wrong.

Although the problem has been considered by the academic side of the profession over a number of years, it has taken the accounting profession a long time to find a practical answer to the problem and one which would be accepted by those who prepare financial accounts and those who use them. Even now, in the face of all the evidence as to the misleading nature of the information contained in financial accounts about the financial position of a company in a period of inflation, there is evidence of great reluctance to change from the familiar, well-tried historical cost system not only in the U.K. but in many countries in the world except, perhaps, in those where the rate of inflation is so high and endemic that it has had to be made painless by the use of government-controlled indexation.

It does appear that resistance to change is such that there needs to be a sustained period of inflation over 10% per annum for there to be a good possibility of acceptance of change in the method of accounting. Because of this, the state of development of inflation accounting in different countries is varied. Those countries which have until now managed to contain rates of inflation well below the 10% rate per annum are perhaps the least advanced in the art. I am not saying, however, that a low rate of inflation obviates the need for inflation accounting—it merely makes it more difficult to persuade people to make the effort to change from a well-tried and familiar accounting convention to a new, untried and unfamiliar one. A rate of inflation of only 5% continuing for 15 years would halve the purchasing power of the monetary unit. An item of plant, therefore, purchased in 1965 for £5,000 would, if the rate of inflation had been contained at 5% per annum, cost in 1980 £10, 395 to replace, over twice the amount of depreciation set aside under the historical cost system to fully write off the cost. In the U.K., we would have been very pleased in the last 15 years to have endured such a steady rate. Our actual experience, using the Retail Price Index of inflation, results in the cost of replacing that asset costing £5,000 in 1965 becoming £22,600 in 1980, more than four and a half times the historical cost depreciation set aside. I believe many countries are now moving closer to the U.K. experience of inflation than a steady five per cent rate.

All systems of accounting have a capital maintenance concept underlying the measurement of profit. The concept underlying historical cost profit is the maintenance of the shareholders' equity capital in terms of the nominal unit of measurement (nominal pounds in the U.K. or dollars in the U.S.). A shareholder of a company who had subscribed, say, £1,000 capital would not be very comforted if after 15 years he found that the purchasing power of his capital maintained throughout in money terms at £1,000 had reduced to £200.

A system of accounting, therefore, which uses a unit of measurement which consistently shrinks in value can be very misleading if used without adjustment in the measurement of profit. The Institute of Chartered Accountants in England and Wales recognised this problem in 1952 when it issued an accounting recommendation, N15. This said: "The Council cannot emphasise too strongly that the significance of accounts prepared on the basis of historical cost is subject to limitations, not the least of which is that the monetary unit in which the accounts are prepared is not a stable unit of measurement. In consequence the results shown by accounts prepared on the basis of historical cost are not a measure of increase or decrease in wealth in terms of purchasing power; nor do the results necessarily represent the amount which can prudently be regarded as available for distribution, having regard to the financial requirements of the business. Similarly the results shown by such accounts are not necessarily suitable for purposes such as price fixing, wage negotiations and taxation, unless in using them for these purposes due regard is paid to the amount of profit which has been retained in the business for its maintenance."

It is now widely recognised, certainly in the U.K., that historical cost accounting does not give a satisfactory answer about profit measurement or the financial position of a company in a period of inflation.

The search for a suitable answer to the problem which is both practical, understandable and auditable has resulted in considerable debate and argument for a number of years. Because sound financial information is the basis of decision making by both investors and management, it is my belief that the most suitable answer to the problem is one which could be useful both to management in managing a business, as well as to shareholders.

There are two main methods which have been advocated. The U.K. accounting profession has now tried to introduce both, and so I would like to discuss the U.K. experience and explain the method which has gained favour and acceptance in the U.K. before discussing the position in other countries.

In addition to the publication of N15 by the English Institute, in 1952 the Association of Certified and Corporate Acountants published a booklet "Accounting for Inflation: A Study of Techniques under Conditions of Changing Price Levels" and the Institute of Cost and Works Accountants published "The Accountancy of Changing Price Levels." Each of these recommended the adoption of replacement cost accounting.

Interest in the subject in practical circles fell away with the fall in the rate of inflation to well below 5% during the remainder of the decade, although academics continued to study and debate the question.

In 1963 the American Institute of Certified Public Accountants published an accounting research study "Reporting the Financial Effects of Price Level Changes," based on the current purchasing power (constant dollar) method of accounting, i.e. adjustment of the historical cost figures by reference to changes in a general index of purchasing power. This was followed in 1968 by a research study published by the English Institute Research Committee "Accounting for Stewardship in a Period of Inflation" which was influenced and largely written by the then President, Edmund Parker.

When, therefore, the rate of inflation began to rise again in 1971, Sir Henry Benson stimulated further action by the Accounting Standards Committee, and the first approach taken was to develop a standard based on the current purchasing power approach. This was the simplest to follow up—it involved no change to the historical cost system and entailed only a restatement of the historical cost profit and loss account and balance sheet in units of current purchasing power. This was done by using the single index of inflation—the Retail Price Index—which was held to be the best available monthly indicator of general inflation.

Although the proposed standard was to require as a supplementary statement to the historical cost accounts a fully restated profit and loss account and balance sheet, a very simplified form of CPP statement can be set out as follows:

	£
Shareholders' equity capital and reserve at beginning of period	10,000
Amount required to compensate for general inflation during year (20%)	2,000
	12,000
Shareholders' equity and reserves at end of period in historical cost accounts before dividends	11,000
Deficit being amount by which shareholders' equity has not been maintained in year in purchasing power terms	1,000

No suggestion was made or intended in the proposed standard that any adjustment should be made to the historical cost profit to take account of the loss in purchasing power illustrated in the CPP accounts. The proposed standard was intended purely as a disclosure standard.

The actual proposals were set out in an exposure draft, ED 8, and caused considerable debate. Before the actual standard could be published, however, the Government stepped in and set up a Government committee to study how best to account for inflation. The ASC was asked not to publish the CPP standard until this committee had reported. Because, however, the rate of inflation was rising and the ASC considered the problem an urgent one, it believed that an attempt should be made to maintain the momentum of progress, and so published the standard SSAP 7 as a provisional one. In the event, it did not achieve a great deal of support and when the Government committee—the Inflation Accounting Committee, which became known as the Sandilands Committee after its chairman Francis Sandilands—reported in 1975 advocating current cost accounting as the way forward, the CPP approach to the problem of reflecting in accounts the effect of inflation was halted in the U.K. and the ASC and accounting profession were pointed firmly in the direction of current cost accounting.

The Sandilands Committee rejected CPP for a number of reasons. They believed it to be the most difficult method of accounting for inflation to understand since it used a different unit of measurement from the uncorrected pound sterling, and moreover a unit of measurement which constantly changed as the chosen index changed. Such an index necessarily covered few items of goods and services normally purchased by any one company and was not appropriate to the needs of management. Since no perfect general index of inflation could be found, it was better to use none. It seems that the committee was opposed to the inclusion in reported profit of any gain arising from the holding of monetary liabilities, and that it also feared that in some way indexation by reference to a general index in accounting measurement was inappropriate in the absence of legal indexation of all debt.

Finally the supplementary nature of the CPP accounts proposed under ED 8 detracted from their usefulness. Being merely a restatement of the historical cost accounts, the supplementary statements would contain all the imperfections of the historical cost accounts.

The Accounting Standards Committee does not believe that CPP is necessarily an alternative to current cost accounting and indeed believes that the most informative solution would be an appropriate combination of current cost accounting and current purchasing power accounting. Since, however, accounts are intended to give the user information which is understandable and useful, it will be some time before understanding of current cost accounting is advanced sufficiently to combine it with another different method also criticised as difficult to understand.

The change of direction from CPP accounting to CCA was advocated in 1975 and a standard, SSAP 16, was only published in March 1980. During that period, considerable and heated debate and argument took place.

The history of those five years would need more than the scope of this article to relate adequately. The five years saw a period of continuously high inflation and a long, fierce argument and debate before it was clear that the proposals in SSAP 16 had gained general acceptance although there are still many managements and accountants who do not fully accept the need for adjusting the method of accounting to take into account the effect of price changes.

The debate was sparked off not so much by the Sandilands Report as by the issue of exposure draft ED 18, giving effect to the proposals for CCA put forward by the Sandilands Committee. This exposure draft was published by the ASC after eleven months of hard and concentrated work by the Inflation Accounting Steering Group and its secretariat. This latter committee was set up, on the recommendation of the Sandilands Committee, and under the auspices of the ASC and Government, specifically to develop a standard on current cost accounting.

The exposure draft was necessarily lengthy and detailed so that those at whom it was directed would be able to understand fully all that was involved. Following Sandilands as it was required to do, it proposed that historical cost accounting should be phased out in favour of current cost accounting and that companies should only publish both historical cost and current cost accounts for two years before abandoning HCA. It also followed Sandilands in that no specific adjustment was proposed to cover the effect of inflation on monetary items, contrary to the CPP proposals, and as a result there was no acceptable definition of profit. Although many accountants disagreed with Sandilands on the monetary item question, many other interested parties agreed at the time with the proposals, but it was not possible to obtain agreement on the issue sufficiently to frame a satisfactory definition of profit.

Although the exposure draft ED 18 seemed to be reasonably well accepted to begin with, the full implications gradually sank in and criticism built up, almost to the extent of a perceptible campaign against it. Members of the English Institute passed a resolution at a special meeting to the effect that they did not want any form of CCA made compulsory. There were over 700 submissions made to the ASC in response to ED 18 and clearly it was bound to take some considerable time for the Steering Group to develop the next stage.

The ASC, in order to keep the momentum going, published an interim guideline (the Hyde Guidelines) asking listed companies voluntarily to produce a simplified supplementary CCA statement. This guideline laid down few rules as to the methods of calculation so that companies had to rely on their own ideas or follow the rules set out in ED 18. A move forward had been made during the debate concerning how to account for the effect of inflation on monetary items, and the proposals in the interim guideline on this were able to be more definitive than ED 18 had been.

The Steering Group had continued to work towards a new exposure draft and it was clear that, in view of events, it was too early to be able to make a standard apply to all companies. Accordingly it was decided to propose only that listed and large companies would be involved, and also that wholly owned subsidiaries of U.K. parent companies would be exempted from publishing CCA accounts.

In addition, it was evident that industry wanted a degree of flexibility during the development phase, at least as far as the measurement rules were concerned. It was decided therefore that the detailed measurement rules, previously set out in ED 18 (the first exposure draft), would be published in non-mandatory guidance notes, leaving the standard itself to set out scope, principles and disclosure requirements.

Finally, it was decided that initially at least a close link still needed to be kept with the historical cost convention and that the CCA adjustments would be shown as being adjustments to the historical cost profit, and that no timetable could be given for any mandatory abandonment of the historical cost accounts.

Exposure draft 24 was prepared and issued accordingly and set out a clear capital maintenance concept underlying the measurement of profit. It was sufficiently accepted for the standard SSAP 16 to be published without major amendment of principle to the proposals in the exposure draft.

An essential element to acceptance has been the general understanding, in a long period of high inflation, of the misleading nature of historical cost accounts. Indications that shareholders, managements, government and trade unions have been misled have been evident, and there was a general will amongst managements of listed companies and many others to accept some change. Accountants and academics will always argue about method, however, and there is still likely to be considerable argument over methods and measurement rules for years to come. Meanwhile, those to whom the standard applies are setting about the necessary effort to report according to the standard, and an increasing number of managements are changing their management information systems on to a CCA basis.

It is worth at this stage considering the basic elements of the CCA system adopted in SSAP 16.

In the first place, it is important to emphasize that SSAP 16 does not extend accounting into assets or liabilities that are not taken into account by a company in its normal historical cost balance sheet. Assets are shown in the current cost balance sheet at their value to the business, except for monetary items which are shown at their nominal amounts. Value to the business is in most cases net current replacement cost. In certain cases, where management recognises that a permanent diminution in value has taken place, value to the business would be the recoverable amount— either what the asset was worth if sold or, if higher, what could be recovered from its continued use. This principle of writing down to recoverable amount in the event of diminution in value is basically the same as for the historical cost system.

An example of the current cost profit and loss account is given below in very simplified form:

			£'000
(i)	Profit before interest and taxation on the historical cost system		2,900
(ii)	Less current cost adjustments		1,510
(iii)	*Current cost operating profit*		1,390
(iv)	Gearing adjustment	166	
	Interest payable less receivable	200	
			34
			1,356
(v)	Taxation		730
(vi)	*Current cost profit attributable to shareholders*		626
(vii)	Dividends		430
(viii)	Retained current cost profit of year		196

It will be noticed that two profit levels are italicised. Each of these profit levels gives important information about the company.

The underlying capital maintenance concept is not concerned with the purchasing power of shareholders' equity, but with the operating capability of the business. This is defined in the standard as the output of goods and services the business is currently able to produce with its existing resources. In accounting terms, the operating assets shown in the balance sheet are the basis from which the operating capability flows so that the current cost adjustments shown in (ii) are concerned with measuring the maintenance of the net operating assets after taking into account the effect of price changes. Net operating assets include fixed assets, inventories and monetary working capital, all of which need to be maintained to protect the operating capability of the business. Current cost operating profit is defined therefore in the standard as "the surplus arising from the ordinary activities of the business in the period, after allowing for the impact of price changes on the funds needed to continue the existing business and maintain its operating capability, whether financed by share capital or borrowing. It is calculated before interest on net borrowing and taxation." This profit level is the one concerned with the success of a business as a trading concern. It is the profit on which is based the return on assets employed.

The current cost adjustments concerned with the maintenance of the net operating assets are three in number.

1. *The depreciation adjustment*—the difference, essentially, between depreciation on the current value to the business of the fixed assets and depreciation charged in the historical cost accounts.

2. *The cost of sales adjustment*—the difference between the replacement cost of inventory and its historical cost at the date of consumption or sale.

3. *The monetary working capital adjustment*—the amount which requires to be set aside to cover the additional financing needs in respect of net monetary assets because of price rises. When sales increase, for example, because of price increases, most businesses need to finance higher receivables.

The current cost adjustments made in arriving at operating profit relate to the whole of the operating assets even though a proportion may be financed by borrowing. To the extent that a business is able to continue to finance that proportion of assets by borrowings it will not need to set aside the full amount of the current cost adjustments for the year.

Accordingly, in arriving at the second important profit level, a gearing (or leverage) adjustment is made which brings back into profit the proportion of the current cost adjustments which do not need to be set aside because the lender is effectively financing that part.

The gearing credit therefore indicates to the shareholders a measure of the benefit the company receives from financing a proportion of its operating assets by borrowings and against that is set the interest on borrowings to arrive at the net benefit or cost to shareholders.

This adjustment gives important information and focuses attention on the leverage ratio. If a large part of the current cost adjustments are credited back to profit through the gearing adjustment, it will indicate that the business might be depending too much on its ability in the future to obtain increased borrowings to maintain its leverage ratio. Dividends partly paid out of credit may indicate that a business may be depending too much on future borrowings to maintain operating capability.

The standard does not deal adequately with making current cost accounts comparable between years since it does not require, as does the U.S. FAS 33, the adjustment of prior years to a common price basis with the current year. This gap is intended to be filled by the ASC which is at present working on an exposure draft on the subject.

The standard also does not focus back on to the shareholders' equity so that a business may be maintaining its physical operating capability in an area where the input prices of its operating assets are going down in price while general inflation continues to rise. However, the standard does encourage a voluntary statement to be given which does focus on shareholders' equity (see page 180). Any deficit shown in that statement, if charged to the current cost profit and loss account perhaps before arriving at profit attributable to shareholders, could restore the position for that company. In the U.K., it may be some time before this latter adjustment is recognised and made mandatory in a standard.

This outline of the U.K. standard is necessarily brief but it is a standard which applies to a broader scope of companies than any other CCA standard. SSAP 16 may therefore be of considerable interest to many countries which are trying to make progress with accounting for price changes.

Development of a standard in any country depends to a great extent on the attitude of business and on management willingness to reveal realistic and lower profits, on the attitude of government towards the subject and, I regret to say, on a longish period of relatively high inflation rates to overcome most people's inevitable inertia and reluctance for change. It is inevitable that the state and direction of development of accounting for inflation should be different country by country. Such differences, however, will increasingly create problems for international business and it is vitally important that harmonisation should take place on this very important topic. The accounting profession may well be blamed if an international consensus of approach cannot be achieved and if multinational businesses are asked to provide inflation accounting information in a number of different ways, according to the various countries in which they operate.

It may well be worth, therefore, taking a look at the state of progress in a number of different countries where the accounting professions have been making strong efforts to make progress towards more realistic accounting in periods of inflation than is offered by historical cost accounting.

In Europe, the German government continues to adopt a hostile approach to inflation accounting, and will not implement the legislation necessary to make accounting for inflation compatible with the EEC 4th Directive dealing with the presentation of financial information. The experience of hyperinflation in Germany has been a strong influence on their attitude towards preventing inflation developing. They have so far been successful at limiting the rate of inflation to very low levels. The Institut der Wirtschaftsprüfer have issued an exposure draft calling for supplementary inflation adjusted information, but this achieved little interest. German industry must certainly be aware of the need to take account of inflation when they venture abroad and experience much higher rates of inflation than they experience at home.

In the Netherlands, replacement cost accounting has been developed over many years and a number of companies of considerable importance have used both for management accounts and for annual financial statements a form of replacement cost (either fully or partially). Companies are able to present either historical cost accounts or replacement cost accounts since there has been freedom of choice of accounting principles. Under the influence of the example, perhaps, of countries like the U.S.A. and U.K. which have recognised the value of accounting standards in the interests of comparability, a Tripartite Committee has been formed, including employers' organisations, unions and accountants, to analyse accounting principles and determine what should be acceptable.

The proposed new law in the Netherlands, to implement the EEC 4th Directive, follows so far as is possible the views of the Tripartite Committee. The idea that pure historical cost data on its own is sufficient in a time of inflation is rejected, while current purchasing power accounting is also regarded as inadequate. While the incorporation of replacement cost data would not be mandatory in all cases, additional information must be disclosed where equity and earnings based on historical cost and current cost vary, and replacement cost data must be incorporated in the annual accounts where to fail to do so would prevent the presentation of a true and fair view.

Little has been done in other countries in the EEC, which are basically not prepared to go beyond the historical cost system, and the accounting professions do not seem to have a standard setting procedure of their own.

In South Africa, the accounting profession started in 1975 with the publication of a discussion paper, which was overtaken by the publication in the U.K. of the Sandilands Report. Still on the table is a "Guideline on the Disclosure of Effects of Changing Prices on Financial Results." This was based largely on the ASC interim guideline and calls for a supplementary statement of a profit and loss account but not balance sheet. The statement is basically a current cost statement where there are only two adjustments, depreciation and cost of sales, to arrive at operating profit, and it provides for a gearing adjustment to reflect the benefit to shareholders of financing a proportion of the assets by borrowed money.

There has been little support for this guideline from industry or government and until the profession produces an acceptable mandatory accounting standard, little further progress seems plausible.

The Australian accounting profession has been very energetic in trying to obtain acceptance of the need for accounting for inflation. Discussion papers were published in 1974 and 1975 and a provisional accounting standard in 1976, although these did not deal comprehensively with the subject. Subsequent exposure drafts were issued dealing with recognition of gains and losses on holding monetary items. The aim was to produce a comprehensive mandatory standard applying from 1978, but this was never published and was replaced by a request for voluntary CCA information.

Such request has not been complied with by many entities in Australia. There are signs of renewed interest, but there is perhaps a need for a mandatory standard before further progress can be made. Businesses do not like voluntary requests—they do not wish to be isolated in giving information which may appear detrimental when compared to others who are not presenting similar information.

The New Zealand Society of Accountants has tried hard to develop current cost accounting. A guideline was issued in 1978, covering additional depreciation charges and a cost of sales adjustment on a CCA basis together with a gearing adjustment to recognise the effect of inflation on net monetary assets. No monetary working capital adjustment was included in the proposals. Unlike the U.K. standard, the New Zealand government has not encouraged the change to CCA by declining to accept the need for any significant tax relief to accommodate the change in profit measurement. Interest has therefore started to wane even amongst companies which have followed the guideline, since many have not and there is a subsequent lack of comparability between those following it and those not doing so.

In Canada, interest in accounting for inflation has not been great, but after an enquiry set up by Ontario into the question, activity has increased and the CCA Accounting Research Committee published in December 1979 an exposure draft on current cost accounting which largely follows the U.K. exposure draft ED 24. This calls for supplementary current cost information with a profit and loss account format almost identical to that in the U.K. standard. It does not call for a balance sheet, but a statement of asset values at the accounting date. It calls for a statement reconciling the changes in the shareholders' equity between the beginning and the end of the year on a current cost basis.

The exposure period was open until 30th June 1980 so it is anticipated that a standard will be published shortly.

In the United States, there is still considerable debate about the need for action on inflation accounting as well as what method should be used. There is still strong support for current purchasing power or constant dollar accounting and it is possible that, if the SEC had not indicated that they would insist on current (or replacement) cost accounts information being produced whatever the FASB standard contained, then the standard might have required only constant dollar information.

However, the FASB standard, FAS 33, was issued in September 1979, applying to public enterprises whose total assets after depreciation are more than $1 billion or whose depreciable assets before depreciation are more than $125 million. The scope of FAS 33 is not therefore as wide as in the U.K. It does however follow the supplementary information route, leaving the historical cost statements as the main accounts, whereas the U.K. standard permits companies to publish CCA accounts as the main financial statements with either full historical cost accounts on a supplementary basis or merely such historical cost inflation as is required by statute.

The standard calls for two supplementary statements, one adjusting the historical cost profit and loss account for general inflation, the other to take account of specific price changes on a current cost basis.

Both these statements deal only with depreciation and cost of sales in arriving at income from continuing operations. The gain from the decline in purchasing power of net borrowings must be shown separately but not as part of income.

The increase in specific prices of assets (holding gains) of the year must be shown analysed between the effect of the general price level increase and specific price level increases. There is no requirement for a balance sheet on a current cost basis, but a five year comparison of selected financial data updated to a common price basis with the current year is required. In the U.K. this is not required but is the subject of an exposure draft being developed for publication in 1981.

The Mexican Institute of Certified Public Accountants has issued in 1979 a Bulletin—B-7—of the Accounting Standards Commission requiring companies to present a supplementary statement for accounting periods beginning 1st January 1980, giving inflation adjusted data which can be either on a general purchasing power basis or a current cost accounting basis. Both methods require calculation of the net gain or loss on net monetary items. Failure to include the inflation adjusted information will require an "except for" qualification in the audit opinion on the financial statements.

Brazil has suffered high rates of inflation going back to before 1964 when the rate was 84% and by 1978 inflation was still running at 41%. It is not surprising therefore that accounting practice and taxation both take account of the effects.

From 1 January 1978, a new method was introduced by law. Under this a company may continue to account internally month by month on whatever basis it likes. It is required, however, to keep monthly memorandum accounts on an inflation adjusted basis. At the end of the company's year, these adjusted figures are required to be incorporated into the published accounts. The intention is that all accounting will eventually only be done on an inflation adjusted basis.

The basis of the adjustments is correction of the assets by reference to a single index whose calculation is based on a Government Treasury Bond unit. The deductions are given for the "depreciation" based on current values and a form of leverage adjustment is also taken into account to cover the advantage of financing assets by borrowed money. Attention is thus focused, as in the U.K., on the extent of a company's leverage.

It is clear from this very brief summary of the situation that the development of accounting for inflation or price changes is gaining pace but that there is still a good deal of resistance to change. Such resistance stems from a number of reasons, such as governments' unwillingness to accommodate the necessary tax changes or to support the changes firmly enough. This is not so in, say, the U.S.A. where the SEC is strongly supporting changes and where LIFO is accepted for tax, or in the U.K., where substantial tax changes have already been made and the Government is supporting the change.

In addition, some countries have not experienced a high enough rate of inflation for long enough to enable those concerned to recognise the extent to which historical cost accounting is misleading. Piecemeal development is not liked by managements who do not wish to be compared on the basis of their voluntary presentation of CCA information with others who are only producing historical cost accounts. There is a need for firm leadership by the accounting profession in producing mandatory standards and a need for major efforts to explain the necessity for a method of accounting which takes into account the effect of changing price levels and how misleading historical cost accounts really are in today's world inflationary environment.

The two alternative methods of current purchasing power accounting and current cost accounting are still being advocated although current cost accounting seems to be gaining credibility on the basis of its relevance to management as well as to the user. It seems to me that these two methods should not be looked on as alternatives but that the ultimate answer may well be a combination of both. At present, I believe that to do this before the implications of either method are fully understood would confuse rather than illuminate. Current cost accounting is the most relevant for most purposes today, even though it is difficult to bring some types of business within its concepts. Further progress should therefore be based on this method. There is an opportunity now for the International Accounting Standards Committee to give a lead rather than follow. None of us must forget that international business will not tolerate a different answer from each country in which it operates. The international investor is fully aware of the prime purpose of accounting standards which is to improve comparability between competing investment opportunities and he will not take kindly to very different answers in different countries.

The job of the accounting profession worldwide is to provide relevant and useful financial information which is understandable by those who need it. We must do so.

ACCOUNTING DEVELOPMENTS IN THE EEC—
THE COMMUNITY'S COMPANY LAW
HARMONIZATION PROGRAMME

Paul J. Rutteman
Arthur Young McClelland Moores & Co.

CONTENTS

ABSTRACT

*Mr. Rutteman explains the background for the European com-
munity's company law harmonisation program and outlines the process
followed in developing a directive. The article summarises the progress
to date and then concentrates on the three directives which are of most
immediate significance to the accountancy profession: the fourth
directive which specifies the formats for the annual accounts of limited
companies and lays down valuation rules and disclosure requirements
to be observed in their preparation: the proposed seventh directive
which sets out the circumstances in which group accounts are to be
prepared and prescribes the accounting principles to be followed: the
proposed eighth directive which sets out minimum standards which
must be met before a person is entitled to carry out the audit of limited
companies in member states. The article concludes by stressing the
importance of accountants taking an interest in the development of
directives.*

The drive for the European Economic Community's (EEC's) company law
harmonisation programme originates in article 54 of the Treaty of Rome:

> In order to achieve a stage in attaining freedom of establishment...
> the Council shall... issue directives... coordinating to the necessary
> extent the safeguards which, for the protection of the interests of
> members and others, are required by Member States of companies
> or firms... with a view to making such safeguards equivalent through-
> out the Community...

This section of article 54 spells out the EEC's aim to afford equivalent
investment opportunities and risks to investors and thus to encourage
the free movement of capital between the Member States.

This need for a company law harmonisation programme, particularly
with regard to accounting, can be put in perspective if one considers the
present legislation in Member States. This ranges, on the one hand, from
the prescriptive, as in France, to the pragmatic, as in the UK; and, on the
other hand, from the detailed as in Germany, to the less stringent, as in
Luxembourg or Italy.

Users of accounts of companies from different Member States would
find great difficulty in making comparisons using those accounts at present.
The harmonisation programme will, ultimately, ease this difficulty, but
because the intention is to set only minimum standards, there will still
be differences at a national level.

THE DEVELOPMENT OF A DIRECTIVE

The proposal for a directive originates with the Commission, often after an external expert has been invited to submit a report on the subject, usually together with a first draft of a proposed directive. After publication, the proposal is considered by the European Parliament and the Economic and Social Committee and in the light of comments received from those bodies and other interested parties such as the Groupe d' Etudes des Experts Comptables (the EEC Accountants' Study Group) the Commission will either issue an amended proposal or forward the original version to the Council of Ministers.

A Council of Ministers' working party, consisting of representatives from the relevant government departments of each Member State, then considers the proposal in considerable detail, making amendments as necessary to reach a text which is acceptable to all states.

The directive will then be adopted formally by the council and the final version published in the Official Journal of the European Communities. The Member States then have a specified time in which to amend their laws to incorporate the provisions of the directive.

The progress of a directive is determined by a number of factors, but its complexity, general acceptability and urgency are those principally affecting the speed with which it is adopted. In some cases the period from first publication to adoption can be very short, while in others it may be a number of years; the Fourth Directive, for example, took seven years to be adopted after its first publication.

PROGRESS TO DATE

So far only a handful of company law directives have been adopted, and even fewer have been incorporated into the legislation of the Member States. There are, however a number which are still at various stages of the adoption process. Despite the relatively small number of directives in the course of preparation, their importance should not be underestimated. Not only do they cover a wide variety of subjects, but also they will cause the alteration of legislation and practice which has been considered perfectly acceptable for some time in one or more Member States.

The table below sets out the status of the more important directives which have been considered to date. Of these, two in particular will have a major impact upon annual financial reporting: the Fourth and Seventh Directives, on company and group accounts respectively. Two other directives will have a substantial effect on the accountancy profession in

TABLE 1

The Company Law Directives

Subject	Status	Published	Adopted	To Be Implemented by
1 Registration and publication	Adopted	1964	1967	In force
2 Company capital	Adopted	1970	1976	In force
3 Mergers	Adopted	1970	1978	1981
4 Company accounts	Adopted	1971	1978	1982
Bank accounts	Proposed	1981	—	—
Insurance company accounts	Unpublished	—	—	—
Interim reports	Proposal	1979	—	—
5 Company structure	Proposal	1972	—	—
6 Prospectuses—listed companies	Adopted	1972	1980	1982
Prospectuses—unlisted companies	Proposal	1980	—	—
Admission to listing	Adopted	1975	1979	1982
7 Group accounts	Proposal	1976	—	—
8 Auditors qualifications	Proposal	1978	—	—
Freedom of establishment of accountants	Proposal	1970	—	—
9 Law relating to groups	Unpublished	— · ·	—	—
Dissolutions and liquidations	Unpublished	—	—	—
Scissions (reverse mergers)	Unpublished	—	—	—
Takeovers	Unpublished	—	—	—

general: the proposed Eighth directive and one on the freedom of establish-ment of practising accountants. The other directives will affect a wide variety of areas of company law.

It is worth noting that, because the intention is to draw together the legislation of the various EEC Member States, some of the requirements of a particular directive are already contained in some countries' laws. Indeed, the initial draft of a directive on a particular subject is often based on the relevant legislation of the Member States, allowance being made during drafting for experience of legislation in practice and, in most cases for the particular needs and difficulties of other Member States.

THE FOURTH DIRECTIVE

The Fourth Directive was first published as a proposal in 1971 and was based on a study produced by a prominent German accountant, Dr. W. Elmendorff, in 1968. Not surprisingly the first proposal owed much to the then recently enacted A G Law of 1965, the essence of the proposal being compliance with reasonably detailed laws relating to the format of accounts and the valuation of items shown therein.

The accession, in 1973, of the UK, Ireland and Denmark saw the emphasis of the Directive change more towards the presentation of a true and fair view. This now overrides the requirements to comply with the law where to do so would result in a true and fair view not being given.

The directive was finally adopted by the Council of Ministers in July 1978 and should be incorporated into the laws of all the Member States by the beginning of 1982.

The accounts of all limited companies published after that date should, therefore, have to comply with its provisions. So far, however, it seems unlikely that most countries will have amended their legislation in time, although in some cases there are fairly clear indications as to the probable nature of the changes to come.

The main consequence of the directive is that legislation will specify the formats for annual accounts and lay down valuation rules and disclo-sure requirements to be observed in their preparation. Cross-border com-parisons of accounts should, therefore, be simpler. However, it could be said that the directive has gone little further than its aim of setting a harmonised minimum standard of accounting throughout the EEC and, indeed, there are a number of areas where substantial differences will still exist. This follows, perhaps regretably, from the number of options, some 50 or so, that were included in the directive in order to obtain the agreement of all the Member States.

Scope of the Directive

The directive applies to the annual accounts of all limited liability companies, although small and medium-sized companies may be exempted from some of its detailed requirements. Banks and insurance companies may also be exempted as separate directives, which are currently being prepared, will deal with their accounts.

The annual accounts are defined as the balance sheet, the profit and loss account and notes on the accounts and are to be drawn up so as to give a fair and true view of the company's assets, liabilities, financial position and profit or loss.

The Accounts Formats

The directive allows a choice of two forms of balance sheet, one vertical and one horizontal, each showing the same information, and four forms of profit and loss account, two vertical and two horizontal, one of each form showing costs by type of expenditure and the other by purpose of expenditure. Member States may either decide which format is to be followed in each case or permit the use of several of the formats, in which case companies themselves will be free to choose which one to use. Each balance sheet format shows assets and liabilities, divided as by main headings (designated by letters), sub-headings (Roman numerals), and detailed items (Arabic numerals). The profit and loss account formats consist solely of items designated by Arabic numerals. Any item may be further sub-divided, while items designated by Arabic numerals may be combined where they are immaterial or where combination results in greater clarity, provided that the items so combined are shown separately in the notes on the accounts. Member States may require the formats to be adapted so as to include the appropriation of profits or the treatment of losses.

In general the layout of the balance sheet and profit and loss account may not be changed from year to year, although changes may be made in exceptional cases. In this event, however, the change must be disclosed in the notes on the accounts and an explanation given of the reasons therefor.

Corresponding figures for the previous year are to be given for each item, but if both are nil the item should be omitted. Where figures for the previous year are not comparable, Member States may require adjustments to be made to them, appropriate disclosure being made in the notes on the accounts.

The Balance Sheet

Whether particular assets are to be shown as fixed or current assets is decided on the basis of the purpose for which they are intended, although fixed assets will generally comprise those which are intended to be used on a continuing basis in connection with a company's activities.

All movements in fixed assets must be disclosed, starting with purchase price or production cost (or the revalued amount if inflation accounting is used) and showing clearly both cumulative and current year's depreciation.

"Participating interests," shown under financial fixed assets, mean rights in the capital of other undertakings which, by creating a durable link with those undertakings, are intended to contribute to a company's activities. A holding of 20% of the capital of an undertaking is presumed to give rise to such an interest but Member States may set a lower percentage.

In order to avoid the creation of secret reserves, the item "provisions for liabilities and charges" may not be used to adjust the value of assets. Instead it is intended to cover losses or debts whose nature is well defined and which are either likely or certain to be incurred, but for which, at the balance sheet date, the amount or date on which they will arise is uncertain. In any event, however, provisions must not exceed the sums which are necessary and material amounts included under "other provisions" must be disclosed in the notes on the accounts.

Commitments by way of guarantee which are not yet liabilities should either be shown at the foot of the balance sheet or in the notes on the accounts, those relating to affiliated undertakings being shown separately.

The turnover figure shown in the profit and loss account should comprise the amounts derived from the sale of products and the provision of services falling within a company's ordinary activities, and should be net of discounts, value added tax and other turnover taxes.

Income and charges arising outside a company's normal activities must be shown as extraordinary items and, unless they are immaterial, must be explained in the notes on the accounts. In some Member States it seems to be difficult to allocate taxes to extraordinary items, so the directive allows a combined amount to be shown as taxes on ordinary activities. Where this option is applied, however, the notes to the accounts must indicate how the taxes affect the ordinary profit or loss and the extraordinary profit or loss.

Valuation Rules (Accounting Principles)

The accounting principles to be used are similar to those already widely used elsewhere, and are based on the following fundamental concepts:

- the company is presumed to be a going concern;
- the valuation methods are to be applied consistently from year to year;
- valuation should be made on a prudent basis;
- account must be taken of all items relating to a particular year;
- items must be valued on the basis of purchase price or production cost;
- the components of each asset and liability item must be valued separately; and
- the opening balance sheet must correspond to the closing balance sheet for the previous year.

Departures from these general principles are permitted only in exceptional cases, when appropriate disclosure must be made in the notes on the accounts.

A number of specific accounting principles are also set out in the directive, mostly applying to fixed and current assets. While fixed assets must, in general, be valued at purchase price or production cost, those with limited useful economic lives must be depreciated systematically and an asset must be written down to realisable value when a permanent change in circumstance results in this being lower than depreciated cost.

The purchase price of a fixed asset is defined in the directive as the price paid plus any incidental expenses. Production cost is the cost of raw materials etc. directly attributable to the item plus, optionally, a proportion of indirect costs to the extent that they relate to the period of production. Interest may also be added to production cost, but its inclusion must be disclosed in the notes on the accounts. Similar general rules apply to current assets. They must, therefore, be valued at purchase price or production cost, although here the option of including interest rests with Member States.

Particular rules are set out for writing off the costs of certain intangible assets. Formation expenses, costs of research and development and goodwill have to be written off over a maximum of 5 years and no distributions may be made until formation expenses and costs of research and development are covered by reserves and profits brought forward. However, Member States may derogate from these requirements in respect of goodwill and costs of research and development. Goodwill, in particular, may be written off over a period not exceeding its useful life by charges to the profit and loss account.

The methods of stock valuation which may be permitted are left to Member States to select from a choice of weighted average cost, LIFO, FIFO or "some similar method," but, whichever method is used, the differences between the value shown in the accounts and market value, if material, must be disclosed in the notes on the accounts.

Inflation Accounting

In addition to setting out valuation rules based upon historical purchase price or production cost, the directive contains a number of provisions relating to inflation accounting. These provisions are, however, optional to Member States and not all states will incorporate them into their law.

Member States may permit or require, in respect of all companies or just particular classes of companies;

- Valuation by the replacement value method for tangible fixed assets with limited useful economic lives and for stocks;
- Valuation by other methods which are designed to take account of inflation for the items in the accounts, including capital and reserves;
- Revaluation of tangible and financial fixed assets.

Where, however, such methods are provided for by law, the law must define their limits, content and application rules. In any event, the extent of the application of such methods must be disclosed in the notes on the accounts.

Where a method of accounting for inflation is adopted, the directive requires the amount of any difference between valuation by that method and by methods based on historical cost to be included in the "revaluation reserve," with all movements during the year being shown in the notes on the accounts. In addition, the balance sheet or notes on the accounts must indicate, for all balance sheet items other than stocks, either a valuation on the basis of historical cost, or the amount of the difference between the valuation made under inflation accounting rules and that under historical cost rules. In general, value adjustments are to be calculated on the basis of the value adopted for an item in the year in question.

The revaluation reserve which arises from the application of these provisions may not, in general, be reduced. It may, however, be capitalized in whole or in part at any time and it must be reduced where the amounts transferred to it are no longer necessary for the implementation of the valuation method. Member States may also allow transfers to be made to the profit and loss account. Such transfers must, however, be disclosed separately in the profit and loss account and may only be made to the extent that they have been entered as charges or reflect realized increases in value. No part of the revaluation reserve may be distributed unless it represents realized gains.

The Notes on the Accounts

In addition to the various disclosures mentioned above, the notes on the accounts must also set out:

- The valuation methods applied to items in the accounts, the methods of calculating value adjustments and the bases of translating foreign currency amounts.
- The name and registered office of undertakings in which the company holds 20% or more of the capital (Member States may specify a smaller figure), together with the proportion of capital held, the amount of capital and reserves and the profit or loss for the latest year.
- The number and nominal value (or accounting par value) of shares subscribed during the year.
- The number and nominal value (or accounting par value) of each class of shares where there is more than one class in existence.
- The Existence of any participation certificates, convertible debentures or similar securities, indicating their number and the rights attached to them.
- Any amounts payable after 5 years together with details of secured debts, shown separately for each item under creditors.
- The total of any financial commitments (other than those shown in the balance sheet) if this information would help in assessing the financial position, with commitments relating to pensions and affiliated undertakings being shown separately.
- The net turnover broken down by category of activity and geographical market.
- The average number of persons employed during the year broken down by category and the staff costs for the year split between wages and salaries and social security costs (unless this is shown in the profit and loss account).

- The extent to which the profit or loss for the year was affected by a valuation of items which was made in order to obtain tax relief, disclosing any future influence if it is material.
- The amount, if material, of the difference between the tax charged for a year and that which will actually be payable. Such amount may be included in the balance sheet as a separate item.
- The amount and totals of the emoluments, advances and credits granted to members of the administrative, managerial and supervisory bodies and any commitments in respect of pensions for former members, or by way of guarantees of any kind. In respect of advances and credits, an indication must be given of interest rates, main conditions and any amounts repaid.

Member States have the option of allowing the list of investments set out above to be filed with the Company Registrar separately or, as with the details of turnover, to be omitted if the disclosure would be prejudicial to any of the undertakings, although omission may be made subject to prior administrative or judicial authorisation. Both separate filing and omission must be disclosed in the notes on the accounts.

The Annual Report

Companies are required to prepare, in addition to the annual accounts, an annual report which is to include a fair review of the development of the company's business and of its position. In addition the report must give an indication of any important events since the end of the year, the company's likely future activities in the field of research and development and details of acquisition of the company's own shares.

Auditing

Companies must have their annual accounts audited by one or more persons authorized by national law to audit accounts. Such an audit also entails ensuring that the annual report is consistent with the annual accounts.

Publication

Once duly approved, the annual accounts, the annual report and the auditors' report must be filed with the company registrar, an act which constitutes "publication." Member States may however permit companies not to publish their annual report in that manner, but companies must then make the report available to the public at their registered office in the country concerned and it must be possible to obtain copies of the report free of charge.

Whenever the accounts are published they must be accompanied by a statement setting out the appropriation of the profit or treatment of the loss unless this information is already disclosed in the accounts.

Whenever the annual accounts and report are published in full they must be reproduced in the form which was used by the auditor in preparing his report, the full text of which must also be reproduced.

If an abridged version of the filed accounts is published it must include a statement that it is an abridged version and also indicating in which register the full accounts have been filed. If filing has not yet occurred, that fact must be noted. In any event, the auditor's report may not accompany the abridged version, but an indication must be given as to whether the report was issued with or without qualification, or whether an opinion was witheld.

Exemption for Small and Medium-Sized Companies

In respect of small and medium-sized companies the directive makes a distinction between the accounts which must be drawn up and sent to shareholders and those which must be published. (The three tiers of company are shown in Table 2.) The distinction, which is at the option of Member States, essentially results in the burden of reporting borne by small companies being reduced when compared with larger companies.

TABLE 2

3 Tiers of Company

Not to exceed 2 out of 3 criteria.

	Small	Medium	Large
Balance sheet total	1 million Eua	4 million Eua	Exceeds
Turnover	2 million Eua	8 million Eua	medium
Employees	50	250	company limits
$ = 0.8	£ = 1.8	DM = 0.4	FF = 0.17

If Member States take maximum advantage of the permitted concessions, small companies need publish only an unaudited balance sheet
(consisting of the items designated by letters and Roman numerals and
showing the amounts of debtors and creditors payable within one and
after one year) and abridged notes on the accounts (setting out, in addition to any matters specified elsewhere, such as exceptional cases etc.,
only details of accounting principles, investments, shares subscribed,
share classes, secured debt and amounts payable after five years). The
accounts for shareholders must also include a profit or loss, and must be
accompanied by the annual report.

For medium-sized companies the concessions are not so generous.
Shareholders' accounts can only be abridged to the extent of omitting
the analysis of turnover from the notes on the accounts and the components of gross profit or loss from the profit and loss account. Some
further concessions are allowed on publication, but these only allow
moderate abridgement of the balance sheet (mainly as regards items
other than debtors or creditors) and the omission of further information
from the notes on the accounts (in particular, details of participation
certificates, etc., an analysis of turnover, details of valuations made for tax
purposes, details of deferred tax and the breakdown of secured debt and
amounts payable after five years).

Special Cases and Transitional Provisions

Two types of company are recognized in the directive as having particular
problems with regard to some of the more detailed points. These are
financial holding companies, such as exist in Luxembourg, and investment
companies. Member States are given powers to prescribe special accounts
layouts for these types of company as long as they satisfy the requirement
to give a true and fair view.

Financial holding companies are defined as those companies whose sole
object is to acquire holdings in other undertakings and to manage such
holdings for profit without actually being involved in the management of
the undertakings. Such companies receive a particular concession in that
they need not be required to publish a list of their holdings of greater than
20% in the capital of another undertaking (note, however, that a lower
figure may be specified here).

The concessions open to investment companies are that these may be
allowed to set off adjustments arising from the revaluation of investments
directly against reserves as long as such amounts are separately shown. This
separate disclosure requirement may be waived, however, if investment

companies are afforded the other concession open to them, that of valuing their investments at market value.

There are also other transitional provisions which are open to Member States to adopt, but which may not continue beyond the introduction into law of the Seventh Directive. These concessions apply in respect of companies in groups; in particular to the dominant and the dependent companies of groups.

Member States need not require dependent companies in a group to comply with the Fourth Directive subject to certain conditions. These are that:

- the dominant company of the group is subject to the Fourth Directive and publishes group consolidated accounts which note the exemption,
- the shareholders of the dependent company have declared their agreement to the exemption,
- the dominant company has declared that it guarantees the commitments of the dependent company and
- the declarations specified above have been filed with the company registrar.

The dominant company of a group similarly need not be required to comply with the directive as regards the auditing and publication of its own profit and loss account. The conditions attached to this concession however are that:

- the dominant company consolidates its accounts with those of its dependent companies,
- it files notice of the exemption with the company registrar, and
- it indicates the fact of the exemption in the notes on the accounts and shows the profit or loss of the dominant company in its balance sheet.

Implementation

The Member States were required to bring into force the laws necessary to implement the directive by early 1982. This deadline may, however, be extended to mid-1985 for a number of special cases, notably for the requirement that a company's accounts be audited. This extension recognises the inevitable difficulty of introducing the audit requirement into countries where there are insufficient trained auditors to carry out the task.

To ensure that the requirements of the directive are kept up to date a Contact Committee, comprising representatives of each of the Member States, has been set up to advise the Commission on any additions and amendments which may be necessary.

THE SEVENTH DIRECTIVE

The Seventh Company Law Directive is currently undergoing its fourth reading by a Council of Ministers' working party. In addition to setting out the circumstances in which consolidated group accounts must be prepared, it will prescribe the accounting principles and accounts formats that should be followed.

This section summarizes the development of the Seventh Directive as far as it is known. Readers should bear in mind, however, that a number of amendments may be made before the directive is finally adopted. The need for a directive on consolidated accounts can be seen readily if one considers the present requirements in respect of group accounting in the EEC. Of the nine Member States, four have no general legal requirement for group accounts, although these are prepared in some instances in response to requests from national institutions, such as stock exchanges. In the other five Member States, while group accounts are required, there are substantial differences in the methods used to prepare them and the information which they contain.

A proposal for a group accounts directive was first considered in the late 1960's, although it was not published until 1976. As a result of comments by a number of interested parties, an amended proposal was published in December 1978. This proposal still retained many of the requirements which had given rise to much of the criticism of the original proposal, particularly by interests in the Anglo-Saxon countries.

These features resulted in a general lack of agreement between the members of the Council of Ministers' working party and have resulted in the directive's adoption being delayed considerably. One of the early difficulties was reaching agreement on a definition of a group. This definition will now be left out of the directive and is expected to reappear in a later directive on group law. The present directive will instead set out the circumstances in which consolidated group accounts must be prepared.

Despite there still being a number of points on which agreement was outstanding it was hoped that the directive could be adopted during 1980, so that countries could anticipate its requirements when implementing the Fourth Directive, but agreement has proved to be so difficult to achieve that it is now unlikely that the directive will be adopted until the latter half of 1981 at the earliest. The Member States will then have approximately 4 years in which to bring into force the directive's provisions.

The Directive's Concept of a Group

The published proposals employ the "economic entity" concept of a group found in Germany, rather than the "legal power of control" concept which is used in the U.K. The "economic entity" concept recognises that a company may be effectively a subsidiary of another even if that other does not have a legal power of control through an outright majority shareholding, or through the ability to control the composition of a company's board of directors.

The principle criterion in this respect is whether or not one company (the dependent or subsidiary company) is managed by another (the dominant or parent company) on a unified basis. If so, then whatever percentage interest is held the accounts of the two companies should be consolidated. If not, equity accounting will generally be appropriate for those companies over which a significant influence is exercised.

Under the "economic entity" concept outlined above it is possible to refute the presumption that one company is dependent on another, even where more than 50% of the capital is held. It may, therefore, be appropriate for a company with, say, a 60% interest in another, perhaps overseas, to equity account for that interest rather than to consolidate.

Alternatively, where a company holds an interest of less than 50% in another, but manages that other on a unified basis, it could be appropriate to prepare consolidated accounts rather than just to equity account for the interest.

The final version of the directive will probably be based on a compromise between the two concepts, but there are still believed to be a number of fundamental areas on which agreement is outstanding.

It is essential to note that the word "undertaking" is used throughout the directive where one might expect to see the word "company." This results from the view that a group in terms of the "economic entity" concept need not consist only of limited companies, but may include any other vehicle through which business is conducted. Indeed, consolidated group accounts could need to be prepared by a parent undertaking which is a partnership or a sole trader, as long as the group contains at least one limited company. Attempts have been made to restrict the application of the directive to groups headed by one of the types of limited company listed in the Fourth Directive, but these have not met with complete success. Such an approach, however, could become an option for the Member States.

When Should Consolidated Accounts Be Prepared?

The proposal specifies three instances in which the preparation of consolidated accounts is required:

- Where one undertaking controls another;
- Where one undertaking is managed on a unified basis with another and
- Where there are two or more undertakings subsidiary to another which is outside the scope of the directive.

Basic Consolidation

Consolidated accounts must be prepared by a parent undertaking such that they include the accounts of all subsidiary undertakings. For this purpose, a parent undertaking is defined as one which:

- holds a majority of the voting rights of another undertaking, *or*
- is a shareholder of another undertaking and has the right to appoint or remove more than half of the board of directors, *or*
- has the right to exercise a dominant influence over another undertaking as a result of any contract entered into with that undertaking or any provision in its articles.

In each case the other undertaking is a subsidiary. Consideration is being given to the inclusion of a provision whereby consolidation would also be required where one undertaking controls another in practice, but does not fulfill any of the conditions above. Such a situation would arise, for example, where one company holds 40% of the voting shares of another but, because of the diversity of the other holdings, is able to exercise complete control.

It is unlikely that such a provision would be mandatory, due to the difficulties of proving in all cases that effective control does exist, but it is possible that it could be retained as an option for Member States in order that agreement can be reached.

In many cases a subsidiary undertaking may also be a parent; in such cases it will also be required to prepare consolidated accounts including all its subsidiaries. There is likely to be an option in the final version of the directive which will reduce substantially the impact of this requirement to prepare sub-group accounts. It would allow a parent undertaking which is also a subsidiary undertaking (not necessarily wholly owned) to be exempted from the requirement to prepare consolidated accounts as long as:

• the accounts of all the undertakings concerned are included in a consolidation of the accounts of a larger collection of undertakings (for example, thé consolidated accounts produced by a controlling undertaking or by the EEC subsidiaries of a non-EEC parent—see below),

• the accounts are drawn up in accordance with the directive or, where they are prepared by an undertaking registered outside the EEC, in a manner "comparable" to consolidated accounts drawn up in accordance with the directive, such comparability being verified by an EEC auditor,

• the accounts are filed with the company registrar,

• the holders of more than 10% of the shares have not requested that consolidated accounts be prepared and

• the fact of the exemption and the name and registered office of the undertaking which has prepared consolidated accounts are disclosed in the notes.

Unified Management

Combined consolidated accounts must be prepared by undertakings which are managed on a unified basis provided that at least one of the under-takings or the subsidiaries is a limited company, but regardless of whether or not there are common ownership links. Unified management in this context would be that arising from a contract or a provision in the articles of association of one of the undertakings.

Member States will have the option to exempt undertakings from this requirement where another undertaking under the same unified manage-ment prepares the accounts. Such an exemption would be subject to those accounts being filed with the Registrar and, where that other undertaking is registered outside the EEC, to the same test of comparability as men-tioned in respect of sub-group consolidated accounts.

Another option will be available which will allow Member States to exempt undertakings under unified management, which are themselves subsidiaries, from the obligation to prepare consolidated accounts, subject to the fulfillment of the same conditions as apply for the sub-group exemption above when the accounts of all the undertakings concerned are included in a consolidation of the accounts of a larger collection of undertakings.

The EEC Consolidation

The directive will also require combined consolidated accounts to be prepared where two or more undertakings, which are registered in the EEC, are subsidiaries of an undertaking registered outside the EEC (see Figure 1).

There are, however, likely to be two options open to Member States similar to those explained above in relation to accounts prepared as a result of unified management.

The effect of requirements will be that an American or Japanese company with, for example, subsidiaries in the U.K., Germany and Italy will either have to ensure its subsidiaries publish combined accounts or

FIGURE 1

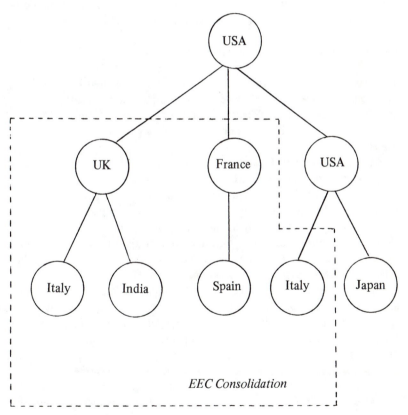

EEC Consolidation

have to file in the EEC countries its own accounts which will have to be verified by an EEC auditor as being "comparable" to accounts prepared in accordance with the directive.

It is not clear exactly what "comparable" means in this context or what would happen if only some and not all Member States were to exercise these options. In the former case, while accounts prepared in accordance with U.S. accounting principles could normally be considered "comparable" to those required under the directive, there may be other instances where it would be difficult for the EEC auditor to verify this comparability, due either to the use of different accounting principles or to the existence of less stringent legal requirements. In the second case, it would be unfortunate if just one country did not exercise its option. This would mean that any non-EEC undertaking with a subsidiary in that country in addition to others would have to prepare EEC accounts, whereas others, with no subsidiaries in that country, would not need to do so. Such a situation could not be considered as being in the best interests of the Community as it could tend to result in a distortion of investment.

Preparation and Presentation of Group Accounts

The group accounts, consisting of the group consolidated balance sheet, the group consolidated profit and loss account and notes, must give a true and fair view of the group's assets, liabilities, financial position and results, and must, in general, be drawn up in accordance with the provisions of the directive.

As with the Fourth Directive, however, departures from the directive's requirements may be made where necessary to give a true and fair view, but they must be disclosed and explained in the notes. The provisions of the Fourth Directive regarding the presentation and valuation of items in company accounts will apply as far as possible to consolidated accounts. However, Member States are permitted to vary the preparation and presentation requirements where insurance companies, banks, or other financial institutions form part of a group.

Group undertakings may be omitted from consolidation only if they are of negligible importance for the true and fair view, but several undertakings, which are of minor importance individually, must be included if they are of significance when taken together. In addition, undertakings may be excluded in the following circumstances:

- where their shares are held exclusively for resale,
- where there are severe long-term restrictions which substantially

hinder either the parent undertaking exercising its right or the exercise of unified management,
- where the information necessary for preparing the consolidated accounts cannot be obtained without undue expense or delay.

Where the undertakings carry on very different activities, such that consolidated accounts would not give a true and fair view, consolidation is effected by activity or the undertakings concerned are treated as associates; i.e. holdings of their shares are valued by the equity method.

Consolidation Methods

The consolidated methods set out in the directive accord closely to those which are generally applied internationally and are subject to the following general principles:

- the methods of consolidation may not be changed from one year to the next;

- consistent accounting principles should be applied throughout the group, unless any differences are immaterial;

- intra-group balances must be eliminated;

- intra-group profits and losses must be eliminated;

- where possible, all group undertakings should have coterminous year ends, interim accounts being required where there is a difference of more than three months;

- where the composition of a group has changed during a year, sufficient information must be given to enable a meaningful comparison of successive sets of accounts to be made (although Member States may allow this obligation to be fulfilled by the preparation of an adjusted opening balance sheet and profit and loss account).

Departures from these general principles are permitted in exceptional cases, but an explanation must be given in the notes, together with an assessment of the effect of the departure on the group's assets, liabilities, financial position and results. Similar information must also be given for the one specific departure which is permitted and which allows profits to be recognised on intra-group transactions involving fixed assets as long as they are concluded according to normal market conditions.

It is notable that the directive does not deal fully with the mechanics of the preparation of combined accounts, i.e. those required where there is unified management or where a non-EEC undertaking controls a number of EEC undertakings. While this omission will probably be rectified, there are a number of attendant problems. It is not clear, for example, exactly which country's accounting principles should be used, or in which currencies the accounts should be prepared and filed. While, in general, this will not give rise to serious problems, there may be instances where accounts prepared in accordance with one country's accounting principles do not comply with the law of another country.

The calculation of goodwill or capital reserve arising on consolidation and the treatment of minority interest is to be made in accordance with the principles generally used internationally. Under these goodwill is the difference between the cost of the shares of an undertaking held and the corresponding proportion of the nominal capital and reserves of that undertaking at the date of acquisition, the reserves being adjusted to reflect the fair value of the undertaking's assets and liabilities at that date. In order to avoid potential problems in some Member States, however, the consolidation difference for the first group accounts drawn up in accordance with the directive may be calculated by reference to the book value of the holdings and the percentage of the capital that they represent.

Consolidation differences will probably be required to be written off over a maximum period of 5 years, although, in line with the Fourth Directive, Member States may be allowed to extend this period to enable such differences to be written off over their useful economic lives. This proposed requirement might suggest that the practice of writing off consolidation goodwill to reserves on acquisition, a common practice in the UK is not allowed in future and this is still under discussion.

Minority interests would continue to be calculated as the relevant proportion of share capital and reserves of the undertakings in which persons outside the group have an interest. The amount to be shown in the profit and loss account, similarly, would be the relevant proportions of the results for the financial period of the undertakings in question.

Associated and Affiliated Undertakings

Associated undertakings will have to be accounted for on the equity basis. The premium or discount on acquisition of interest in an associated undertaking will, however, have to be written off in the same way as other consolidation differences.

As an alternative to equity accounting, Member States may be given the option of allowing proportional consolidation where one undertaking is managed jointly by two or more other undertakings which together do not form part of a group; i.e. where there is effectively a consortium or a joint venture.

It is understood that the exact definition of an associate to be used in the directive has not been agreed upon yet but it will almost certainly incorporate the principles of a minimum holding of shares and involvement in the affairs of the undertaking which are normally applied.

The directive will set out a definition of affiliated undertakings for the purpose of disclosures in both group and company accounts. It is believed, however, that this definition has yet to be agreed upon but is likely to encompass at least all undertakings forming part of any group which includes the undertaking whose accounts are being considered.

Notes to the Accounts

The directive will specify a certain minimum amount of information to be included on the notes on the group accounts. Particular disclosures additional to those required for company accounts that will probably be required include:

- the name and registered office of all consolidated undertakings, together with the proportion of capital held and the legal relationship between them;

- equivalent information in respect of undertakings which have not been consolidated because of their minor importance, together with an explanation for their exclusion;

- the name and registered office of the immediate parent undertaking, where appropriate, and the proportion of capital it holds;

- the names and registered offices of other EEC subsidiaries of a non-EEC parent undertaking (i.e. those which would be included in the EEC consolidation referred to above);

- the names, registered offices, and proportions of capital held of associates and those undertakings consolidated on a proportional basis;

- the total amount of financial commitments outside the group in so far as is necessary to assess the financial position of the group as a whole. Commitments in respect of pensions and with regard to affiliates which do not form part of the group are to be shown separately;

- the group's turnover, broken down by activity and geographical market, in particular between trade inside and outside the EEC.

Audit and Publication

The parent company of the group will be responsible for ensuring that the group annual accounts are audited by one or more persons authorised by national law to audit accounts. The auditor will also be required to verify that the group annual report, which will contain information similar to that required for a company's annual report, is consistent with the consolidated accounts.

Publication of the group accounts will be required in the same way as it was in the Fourth Directive for companies' annual accounts.

Possible Exemptions

It is understood that the directive may contain some exemptions for smaller groups. While it is not yet clear what form these will take, it is likely that smaller groups will need to prepare and publish only abridged accounts, roughly in line with the abridgement permitted under the Fourth Directive and possibly using size criteria similar to those contained in that directive. It is also possible that there could be some form of audit exemption for small groups.

Another matter, which it is believed, is yet to be resolved is the fate of Articles 57, 58 and 61 of the Fourth Directive. These permit the accounts of subsidiaries, the profit and loss accounts of parent companies and the note disclosure of the financial details of subsidiaries and associates not to be published when the undertakings concerned are included in consolidated accounts. The amended proposal for the directive suggested that these exemptions would be allowed to continue only for 30 months after the directive was adopted. It is understood however, that several interested parties would prefer the exemptions to be available permanently and it is possible that this may become an option to be taken by the Member States.

EIGHTH DIRECTIVE

The proposed Eighth Directive is of some interest to accountants in the EEC as it sets out minimum standards which must be met before a person is entitled to carry out the audits required by the Fourth Directive. Indeed, considerably more interest would probably have been shown were it not for the significant amount of time which can elapse before a directive is finally enacted by the individual Member States. The Eighth Directive was originally published in April 1978 and a revised draft in November 1979. It is currently in its second reading with the Council of Ministers working party but even when it is adopted by the Council of Ministers Member States will have up to five years to implement its provisions.

The proposed directive is aimed at harmonising the qualifications of auditors throughout the community so that the accounts required to be prepared by the Fourth Directive, and eventually the Seventh, will be subject to a consistent review. It does not cover the mutual recognition of auditors throughout the European Community. This is to be the subject of a subsequent directive on mutual recognition. Although some work has been done here it is unlikely that a definite proposal will be published until the requirements of the Eighth Directive have been finalised. Indeed the original version does not even cover auditing. It is limited to the provision of other accountancy services.

The Eighth Directive is concerned with the setting of common minimum qualification standards throughout the community and doesn't go so far as to actually establish uniform qualification standards. Countries which have more stringent requirements at present will no doubt retain them.

Training Requirements

The directive sets out a basic route to be followed in obtaining approval to act as auditor which is not dissimilar to that which presently exists in a number of European countries. Having attained an education to university entrance level a person wishing to be approved as an auditor would then commence a period of professional study which would cover the following subjects:

- Auditing
- Evaluation and critical appraisal of balance sheet and profit and loss accounts
- General accounting
- Provisions relating to group accounts
- Cost and management accounting
- Internal control
- Accounting Standards and methods of evaluating balance sheet items and of determining results
- Company tax law
- Company criminal law
- Company law

In addition studies cover, in so far as they are relevant to auditing the following:

- — Principles of law
- — Information and computer systems
- — Business, general and financial economics
- — Mathematics and statistics
- — Basic principles of financial management of business undertakings.

One of the points which has been the subject of debate in respect of this syllabus is the inclusion of such a broad legal study requirement in the first category of subjects. There is a strong feeling that the three legal subjects should more logically be included in the second part of the syllabus, in other words that studies should be restricted to the elements of the law which relate to auditing and that only the legal requirements specific to auditing should be included in the first category.

Having completed his professional studies the student would then spend a practical training period of at least three years with an approved auditor and this training would principally relate to statutory audits. At the end of this period the candidate would have to pass an examination of both his theoretical knowledge and his ability to apply the knowledge in practice before being granted approval.

The requirement that the practical training is to relate principally to statutory audits is viewed in some countries as being too restrictive. They believe that it is desirable for the training programme to develop a highly qualified all round accountant who has the knowledge and training necessary to be able to carry out auditing as part of his skills but not as his only skill.

In some countries exams are held at present throughout the training period and theoretical and practical training can also be mixed rather than running consecutively. It is likely that these approaches will be permitted in the final directive.

Indeed although the above route represents the basic path to qualification the proposed directive already envisages certain variations. For instance if a person holds a university degree in one of the subjects included in the second part of the syllabus Member States may exempt him from the test of theoretical knowledge in that subject. In addition persons who have not attained the level of study generally required may sit the examination if they have spent fifteen years engaged in activities which have enabled them to acquire sufficient experience in the field of finance, law or accountancy or if they have spent seven years in such activities and also meet the practical training requirement.

Accounting Firms

The draft directive covers not only individuals but also accounting firms. In the case of the latter it sets three requirements:

- That the persons responsible for the audit and signing of accounts meet the standards set in the directive.
- That the majority of the capital or voting power in the firm be owned by individuals who meet the standards set in the directive.
- That the persons who do not meet the standards set in the directive shall neither be involved in the choice of the persons responsible for an audit nor issue any instructions in respect of that audit.

The above requirements, whilst feasible perhaps at first glance, pose a number of problems. In Germany some auditing firms are owned by banks or indeed the State and in Denmark there is a publicly listed audit company, these situations could presumably no longer continue once the directive is in force unless an extension were to be granted here. The same would presumably apply in the case of international partnerships. In addition international firms would, given the restriction on the issuance of instructions by unapproved persons, find it difficult to coordinate the audit of multinational corporations (in particular, their subsidiaries in the European Community) and to take steps to ensure that the audits were being carried out to auditing standards set by, for instance, a head office in the U.S.A.

If the above problems are not to apply within Europe as well it would be desirable for it to be clarified that any requirement to meet the standards set in the directive is met by a person who is approved to carry out audits in any Member States in which the directive has been implemented. If this is not done a Member State may choose to declare when implementing the directive that only partners who personally fulfill the conditions which have been laid down in that particular state may exercise any influence over statutory audits in that state.

Independence

The approval of a person is subject to his being of good repute and not carrying out an activity which casts doubt on his independence. The vague wording of this requirement raises questions as to precisely which activities are envisaged as casting doubt on independence. Countries have, not unnaturally, interpreted this requirement in different ways depending on the nature of any similar requirements to which the profession in their country is already subject. Certain countries' auditors do not provide any form of service other than actual audit work. In others, such as Germany and France, a person loses their right to practice as an auditor should they move out of the profession into Industry.

It is to be hoped that the above general independence requirement will be shelved and that the independence requirements will be restricted to those relating to individual clients. Failing this the question must be asked as to whether any profession which has traditionally supplied a number of services to clients such as tax advice or consultancy services will need to be irrevocably split with a chasm separating auditing from all other activities.

The more specific independence requirements are that an auditor be independent from any majority shareholder and board members of the company he audits. The auditor is also barred from receiving loans or security from the company, affiliates, majority shareholders or board members. Finally he is precluded from any shareholding in the company or an affiliate.

Member States are required to set up, if they do not already exist, the measures required to supervise compliance with the requirements of the directive and, in particular, to ensure that there are disciplinary sanctions if an approved person fails to carry out his duties with due professional care. Regular updated lists of approved persons must be maintained and be available to the public.

Transitional Measures

There are a number of transitional measures designed to ease the implementation of this directive in the individual countries. These measures are optional and contain some ambiguous points.

Persons who were previously entitled to carry out audits in a country and had been doing so may be approved before the implementation of the directive despite the fact that they do not meet the standards it sets. The present wording could therefore imply that a person can only be approved in these conditions if they had in fact exercised that right. In addition there is a provision for a Member State to approve persons after the implementation of the directive where they had been carrying out the audit of a body not previously subject to statutory audit requirements but which becomes so through new legislation.

Member States may also adopt transitional measures for a period of up to three years after the implementation of the directive in respect of students undergoing professional training at the time of implementation.

The provisional measures above are all accompanied by the proviso that approval will only be granted to persons who are of good repute and not carrying out any activity which casts doubt on their independence and that they are judged by the competent authorities fit to be auditors on the grounds that the standard which they have attained is compatible with that required by the directive. The present wording of the directive is not clear, however, as to whether persons approved under the transitional measures are deemed to meet the requirements of the directive for the purpose of determining whether they are entitled to hold a controlling interest in a professional firm.

The Eighth Directive only applies to the audits required under the Fourth Directive although it will no doubt be extended to cover the entities which might need to be audited as a result of the implementation of the Seventh Directive and it does not address the problem of the qualification of auditors performing the statutory audit of any other bodies. There is a fear, therefore, that in certain countries where there are at present auditing bodies with training requirements which do not comply with those of the Eighth Directive, such as in Denmark, that one will see the development of a two tier profession rather than one in which different bodies intermingle.

Recognition of Non-EEC Qualifications

There is provision in the Directive for the recognition of non-EEC qualifications by a Member State provided that these are deemed to be equivalent in standard to a qualification meeting the requirements of the directive. In addition, however, a person with such a qualification will be expected to prove that they have sufficient knowledge of the law of the country in which they wish to practice. European law prevents discrimination on the basis of a language test and there is some concern that a proof of legal knowledge might be used as a language barrier should a Member State be over protective in respect of its own accounting profession.

In addition it would be highly desirable if the mutual recognition directive could be implemented at the same time as the Eighth Directive. If this is not done any freedom of establishment which is already enjoyed in the Community may cease on the implementation by a Member State of the Eighth Directive. An English accountant practicing in another Member State may for instance suddenly find that he is no longer entitled to.

CONCLUSION

The EEC company law harmonisation programme is already effecting the work of the European accounting professions. The implementation of the

Fourth Directive in national law will have a very noticeable impact on the reporting requirements throughout the Community. The Seventh and Eighth directives may not be implemented for some time yet but accountants ignore them at their peril. Indeed if they do not take an interest in the development of directives at an early stage they may find when these are implemented that they have a far wider impact than they realised and, by then, it will be too late to change them.

It is obviously desirable for accounting requirements throughout the EEC to be harmonised and if the price which has been paid by the accounting profession in certain countries is the surrender of a certain degree of previously enjoyed self-regulation as more prescriptive legislation is introduced this does not mean that these professions can no longer influence the rules by which they operate. There is scope for playing a part in the development of EEC legislation and the ideal would obviously be that at the end of the day an exchange of the lessons learnt in the different countries will lead to a stronger, healthier and more dynamic European profession. But there is still a long way to go before accounting requirements in the EEC are near to being truly harmonised. Efforts to date, considerable as they have been, have substantially been limited to agreeing approaches to the setting of minimum standards.

IS THERE MORE THAN ONE ACCOUNTING PROFESSION?

Michael Shirley-Beavan

Binder Dijker Otte & Co.,
London

CONTENTS

ABSTRACT

Mr. Shirley-Beavan examines the forces of change that could divide the UK accounting profession, and states that the principal concern is with dual standards. He examines the size of firm as a factor and notes the increasing involvement of the larger firms in smaller-client work. He reviews the necessity for compulsory audit of smaller enterprises, and questions whether it can be justified on a cost-benefit basis. Compulsory review is not a substitute for audit but standards of (voluntary) review and compilation would "do much to enhance the prestige of the smaller practitioner". Practices must adhere to adequate standards of education and training, independence, discipline and self-regulation. The maintenance of such standards is expensive and firms must charge adequate

fees and make adequate profits. Finally, he concludes that larger prac-
tices with their spread of both small and large clients can be an impor-
tant voice for unity.

INTRODUCTION

The accounting profession in the United Kingdom has undergone a rapid transformation in the last few years, to the extent that the question is increasingly being asked whether the forces of change are not now greater than those that have historically held together the wide spectrum of knowledge, training and experience that together form "The Accounting Profession". This article seeks to examine some of these forces. It is written primarily from the UK standpoint because the pace of change in this country has recently been so great that the UK is to a considerable extent a microcosm of what is happening elsewhere in the world.

The "Accounting Profession" Defined

In the UK there are several accountancy bodies. There are the two Institutes of Chartered Accountants (in England and Wales and in Scotland). There is the Association of Certified Accountants, The Institute of Cost and Management Accountants and the Chartered Institute of Public Finance and Accountancy. Together with the Institute of Chartered Accountants in Ireland, they form the Consultative Committee of Accountancy Bodies, (CCAB).

If the number of bodies is anything to go by, there is clearly more than one accounting profession. It is not, however, the purpose of this Article to examine in detail the different roles of these bodies or to reflect upon the scheme to integrate them which was thrown out by the members of the English Institute in 1970. That was part of a broader attempt to update training methods, examination standards and professional standards generally. Too much was bitten off at once and since that time the bodies have remained apart, but have worked together under the CCAB.

Neither is it the purpose of this article to consider the current debate in the English Institute about industrial training. A large number of members believe that the Institute's practice-based training fails to provide for the central social need to meet the requirements of future finance directors. This is a view that has long been held to a greater or lesser degree by many of the members of the other accountancy bodies whose training is essentially non-practice based.

This article will concentrate on the practising profession; not, however, to examine in any depth the various specialisations embraced by the profession. It would be too facile to observe that, in this respect as well, there is more than one profession. The true concern is that the profession may find itself applying dual standards—perhaps one for the large and one for the small, or one for the public enterprise and one for the private. This is the real debate.

Historical Background

Twenty years ago—perhaps not much more than ten—it was rare for the UK accounting profession to make any headlines. It pursued its traditional role of invisible guide and mentor, the epitome of solidity and reliability. As already noted, there was more than one branch of the profession, more than one specialisation and more than one size of firm. Essentially, however, accountants were all cobblers at the same last. Although closely involved with the public, the accounting profession was nevertheless a relatively private one. It did not open itself to public scrutiny, nor in truth was such scrutiny much in demand.

Viewed against the historical background, the change in the last decade or so has been dramatic, as a few salient dates will demonstrate. The English Institute was formed in 1880 (some twenty-five years after the Scottish Institute), two years after the notorious failure of the City of Glasgow Bank and one year after the Companies Act made compulsory the annual audit of all banking companies. The following year the first important text on auditing was published.[1] It was, however, over sixty years later, in 1942, that the English Institute issued its first "Recommendations on Accounting Principles".[2] Over twenty years passed by before the profession started to gain increasing prominence as a result of disputes arising from takeovers, the most notable occurring after AEI, who in October 1967, during its unsuccessful defence against a takeover by GEC, had forecast a pre-tax profit of £10 million for 1967, in the event turned in a loss of £4.5 million. Of the £14.5 million shortfall, roughly £5 million was subsequently attributed to adverse differences which were matters of fact rather than judgment, and the balance of some £9.5 million to adjustments which remained substantially matters of judgment. After many decades of quiet obscurity, the profession was well and truly in the firing-line.

As a result of these disputes, the City Panel on Takeovers and Mergers was established in 1968 and published the "City Code",[3] and shortly after, in 1969, the English Institute appointed its first technical director. In January 1970 it formed the Accounting Standards Steering Committee, joined by the Scottish and Irish Institutes later that year and by the other UK accounting bodies as associate members in 1979. (The Committee was re-named the Accounting Standards Committee in 1976). In the last decade the accountancy bodies have, at the time of writing, issued eighteen State-ments of Standard Accounting Practice (SSAP's), with several more at the exposure draft stage; the first set of definitive audit standards, and several versions of a basis for inflation accounting, culminating in SSAP 16. The Cross[4] and Grenside[5] Committees have reported on self-regulation in the profession; a new guide on professional independence has been issued; the Solomons Committee has reported on educational and training standards;[6] a paper setting out objectives of, and recommendations for, corporate re-porting was published in 1975.[7] On top of this there have been two new Companies Acts with at least one more to come, EEC directives, Interna-tional Accounting Standards, International Auditing Standards, and so it goes on. After ninety years of quiet progress out of the public gaze, there have been ten years of great activity, even if there has often seemed to be too much debate and not enough decision.

The Profession in the Future

The AEI affair was not in itself sufficient to rock the accounting boat—it was merely the catalyst. As the nineteen sixties drew to a close, in society generally a younger post-war generation was beginning to assert itself, a generation not content to accept without question the philosophy of its predecessors; a generation more politically aware and questioning and, above all, one demanding greater accountability from all those whose ac-tions affected its way of life. The accounting profession was by no means alone in being caught up in the tide of opinion demanding greater regulation in public matters.

The fact is that there had been, and there is continuing, a massive change in the environment in which modern society exists. The computer revolu-tion has meant that information is available and can be transmitted on a scale undreamt of a few years ago. Travel is quicker and easier. Multina-tional corporations have grown as international barriers have been broken down. Today, there is a greater degree of interdependence amongst the constituent parts of modern society than ever before. Life is infinitely more complex and the demand for greater accountability in matters of public interest is not going to abate.

Greater accountability brings with it a need for effective and indepen-dent monitoring and reporting. This has traditionally been the accountant's role and pressures have been mounting for an expansion of that role into new fields. There are demands for auditors to assume responsibility for an increasing amount of non-financial information in annual reports; for them to conduct efficiency audits; for greater involvement in the auditing of public sector bodies such as local authorities, and so on.

As we enter the eighties therefore, it is in the knowledge that the accounting profession will be increasingly involved in matters of public concern and on an ever widening front. At the same time it will come under greater scrutiny itself than ever before.

THE SIZE FACTOR

The profession in many countries has increasingly been polarising into the large and the small firms. This polarisation has not happened merely as a result of the changes in the profession in the last decade. It had started well before that. As investment flowed from the USA into Europe and from the developed world to the developing countries, as businesses became increasingly international and takeovers and mergers flourished, so the call for international accounting, principally auditing, services grew. Accounting firms had to keep pace with the growth of their clients. In particular, they had to set up credible international organisations. Those that did survived; those that did not found it increasingly hard to hold on to their large clients and many have ceased to exist as independent firms. Some of the more far sighted have re-thought their role and built up substantial practices orientated towards the smaller client.

At the same time, the increase in activity within the professional bodies, and the emphasis on public accountability, has inevitably meant that a large share of the burden for accounting development and standard setting now falls on practitioners from the large accounting firms who can more easily afford the time and expense of substantial non-client activity. This in turn has increased the concern felt by the smaller firms that official pronouncements are very often irrelevant, or inappropriate, to their needs and to those of their clients. But are the large firms deaf to the needs of the smaller practice and its clients?

In the last few years, it has generally been true that the dozen or so largest firms, sometimes referred to in the UK as the "Reporting Accountants"—that is the firms principally used by the merchant banks and issuing houses to prepare Accountant's Reports for prospectuses—have been heavily involved with public enterprise auditing and reporting. Figures disclosed by such firms show that a major part of their income derives from this source. Small firms, on the other hand, have been principally involved with counselling their predominantly private clients, both corporate and individual, providing day to day taxation, accountancy and general financial and management accounting advice. This all-round service demands a different, and more sensitive approach, and hitherto the big firms have, arguably, not been particularly successful in providing it at a reasonable cost.

There are, however, signs that the trend is changing. The larger firms now have an overwhelming share of the quoted and large private company market. They are increasingly looking to the smaller clients for their future growth. Outside the main cities, many have offices with a substantial volume of small client work. Consequently, it is not so much the size of firm that matters, but the size of the individual office.

The involvement of the large firms in the smaller end of the market, and the mergers of smaller firms into larger small-client practice units, undoubtedly poses a challenge to the small practice, but not necessarily a threat. If many small practices feel threatened, we need to look further than sheer size.

THE SMALL AUDIT DEBATE

It would be wrong to suppose that small practitioners together form a cohesive group that speaks with one voice. The revolt against the CCAB's proposals on Current Cost Accounting, largely led by small practitioners and which in 1977 ended with the carrying of a motion against the compulsory implementation of Current Cost Accounting by a majority of the voting members of the English Institute, has probably been the only real public evidence of a majority on any major issue affecting the smaller practice. In a way, that was an unfortunate issue on which to make a stance at all; historic Cost Accounting so clearly fails to give a full picture of what is happening to a business in times of high inflation that some form of inflation accounting was inevitable. What was in fact a reaction against an arguably ill-conceived, but undoubtedly too hurriedly prepared and imposed, set of proposals may have given the impression of reactionary forces in the profession seeking to stem the tide of progress.

The profession is currently debating the need for compulsory audit of certain smaller companies. There is a risk that this debate could give the same impression of the same reactionary forces at work. Fears have been expressed in some quarters that the abolition of compulsory audit for small companies might have an unfavourable impact on the smaller practitioner. Not everyone would agree. In any event these fears must be kept in check since it cannot be acceptable that the profession appears to be acting out of self-interest. The first priority must be the needs of the community.

Because the debate is of great importance to the UK profession, it is worth examining in some detail the facts and issues involved. Until recently, there has been an uneasy silence about the quality and scope of the audit of smaller companies. Such companies seldom received audit qualifications solely on account of the scope of audit work. In May 1978, however, the exposure drafts of the new "Auditing Standards and Guidelines" were issued. These were finalized with one major modification and published in April 1980.[8] The fears about the audit of smaller companies are expressed in the Standard on Qualifications in Audit Reports.

> ... the operating procedures and methods of recording and processing transactions used by small enterprises often differ significantly from those of large enterprises. Indeed, many of the controls which would be relevant to the large enterprise are not practical, appropriate or necessary in the small enterprise. The most effective form of internal control for small enterprises is generally the close involvement of the directors or proprietors. This involvement will, however, enable them to override controls and purposely to exclude transactions from the records. This possibility can give rise to difficulties for the auditor not because there is a lack of controls, but because of a lack of independent evidence as to their operation and the completeness of the records.

The Audit guidelines put forward a qualification to deal with these circumstances.

> We have audited the financial statements on pages ... to .... Our audit was conducted in accordance with approved Auditing Standards having regard to the matters referred to in the following paragraph.
>
> In common with many businesses of similar size and organization, the company's system of control is dependent upon the close involvement of the directors/managing director (who are major shareholders). Where independent confirmation of the completeness of the accounting records was therefore not available we have accepted assurances from the directors/managing director that the company's transactions have been reflected in the records.
>
> Subject to the foregoing, in our opinion the financial statements, which have been prepared under the historical cost convention, give a true and fair view of the state of the company's affairs at 31st December 19.. and of its profit and source and application of funds for the year then ended and comply with the Companies Acts 1948 and 1967. (Now 1948 to 1980)

It should be noted that under the exposure draft a disclaimer would have been required. This major modification resulted from pressure from the smaller practitioners.

If the phrase "in common with many businesses of similar size and organisation" is accurate it would be reasonable to expect that a substantial number of the 600,000 or more companies registered in the UK will now have their statements qualified. But the public, it is argued, is already growing cynical about the number of "technical" qualifications that have been given since Statements of Standard Accounting Practice were introduced. Might not a further spate further devalue the report to the extent that when something really is amiss, the qualification will have little impact?

Under UK company law all enterprises incorporated under the Companies Acts are required to have their financial statements audited by qualified accountants who must report whether or not the statements show a true and fair view. As already noted, there are over 600,000 such companies comprising a complete range of entities; large public companies; their subsidiaries; dormant subsidiaries with no assets or liabilities; family companies; the corner shop; individuals incorporated for tax purposes, and so on.

The EEC Fourth Directive which must eventually be incorporated into UK Company Law requires member countries to legislate for companies to have their financial statements audited but permits them to exempt certain small companies from the requirement. In September 1979 the British Government published a "green paper" on company accounting and disclosure.[9] After repeating the problem stated in the Auditing Standards it goes on:

> ... It has therefore been suggested that this position should be recognised by removal of the statutory audit requirement...
>
> The government welcomes the proposals of the accountancy profession to improve auditing standards, particularly regarding large companies, and recognises that it would be undesirable if the new and more stringent standards, if applied to the proprietary companies, led to either a considerable increase in qualifications in audit reports or to significantly increased audit fees, or both.

The arguments for and against compulsory audit are by now very familiar, since the UK is the only country in the western world requiring independent full audit and disclosure for the smaller company. The arguments were fully set out and discussed in an excellent paper published by the Auditing Practices Committee of the CCAB in October 1979.[10] Briefly, the arguments put forward in favour of the compulsory audit are that:

Shareholders	-	need reassurance that their interests are being protected.
	-	need audited statements to enable a value to be placed on their shares.
Banks and other lenders	-	need audited statements as a basis for lending decisions.
Trade Creditors	-	seek assurance that the businesses they supply are financially sound.
Taxing authorities	-	rely on audited statements.
Employees	-	need reliable financial information for collective bargaining and to assess the prospective viability of an employer's business.
Management	-	is helped by an independent check on a business's performance and on the company's procedures and staff.

The contrary view can be summarised as follows:

Shareholders	-	let them decide. If even a significant minority want an audit, let them have one; but why impose it?
Banks, etc.	-	again, let them demand it when necessary. Why impose it on companies with no borrowings? In any event banks rely as much on the way the account is conducted, on management accounts and other "timely" information, on cash flow projections and on out-turn against these projections, as they do on an out of date balance sheet.
Trade creditors	-	statements are filed too late to be much use to creditors or for credit ratings.

Taxing authorities	–	have always been prepared to rely on unaudited statements and have stated that they would not hold out for an audit.
Employees	–	in a small company employees are very unlikely to rely on audited statements, the profit shown by which is heavily dependent on director's remuneration, low interest loans from directors, etc.
Management	–	again, let them decide. In any event, the whole debate stems as much as anything else from the concern that the statements frequently reflect only the information supplied by management. Further, without an audit fee, management could afford to make better use of the accountant's other advisory services.

The abolitionists' arguments are essentially pragmatic—where there is a need, let those concerned make the appropriate decision. The arguments of the advocates of the status quo are more essentially theoretical and are enshrined in the concept of "the price of limited liability", as if the recipients of this public privilege must pay for it in the time-honored way, an audit, whether or not such form of payment is relevant to Society's needs.

The advocates of the status quo claim that there is no mandate for making any change. This attitude, however, does not take account of the main philosophical issue involved. In a free enterprise system, it must surely be argued that regulation is only justified if it passes a cost-benefit test; that is, the costs to be borne by those being regulated are outweighed by the benefits to Society of imposing or, more particularly in this instance, retaining the regulation. This argument would say that, if there is no clear balance of advantage in retaining compulsory audit for certain classes of company, it should be done away with.

From soundings and straw polls made, there is clearly no evidence of a strong majority either way, even, surprisingly, amongst the smaller practitioners themselves. It may, however, be noted that the English Institute has come out against abolishing the audit and against review as an alternative in the event of abolition.

Compulsory Review is not the Answer

Although a novel concept in the UK, the idea of a review has operated in the US and Canada for some while. The concept is now established in the US in SSARS 1, issued in December 1978.[11] The UK proposals are similar, and will not be repeated here, except to note that the review report would make it clear that an audit was not being carried out and would express no opinion. It would give a negative comfort to the effect that nothing had been found to suggest that material adjustments would be necessary for the financial statements to be in conformity with generally accepted accounting principles.

The concept of a compulsory review has a certain seductive attractiveness. It allows one to hedge one's bets—to sit on the fence. But when examined more closely it can also be seen to fail the cost-benefit test. There is no real evidence to suppose a review will be significantly cheaper than an audit. If public interest dictates the abolition of the compulsory audit, why should it require a compulsory review? By pushing for compulsory review, does the profession not run the risk of giving way to self, rather than public, interest?

This is not to argue that review has no place, provided it is voluntary. One of the arguments put forward to oppose compulsory review—that it would be confused with audit—is not persuasive. Why should it be confused? Other countries have successfully adopted review on a voluntary basis and without any apparent difficulty. Perhaps a period of public education would be necessary. So be it. Experience in the US and Canada suggests that a review can be a very effective exercise. So far the U.K. accountancy bodies have not really grappled with the much wider problem of an accountant's association with unaudited financial statements. If compulsory audit is abolished, there will be many more such statements. Many will be prepared by accounting firms and clients will expect some form of assurance. They are entitled to a uniform approach and standard. Accountants will have to decide how, and in what circumstances, such assurance can be given. The US and Canada have standards of review and the former has standards of "compilation", i.e. preparation, of statements as well. We have a very real need for standards of non-audit work in the UK. The existence of such standards would do much to enhance the prestige of the smaller practitioner.

Abridged Accounts

It should be noted here that there is another issue which has so far received less prominence. The EEC Fourth Directive would permit small companies to prepare and send to shareholders an abridged balance sheet and profit and loss account. Alternatively, the UK could retain the existing requirements for accounts which are to be sent to shareholders, merely preparing abridged accounts for filing purposes. Such abridged accounts would not even include a profit and loss account.

The CCAB has come out against the suggestion. It can perceive no real demand. Costs would not be reduced and such abridged accounts might be positively misleading. Consequently, they have suggested that, should the Government decide in favour of abridged accounts, no audit opinion could be given. The report would confirm that the abridged accounts have been extracted from "the (audited) accounts" and comply with statutory requirements. It would also confirm that the auditors had reported on "the accounts" and would reproduce the report in full.

It is difficult to see what would be achieved. Unwillingness on the part of small companies to disclose information about themselves does not seem to be a major issue. If audited accounts are prepared, they might as well be filed. Again the cost-benefit test is not passed. The only advantage might be that most of the published qualifications referred to earlier would be in respect of abridged accounts. Thus, as far as full accounts were concerned, an audit qualification would be more likely to mean something. A plus factor certainly, but hardly sufficient of itself to merit introducing a whole new tier of regulation.

Dual Standards

At this point, let it be clearly stated that the idea of exempting certain companies from the statutory audit requirement is not in any way bringing in dual standards. Many argue passionately that there can be only one standard of audit—one cannot impose a different standard *of audit* on smaller companies. Others have argued, misguidedly, that one can. This must be wrong. The audit opinion is ultimately a matter of judgment. It is often hard enough to decide what is "true and fair". One cannot impose a lower judgmental level, an attainment of a "reasonably (or nearly) true and fair view". In this respect, it is all or nothing. For this reason, the review report does not pretend to express an opinion.

One can, however, define the various parameters that determine the need for audit. These parameters are capable of objective assessment and a decision can be made where to draw the line. This is not dual standards.

The small audit debate has drawn into focus the real issue lying behind the title to this article—it is not so much the existence of two professions, but the existence of two sets of standards within the profession.

PROFESSIONAL STANDARDS

There are three aspects of U.K. professional standards in which there have been important developments in the last few years. Education and training, independence and professional discipline.

Education and Training

One current source of tension in the UK profession is the ability of firms to recruit, train and hold suitable staff. New and more complex legislation demands better academic attainment; the increased emphasis on professional standards demands more training and greater expenditure on quality control. In 1974, the Solomons report[6] proposed, inter alia, a movement towards an all graduate entry to the profession and a greater emphasis on relevant education. The practising profession's examinations now comprise not only tests of professional competence but also of intellectual capability. Consequently, there has been an increasing demand for the academically well qualified graduates and an enormous increase in the money spent training them both before and after qualifying.

Widespread concern exists amongst the smaller firms that they are increasingly finding they cannot recruit and train suitable new students. The pressure on fee income is a restraint upon their ability to pay competitive salaries and to invest in the necessary training facilities. Neither can they easily afford the investment in the development of professional standards and quality control demanded by the public, at least for public client work.

On the other hand the smaller firms assert, with much justification, that the better training claimed to be obtained by students in the larger firms is to a significant extent a misrepresentation. One of the major international firms recently announcing its results disclosed that over 75% of its worldwide income comes from auditing. As non-audit services are to a large extent provided by specialist senior staff and partners, it can confidently be reckoned that the proportion of a trainee's time spent on audit work is considerably higher. The English Institute has fairly recently agreed that practical experience in, say, taxation, acquired in the lecture room in simulated field conditions, will be accepted where necessary as an adequate substitute for on the job training acquired under supervision in the field— training which the smaller firms feel able to provide as a matter of routine. Such firms can, and do, provide admirable basic on the job training in accountancy, small company auditing and taxation. They can enable their students to "see the whole job" at an early stage. Many of them have clubbed together to provide classroom training resources they could not have provided on their own. They have together, or singly, devised sound audit methods and procedures, often based on the instructional material increasingly provided by the Institute. In short, it is argued that many small firms provide a better all-round training and yet find it increasingly difficult to find adequate students to train. Meanwhile, the big firms are tending to produce highly skilled "Chartered Auditors". There is some truth in it. Equally there is, of course, the other side to the argument. However good their methods and training, the small firms can provide only very limited experience in auditing and reporting on large companies; and the trend is increasing. What is more, it is in respect of this type of work that the profession is really under scrutiny.

The inability to recruit students is a potentially very devisive state of affairs. Some smaller firms of Chartered Accountants are concentrating on students studying for the Certified Accountants' exams. These exams, they argue, are more practical and relevant to their needs, and are spread over a longer period without demanding the long periods of absence on study leave. If this continues we clearly will have two professions. What is to be done? A start might be made with greater recognition that the demands made upon the smaller practice require no less skill than those made upon the larger. The main characteristic of a professional man is his ability to exercise judgment in any given situation and to reach a conclusion from which he can give his opinion, or his advice. The more regulation, the more the role of judgment is reduced—ultimately to the extent of reducing the professional to a technician. The large audit is today a pretty well regulated operation. In addition to company law, accounting standards and auditing standards, each large firm has its audit manual, standard working papers and so on. Again, the smaller clients very often require advisory help on a broader front than most of the big clients do. Drawing a parallel from the medical profession—being a general practitioner is a very specialized form of medicine. Looking after the smaller business requires a range of expertise, training and experience that is no less, and arguably greater, than that required for the large company.

Secondly, the smaller practitioners may have to realize that it is not necessary to be small to give a personal service. It has already been observed that many medium-sized firms are successfully running substantial smaller client practices. By clubbing together they are also providing excellent training facilities. If a practitioner wishes to remain in the top grade, he will have to have capable and well-trained staff and apply the relevant standards.

Ultimately, it is likely that the profession will have to accept some form of secondary specialist training and examination. The widening demands being made upon it, as observed at the start of this article, cannot be easily satisfied solely by one general set of examinations combined with a variety of basic field experience. Regulation creates a need for greater experience and specialist knowledge. The public needs to be confident that the necessary experience and specialist knowledge is being acquired.

Independence

There is a risk that a further strain may be placed on the small firm by the development of the ethical code of conduct, and particularly of the concept of independence. Formerly, it was acknowledged that independence was a state of mind (it still is) and it was sufficient merely to *be* independent.

If one acquired anything during one's training, it was that degree of integrity demanded of the professional person. That hasn't changed; but it is now just as necessary to be *seen to be* independent, and that can be rather different.

No longer can a firm act as company secretary to an audit client. No longer can it act as auditor where a partner or employee of that firm has any beneficial shareholding in the audit client company. Neither can a partner who is a trustee shareholder take any part in the audit assignment. These provisions are not in themselves unduly onerous. They are, however, indicative of the growing concern about the propriety of auditors providing other advisory services to their audit clients. Significant restrictions in this respect would strike at the very heart of the smaller firm's practice since a professional accountant is more often than not engaged by the smaller client not because of the quality of his audit service, but because of all the other services, notably accounts preparation and tax, that he can provide. The USA, and indeed, much of continental Europe, have for some time imposed a greater degree of limitation on the provision of these other services to audit clients, without impairing independence, than that imposed in the UK. There has, however, been one major difference. Most of the client companies of the smaller firms outside the UK are not subject to compulsory audit.

There cannot be dual standards of independence any more than there can be dual standards of work. Prima facie, therefore, the smaller practice could have a problem, particularly if compulsory audit for the smaller company is not abolished. However, there is a danger that the "other services" aspect of independence will be taken too far. The public cannot have it both ways. If it wants the profession to apply its skills and expertise to areas other than auditing and reporting, it will have to relax in its concern that rendering non-audit services to audit clients poses a risk of impairment of independence.

Discipline and Self-Regulation

Ultimately, if a professional firm wishes to be considered to be in the top grade, it must submit itself to an acceptable standard of discipline and self-regulation. A major advance was made in this area with the publication of the Cross Report,[4] and the proposals for implementing its recommendations contained in the Grenside Report.[5] The Grenside proposals have broadly been adopted by the three professional bodies to whom the two reports were addressed—The Chartered Institutes of England and Wales and of Scotland, and the Association of Certified Accountants. In summary they were:

(a) the extension of disciplinary jurisdiction to include inefficiency and incompetence to such an extent or on such a number of occasions as to cause concern about its effect on the standing of the profession;

(b) the establishment of joint machinery to inquire into and make findings upon the professional conduct, efficiency and competence of members and of member firms in circumstances which give rise to *public* concern;

(c) the inclusion of a lay observer in the domestic (i.e. *private*) investigation process;

(d) the importation of lay representation at all levels in the disciplinary process;

(e) the creation of Practice Advisory Services by each body;

(f) the need for stricter control over practising certificates;

(g) the need for development of a programme for continuing professional education;

(h) the need to recognise the separate responsibilities of members not in public practice.

A joint scheme has been set up for investigation and regulation of the professional conduct, efficiency and competence of any member and member firm involved in a matter of public concern, in accordance with (b).

It is important to note that "public" and "domestic" apply to the nature of the case being investigated, and not to the firm. All firms from sole-practitioners to the very largest are treated in the same way by the new disciplinary arrangements. No attempt has been made to segregate the firms.

Peer review and the US Division for CPA firms. Matters have taken a rather different course in the US. In 1977, following Congressional criticism of well-published audit failures, the AICPA created the Division for CPA firms with its two sections—the SEC Practice Section and the Private Companies Practice Section. Those joining the Division had to submit to peer review every three years, and those joining the SEC Practice Section had to comply with further requirements, including the rotation of engagement partner every five years.

The formation of the Division has caused considerable concern in the US profession to the extent that a "National Conference of CPA Practitioners" has been formed, whose membership comprises many smaller practitioners who oppose the whole concept. They point out the enormous cost of running the two sections and of peer review, costs they can ill-afford. Ultimately their concern is to prevent the split of US accounting firms into first and second grades. They point out that Congressman Moss, the leading protagonist of federal regulation of the profession, considered at the time the Division was formed that dividing the Institute into separate classes of membership would not be a useful reform, since it would tend to promote further concentration in the accounting profession.

Seen from the UK, one can well perceive that the Division could have a damaging effect on the smaller practice. At the time of writing, the report by Sam Derieux commissioned by the AICPA, known as the "Report of the Special Committee on Small and Medium Sized Firms" is circulating in draft. It is understood that it may contain proposals that the FASB should give more thought to the needs of the small enterprise when issuing accounting statements, and even that the statements of small enterprises be drawn up on a totally different basis. These are dangerous waters. If the public need is served by having two different but acceptable *bases,* that is one thing; it is, however, but a small further step to accepting lower *standards,* and that is very different.

For the time being the UK profession is concerned with raising the standards of the whole profession at a cost it can afford. It is partly for this reason, and a desire not to allow the UK profession to become too US dominated through the "big eight," that the UK practising bodies have shied away from the heavy costs of compulsory peer review.

SUMMARY AND CONCLUSION

We have noted that society is placing an increasing reliance on the accountant and requiring greater accountability in public matters. We have also observed the necessity to provide the smaller or private client with a service relevant to his needs and to set adequate standards for the provision of that service. But standards cost money—and that means adequate fees.

Surveys carried out by the English Institute have revealed that a significant number of small practices actually make losses after allowing a reasonable salary for the partners. It is very doubtful whether these losses result from the cost of maintaining adequate standards. More probably the opposite is true—low profitability means poor staff; poor staff means low standards; low standards means low fees—a downward spiral.

The profession will have to educate the public that it must pay for a high standard of service. It will have to persuade its members to charge adequate—not unreasonable—fees for the job. Small practitioners will have to consider whether their firms are viable at their present size or whether a more effective service could not be provided from a larger client base.

Finally we have noted that the large firms who dominate the public reporting market are beginning to move more into the smaller client area. At the same time, small practices are merging to form larger units structured to service the smaller client. This trend could well be a unifying force since the needs of the smaller client, and of the firms that service them, will be increasingly the concern of those with a powerful voice. It will be very important how this voice is used.

REFERENCES AND NOTES

1. F.W. Pixley—"Auditors, Their Duties and Responsibilities."

2. On accounting for tax reserve certificates.

3. "The City Code on Takeovers and Mergers," issued on behalf of the City Working Party.

4. "Report of a Committee under the Chairmanship of the Rt. Hon. The Lord Cross of Chelsea."

5. "Report of the Joint Committee appointed to consider the Cross Report and related matters."

6. "Prospectus for a Profession—The Report of the Long Range Enquiry into Education and Training for the Accounting Profession."

7. "The Corporate Report." A Discussion Paper published in 1975 for comment by the Accounting Standards Steering Committee of the Institute of Chartered Accountants of England and Wales (in association with the other accounting bodies).

8. "Auditing Standards and Guidelines" issued by the Auditing Practices Committee of the Consultancy Committee of Accounting Bodies.

9. "Company Accounting and Disclosure—A Consultative Document" Cmnd 7654, September 1979.

10. "Small Companies—the need for Audit."

11. "Statement on Standards for Accounting and Review Services," issued by the AICPA in December 1978.

SOME THOUGHTS ON AUDITORS'

RESPONSIBILITY FOR FALSE AND

MISLEADING FINANCIAL STATEMENTS

Donald R. Ziegler
Partner, Price Waterhouse & Co.

CONTENTS

ABSTRACT

In this article, Mr. Ziegler distinguishes between fraud in general and fraud which results in false and misleading financial statements. He acknowledges the auditor's responsibility, in conducting an examination, to look for errors and irregularities which could materially affect financial statements and says that he believes that such responsibility is nothing new; that it has been implicit in authoritative pronouncements for quite some time. He comments on recent pronouncements

241

and activities of the AICPA and the SEC and gives his view as to their significance. He also discusses auditors' performances in the area of fraud detection and states that, on the whole, they have performed commendably. In concluding, he expresses confidence that the auditing profession will continue to willingly assume as much responsibility as can reasonably be expected of it.

INTRODUCTION

When it comes to false and misleading financial statements, one case seems to stand out above the rest (if the number of times it has been mentioned to me is any indication). While many people know the name of the company involved, I get the impression that knowledge of what the case was all about is not so widespread.

The case concerns an old, well-established name in the drug industry. By 1929 it included almost half of the largest and soundest wholesale jobbing houses in the United States. In 1937 its total consolidated assets were stated at $87 million and shareholders' equity was $46 million.

Control of inventories had been made difficult by the complexity of the consolidation and the type of merchandise sold (between 40 and 50 thousand items were stocked). Further, the president of the company had expanded operations in the late 1920's to include trading in crude drugs from abroad (e.g., wood oil from China, camphor from Japan and quinine from Java). He worked sixteen hours a day and appeared to be completely devoted to making a success of the business for the benefit of the shareholders. As later events showed, he had conceived an amazing plan. The plan involved placing two of his brothers in key managerial posts, using fictitious names. Forged Dun & Bradstreet reports and numerous other forged documents were skillfully prepared by a third brother, who was not an employee of the company. The plan also involved dummy companies, fictitious warehouses, and nonexistent assets of $19 million: $10 million in inventories and $9 million in accounts receivable.

Nonexistent inventories proved to be more easily increased than reduced. The company's directors had voted to reduce inventories by $4 million, and the treasurer of the company began in 1938 to observe certain strange phenomena. The crude drug operations showed the best profits of all the divisions, but these profits were always plowed back into new purchases. When the treasurer asked the president for proof of the physical existence of the assets in the crude drug division, the scheme began to collapse. Warrants were obtained for the arrest of the president and two of his brothers, and on December 16, 1938, just as the U.S. marshal reached his home to arrest him, the president committed suicide. His brothers were later sentenced to prison terms.

After a thorough investigation, it was discovered that over a twelve-year period the president and his confidants had managed to defraud the company of some $2,900,000 in cash. The crude drug division had been separated into two parts: one domestic and legitimate, the other wholly fictitious. The fraud consisted of pretending to purchase crude drugs, making actual payments to fictitious companies, pretending to sell the drugs to genuine foreign dealers and paying the company back part of its own money through dummy corporations.

To conform with the company's accounting procedures, semi-annual inventory reports had to be prepared and an accounting and check disbursement system maintained. These requirements were met by the two brothers on the payroll. The dummy corporations were operated by the non-employee brother. In addition, a dummy banking firm was set up to act as fiscal agent for all the crude drug department's purchases and sales. Every month statements (prepared by the non-employee brother) were received showing the funds collected and paid and balances to the credit of the company.

Prior to 1935 (when crude drugs were supposedly stored in Connecticut, rather than being held by Canadian suppliers) the auditors, carefully following the auditing procedures generally accepted at that time, were furnished inventory sheets signed or initialed by company employees. They test-checked the items to the perpetual inventory records and checked the inventory sheets for clerical accuracy. After 1934, the auditors obtained confirmations of the quantities supposedly held by suppliers. In addition, they checked the prices shown in the inventory sheets by reference to purchase invoices covering a substantial portion of the quantities of each item and comparison with quotations published in trade journals and selling prices indicated by duplicate sales invoices. The auditors obtained certificates, signed by two or more company officials, covering the quantity and condition of inventories presented in the balance sheet. The Federal Reserve Bulletin, *Approved Methods for the Preparation of Balance Sheet Statements*, published in 1918, included the following statement with respect to inventories:

> Obtain a clear and detailed statement in writing as to the method followed in taking stock and pricing it; also, a certificate from a responsible head as to the accuracy of the inventory as a whole.

The 1929 revision of that bulletin contained the same line, while the 1936 Bulletin, published by the AICPA under the title of *Examination of*

Financial Statements by Independent Accountants, made only slight revisions to this directive.

Early in 1939, in the aftermath of this case, the AICPA reviewed then customary auditing procedures to determine whether the procedures, which had been generally accepted for many years, should be changed. While concluding that it was the ultimate responsibility of practitioners to perform such procedures as, in their professional judgment, they considered appropriate, the AICPA recommended that confirmation of receivables and observation of inventories (where practicable and reasonable) should be established as generally accepted auditing procedures where such assets are material to financial position or results of operations. This recommendation was adopted by a vote of the AICPA membership later that year.

It is unlikely that the endorsement of these procedures by the AICPA membership will be recognized as a great moment in history. Yet, I believe that their adoption as generally accepted auditing procedures was one of the more significant developments in the evolution of auditing as we know it today. Their role as a deterrent to the preparation of false and misleading financial statements has undoubtedly been an important one, one that is often taken for granted.

DIFFERING ASSUMPTIONS

Neither the title of this article nor the comments in the preceding paragraph mention the word "fraud." Both, however, focus on false and misleading financial statements, which is where I believe the focus belongs.

While all false and misleading financial statements involve an element of fraud, all frauds do not result in false and misleading financial statements. The distinction between fraud in a broad sense and fraud which results in false and misleading financial statements is an important one. Fictitious transactions and actual transactions, in which substance differs from form, could, if material, result in false and misleading financial statements, as could undiscovered embezzlements, in material amounts. Conversely, while the embezzlement of $100,000 by a divisional employee of a large conglomerate would fall within the definition of fraud, it would ordinarily not result in false and misleading financial statements, whether or not discovered and regardless of the eventual accounting for it.

Why the distinction? Let's take a look at the auditor's standard, unqualified opinion, as illustrated in Statement on Auditing Standards No. 2:

> In our opinion, the financial statements referred to above present
> fairly the financial position of X Company as of (at) December 31,

19xx, and the results of its operations and the changes in its financial position for the year then ended, in conformity with generally accepted accounting principles applied on a basis consistent with that of the preceding year.

A reader of this opinion would be justified in assuming that, in the auditor's professional judgment, the financial statements to which it relates are presented fairly in conformity with generally accepted accounting principles consistently applied—no more, no less. There is no basis in the auditor's opinion for an assumption that the business activities of the entity have been conducted effectively, efficiently or in the best interests of its shareholders.

DIFFERING PERCEPTIONS AND EXPECTATIONS

The extent to which auditors can or should be held accountable for failure to detect fraud has been the subject of much discussion and controversy over the years. Just what is the auditor's responsibility for the detection of fraud? The answer to that question depends upon the person of whom it is asked. Ask certain judges, Congressmen or regulatory agency officials and the answer is likely to be that auditors are responsible for the detection of *all* fraud. Ask some auditors and they'll contend, in all sincerity, that they have no responsibility for the detection of fraud. Their position is based on the following commentary from Statement on Auditing Procedure No. 30, *"Responsibilities and Functions of the Independent Auditor in the Examination of Financial Statements"* which became part of the authoritative auditing literature in 1960 and endured as such, essentially unchanged, until 1977:

> However, the ordinary examination incident to the expression of an opinion on financial statements is not primarily or specifically designed, and cannot be relied upon, to disclose defalcations and other similar irregularities, although their discovery may result. Similarly, although the discovery of deliberate misrepresentations by management is usually more closely associated with the objective of the ordinary examination, such examination cannot be relied upon to assure its discovery. The responsibility of the independent auditor for failure to detect fraud (which responsibility differs as to clients and others) arises only when such failure clearly results from noncompliance with generally accepted auditing standards.

Unfortunately, the sentence which preceded the "However," was often overlooked. In my view, this is the sentence that said it all, so far as responsibility for detection of fraud goes. It read:

The auditor recognizes that fraud, if sufficiently material, may affect his opinion on the financial statements, and his examination, made in accordance with generally accepted auditing standards, gives consideration to this possibility.

Giving consideration to the possibility of fraud, in this context, has always meant to me identifying the kinds of fraud that could materially affect the financial statements being examined and maintaining an alertness for conditions that may indicate the presence of such fraud. The identification process originates during the planning phase and continues throughout the examination by giving consideration to conditions observed and information developed as the examination progresses.

REAFFIRMATION OF PREVIOUSLY ACKNOWLEDGED RESPONSIBILITY

In 1977 the Auditing Standards Executive Committee (of which I was then a member) issued Statement on Auditing Standards No. 16 ("SAS 16") entitled *The Independent Auditor's Responsibility for the Detection of Errors or Irregularities*. SAS 16 superseded prior pronouncements concerning the auditor's responsibility for fraud detection. Irregularities are defined in SAS 16 as "...intentional distortions of financial statements, such as deliberate misrepresentations by management, sometimes referred to as management fraud, or misappropriations of assets, sometimes referred to as defalcations."

SAS 16 states that "...under generally accepted auditing standards the independent auditor has the responsibility, within the inherent limitations of the auditing process, to plan his examination to search for errors or irregularities that would have a material effect on the financial statements, and to exercise due skill and care in the conduct of that examination." What does SAS 16 require that was not required by prior pronouncements? In my judgment, SAS 16 requires *nothing* that was not required by prior pronouncements.

DIFFERING VIEWS AS TO SAS 16 REQUIREMENTS

SAS 16 has been read by some, however, as requiring auditors to do something new in order to detect irregularities which could materially affect financial statements. The "something new" that they see in SAS 16 is the requirement to *search* for material errors or irregularities. It all depends upon how one interprets the word *search*. In this regard, dictionaries may not be of much help. Definitions run from "look for," which is what SAS 16 says to me, to "painstakingly examine." Those who view SAS 16 as requiring auditors to do something new apparently base their view on something closer to the latter definition.

SAS 16 clearly states that "[t]he auditor's search...ordinarily is accomplished by the performance of those auditing procedures that in his judgment are appropriate in the circumstances to form an opinion on the financial statements..." It also provides that "...extended auditing procedures are required if the auditor's examination indicates that material errors or irregularities may exist." This latter requirement (which has long existed) was incorporated into SAS 16 to clarify the auditor's responsibility. It appears, however, that, rather then being helpful, it may have added to the confusion. Obviously, an auditor must satisfactorily resolve *all* significant questions which come up during the course of his examination. The extended auditing procedures referred to in SAS 16 are simply additional procedures not contemplated at the time the examination was planned.

NO INTENT TO INCREASE RESPONSIBILITY

SAS 16 was adopted by the assenting vote of nineteen members of the Auditing Standards Executive Committee. Four of the nineteen qualified their assents and two members cast dissenting votes. The qualifications and dissents can be attributed to a lack of clarity in the document, in that it did not explicitly state that it was not intended to require auditors to do anything more with respect to the detection of errors and irregularities than they were already required to do.

In substance, no committee member believed that auditors should assume any greater responsibility than they already had. As one who cast an unqualified vote assenting to its adoption, I did not then, and do not now, see any reason for modifying the text of SAS 16. At the same time, if the substitution of the words "look for" for the words "search for" would take away some of the confusion (as I'm led to believe it might), I would be all for it.

RISKS INHERENT IN SELECTIVE TESTING

Application of the generally accepted concept of selective, rather than exhaustive, testing in an examination of financial statements carries with it the risk that material errors and irregularities, if they exist, may not be detected by the auditor. For example, while the auditor may be alert to the possibility of unrecorded transactions, collusion between client management and outside parties and management override of internal accounting controls, these conditions could exist and not be detected by the most competent of auditors. SAS 16 recognizes this possibility and reaffirms the conclusions (expressed in prior announcements) that an auditor is neither an insurer nor a guarantor and that "...if his examination was made in accordance with generally accepted auditing standards, he has fulfilled his professional responsibility."

RECOGNITION OF EVENTS OF THE 1970's

Although generally accepted auditing standards have long required auditors to give consideration to the possibility of errors and irregularities, authoritative pronouncements placed little emphasis on such possibility until recent years.

Several events that occurred in the 1970's put fraud and its detection on center stage: investigations by the Securities and Exchange Commission of alleged frauds, discovery of illegal campaign contributions (facilitated by "off book" slush funds) during the course of various Watergate investigations, passage of the Foreign Corrupt Practices Act, the Equity Funding saga, Congressional investigations and hearings involving the auditing profession and the study and report of The Commission on Auditors' Responsibilities, the "Cohen Commission," established by the AICPA, to name the more prominent ones.

The AICPA and its Auditing Standards Division have closely monitored these developments to determine whether generally accepted auditing standards continue to be adequate in view of changing times and circumstances. Thus far, recognition given to the events of the 1970's has not resulted in major modification of auditing standards. The emphasis has been placed, rather, on providing guidance as to the application of existing standards in situations encountered or expected to be encountered by auditors. This guidance has, in some instances, included an articulation of procedures which should be applied or considered, depending upon the circumstances.

TRANSACTIONS WITH RELATED PARTIES

In 1975, Statement on Auditing Standards No. 6 ("SAS 6"), *Related Party Transactions*, was issued in recognition of a significant number of widely publicized situations in which related party transactions were involved in allegedly fraudulent activities. SAS 6 provides auditors with information as to procedures to be considered for identifying related parties and related party transactions. It illustrates conditions which might motivate management to execute transactions (with related parties) for the sole or principal purpose of portraying a financial picture unwarranted by actual conditions and the substance of the transactions. It also effectively establishes disclosure requirements that would more appropriately fall under generally accepted accounting principles, but as to which generally accepted accounting principles are silent.

ILLEGAL ACTS

Statement on Auditing Standards No. 17 ("SAS 17"), *Illegal Acts by Clients*, was issued in 1977 to provide guidance in situations in which information obtained by an auditor during the course of an examination leads him to believe that a particular act is or may be illegal. Like its immediate predecessor, SAS 16, it imposed no new obligations on auditors. It merely sets forth a course of action which should be considered by the auditor in situations to which it applies.

ACCOUNTING SERIES RELEASES

Since its inception, the Securities and Exchange Commission ("the SEC") has issued numerous Accounting Series Releases alleging that auditors have failed to comply with generally accepted auditing standards. Most of these releases discuss situations in which the SEC concluded, but did not necessarily prove, that specified financial statements were materially false and misleading. Interestingly, in charging the auditors with failure to comply with generally accepted auditing standards, the SEC in many instances cited omission of what appear (admittedly, on the basis of twenty-twenty hindsight) to have been simple, rather than complex or unusual, auditing procedures. Also, the text of a number of the releases indicates that the auditors had knowledge of pertinent information, which, if properly evaluated or acted upon, would likely have caused them to conclude that the financial statements were false and misleading.

Except, perhaps, for the case which introduced this article, I am not aware of any situation in which the SEC has attributed an auditor's failure to detect fraud to deficiencies in generally accepted auditing standards or procedures. In other words, although the SEC's Chief Accountant and its staff have, from time to time, made suggestions as to areas in which guidance should be provided to auditors, the Commission itself has not taken issue with the adequacy of existing standards or procedures.

QUALITY OF FINANCIAL STATEMENTS

An important point to keep in mind is that the quality of financial statements may not necessarily be influenced by the quality of the auditor's examination of them. As the representations of management, the quality of financial statements is dependent primarily upon the integrity and competence of management. If financial statements are, in fact, prepared in conformity with generally accepted accounting principles, the auditor's opinion to that effect does not enhance their quality. It simply provides the user with a basis for placing greater reliance on management's representations than might be placed on them in the absence of such an opinion. If, however, financial statements in their preliminary stages are materially false and misleading or fail to conform with generally accepted accounting principles because of errors, irregularities or inadequate disclosure, the prospects of a qualified or adverse opinion will likely go a long way toward encouraging management to improve the quality of the final product. What this says is that a well planned and executed audit can and frequently does have a significant influence on the quality of financial statements.

On the other hand, an audit planned and performed in accordance with generally accepted auditing standards may not detect instances of management fraud or defalcations that materially affect the financial statements. Management's override of internal controls, collusion, forgery and unrecorded transactions are frequently extremely difficult, if not virtually impossible, to detect; which is why alertness for evidential matter having a bearing on the integrity of management is an essential ingredient of every examination of financial statements. An unqualified opinion issued in these circumstances may lend credibility to management's financial statement representations but certainly does not improve their quality.

Now let's turn to situations in which auditors clearly fail to conduct their examinations in accordance with generally accepted auditing standards to such an extent that there is an inadequate basis for the expression of an opinion and, yet, an unqualified opinion is expressed. How do these situations impact the quality of the financial statements to which they relate?

If the financial statements are, in fact, prepared in conformity with generally accepted accounting principles, their quality is unaffected by the auditor's opinion to that effect, which turns out to be an appropriate one, despite the fact that there is an inadequate basis for expressing it. Inasmuch as the financial statements are not false and misleading, third party users can hardly claim to have been damaged by the auditor's inadequate performance.

If it turns out, however, that the financial statements are false and misleading or otherwise not in conformity with generally accepted accounting principles, an auditor who expresses an unqualified opinion on them must be prepared to demonstrate conclusively that remedying all of the significant deficiencies in his examination prior to the expression of his opinion would not have caused him to change it. In effect, he would have to show that an adequately planned and executed examination would not have influenced the quality of the financial statements prior to their finalization.

QUESTIONS AS TO THE QUALITY OF AN EXAMINATION

When financial statements on which an auditor has expressed an unqualified opinion are subsequently found to be false and misleading, there is a strong likelihood that the quality of the auditor's examination will come into question. With the knowledge of what happened and how it happened, it may not be too difficult for an injured party's counsel to identify a simple audit procedure or test that would, or should, have brought the problem to the auditor's attention before, rather than after, issuing his report, and to claim that failure to perform the procedure or test resulted in a failure to comply with generally accepted auditing standards.

To refute such a claim, the auditor may have to explain why he did not perform the particular test or procedure. While it might be reasonable to expect that the matter would be put to rest by showing that the auditor, at the time of his examination, had no way of knowing or reason for suspecting what happened, it is not always that simple. The auditor may also have to demonstrate to the satisfaction of a judge or jury that his examination included adequate procedures for the detection of errors and irregularities which might reasonably have been expected to occur in the circumstances in which the company operated.

AUDITING BY OBJECTIVES

If it were possible to develop manuals and programs setting forth in detail all procedures which would be necessary for the detection of all material errors and irregularities in all circumstances, production of documentation showing that the auditor had adequately performed all of the procedures in the manuals would probably be accepted as indisputable evidence that sufficient attention was given to the possibility of material errors and irregularities. The fees that would be involved, however, could bankrupt many companies and would be difficult to cost justify for others.

Using a set of unmodified, standardized audit programs as the framework for each examination has resulted in more than one auditor getting into difficulty. Despite whatever merits they may have, untailored, standardized programs tend to make the auditor lose sight of the objectives of his examination. Auditing by objectives, on the other hand, stimulates the thought processes by requiring the auditor to continually answer (consciously or instinctively) two questions:

What am I trying to accomplish?
and
How am I going to accomplish it?

Answering these questions is easier for the experienced, more knowledgeable auditor than it is for the relatively inexperienced, less knowledgeable auditor.

KNOWLEDGE OF THE BUSINESS

Statement on Auditing Standards No. 22 ("SAS 22"), *Planning and Supervision*, discusses, among other things, the level of knowledge of an entity's business that an auditor should have to be able to plan and execute his examination in accordance with generally accepted auditing standards. SAS 22 states that "[t]he auditor should obtain a knowledge of matters that relate to the nature of the entity's business, its organization, and its operating characteristics..." and provides examples of such matters. It was issued to provide guidance in applying the first standard of field work, which requires that "...the work is to be adequately planned and assistants, if any, are to be properly supervised." The concept of knowledge of an entity's business is not new; it was implicit in generally accepted auditing standards long before the issuance of SAS 22.

Attaining and maintaining auditing proficiency involves a never ending educational process. This fact is evidenced by the increasing number of jurisdictions which have established continuing education as a criterion for renewal of an auditor's privilege of practicing as a certified public accountant.

In today's environment, the level of knowledge required to effectively audit the financial statements of most large and many not-so-large enterprises is significantly greater than that which may be necessary to pass the CPA examination. The auditor's ability to incorporate into his audit plan procedures adequate to detect material errors or irregularities is necessarily enhanced by experience with and/or knowledge of situations in which past errors and irregularities have occurred or been attempted. In this regard, many firms include in their basic and continuing education programs material based on actual experiences and knowledge obtained from the public record.

CONTRIBUTING FACTORS IN
PAST FRAUD SITUATIONS

In March 1979, a subcommittee, established by the AICPA to study methods by which frauds have been perpetrated and means by which they have been detected, compiled and published in *The CPA Letter* a list of sixteen conditions and events which were or may have been contributing factors in past fraud situations and which could very well contribute to future fraud attempts. The list was compiled from information provided by various accounting firms and others. It was published as a preliminary list with the intention of later publishing a more comprehensive list based on responses to an invitation to comment and provide additional examples. It was prepared and distributed not as something new or unique, but simply as a means of providing all auditors with information already possessed by many of them.

It illustrates conditions and events which *could* motivate management to engage in fraudulent activities or prepare false and misleading financial statements. Also included are conditions which provide management with greater opportunity to engage in such activities that might ordinarily exist. Finally, there are illustrations of unusual conditions, events and transactions which should be recognized as having fraud potential when they come to the auditor's attention in the ordinary course of his examination.

The items included in the list are referred to as "warning signals" in *The CPA Letter*. Since their publication, I have also heard them referred to as "danger signals" and "red flags." Each of these descriptions tends to lead to the unwarranted conclusion that if one or more of the items are present, the auditor must somehow extend the scope of his audit. More dangerous, perhaps, is the false sense of complacency which may result from the determination that none of the items on the list are present and the conclusion, therefore, that the possibilities for fraud are minimal. The audit objective of obtaining reasonable assurance that the financial statements are not materially false and misleading *requires* the auditor to consider the kinds of errors or irregularities that could occur and to plan his examination in light of such considerations. This must be done in *all* cases, not just those in which he believes there is a strong potential for fraud. The conditions and events illustrated in the list may be of assistance to some auditors in planning their examinations. Without question, they have been given consideration by many, if not most, auditors long before they appeared in *The CPA Letter*.

A LOOK AT THE RECORD

There seems to be popular belief that auditors have been "asleep at the switch" on too many occasions in the area of fraud detection. I disagree with this contention and, while I cannot prove it, I am convinced that on the whole auditors have performed commendably as far as fraud detection is concerned.

Concluding that a perfect baseball game has been pitched is a relatively simple matter. If the winning pitcher goes a full nine innings, during which his team has scored at least one run, and the first twenty-seven batters on the losing team fail to reach first base, we have a "perfect game." A single hit ruins a "perfect game" and even though the pitcher can claim 96.4% effectiveness, few people will long remember his performance.

It's quite the opposite where auditors and management fraud are concerned. Turn in a "perfect record" and get no credit for it—that's what auditors are paid for, isn't it? But turn in a 96.4% performance and you've made it into the Hall of Fame.

When it comes to detection of management fraud, what is a perfect record? In its strictest sense, it can only mean that every attempted fraud situation has been thwarted by the auditor. Similarly, an imperfect record is one in which an attempted fraud was successfully perpetrated without detection by the auditor.

Until such time as would-be perpetrators of fraud are somehow compelled to report each attempt (perhaps to some governmental agency), there is no way to determine how perfectly or imperfectly auditors have performed. In the meantime, auditors may be presumed to have perfect records in the absence of evidence to the contrary.

Undoubtedly, a number of management frauds have been successfully perpetrated without detection by auditors or others. It is only when a fraud comes to light that the possibility of audit failure becomes an issue. What this means is that some apparently perfect records may not be so perfect after all.

While alleged audit "failures" have received widespread publicity in recent years, little has been written about audit "successes." The reason is quite simple; unless fraud or alleged fraud becomes a matter of public record, the auditor gets no public recognition for its detection. Frauds or attempted frauds that have been detected by auditors during an ordinary examination (directed at the expression of an opinion on financial statements) rarely become part of the public record. This is because remedial action is taken prior to the time the audit report is issued. Since their reports are directed to the integrity of the financial statements and not (at least at the present time) to the integrity of management, auditors have no basis or requirement for publicly reporting that a fraud was perpetrated or attempted. Similarly, management that has perpetrated or attempted to perpetrate a fraud can hardly be expected to come forward and report that alert auditing detected it.

THE FUTURE

While not probable, it is not beyond the realm of possibility that the day will come when auditing, as a profession, will cease to exist. Its demise could be brought about by the evolution of a society in which there are no such things as dishonesty, unintentional errors, estimates, uncertainties or complex, authoritative accounting pronouncements.

Until such time, I am confident that the auditing profession will continue to provide society with a useful service, willingly accepting as much responsibility as can reasonably be expected of it, keeping in mind that auditors are people too—no more or less perfect than those who read their reports.

REFERENCES

American Institute of Certified Public Accountants (1939). *Statement on Auditing Procedure No. 1*, "Extensions of Auditing Procedure." New York: AICPA.

American Institute of Certified Public Accountants (1960). *Statement on Auditing Procedure No. 30*, "Responsibilities and Functions of the Independent Auditor in the Examination of Financial Statements." New York: AICPA.

American Institute of Certified Public Accountants (1974). *Statement on Auditing Standards No. 2*, "Reports on Audited Financial Statements." New York: AICPA.

American Institute of Certified Public Accountants (1975). *Statement on Auditing Standards No. 6*, "Related Party Transactions." New York: AICPA.

American Institute of Certified Public Accountants (1977a). *Statement on Auditing Standards No. 16*, "The Independent Auditor's Responsibility for the Detection of Errors or Irregularities." New York: AICPA.

American Institute of Certified Public Accountants (1977b). *Statement on Auditing Standards No. 17*, "Illegal Acts by Clients." New York: AICPA.

American Institute of Certified Public Accountants (1978). *Statement on Auditing Standards No. 22*, "Planning and Supervision." New York: AICPA.

AICPA Standing Subcommittee on Methods of Perpetration and Detection of Fraud (1979). *Warning Signals of the Possible Existence of Fraud*. The CPA Letter, March 12, 1979. New York: AICPA.

Hoffman, R.A. (1967). *Inventory Frauds.* The Price Waterhouse Review Summer 1967. New York: Price Waterhouse & Co.

Ziegler, D.R. (1980). *A Look at the Record on Auditor Detection of Management Fraud.* 1980 Touche Ross/University of Kansas Symposium on Auditing Problems. School of Business, University of Kansas.

CONTENTS OF ANNUAL ACCOUNTING REVIEW, VOLUME 1

CONTENTS OF ANNUAL ACCOUNTING REVIEW, VOLUME 2